# Changing Sea-Level along the North Coast of Kuwait Bay

# Changing Sea-Level along the North Coast of Kuwait Bay

Taiba A. Al-Asfour

Kegan Paul International
London, Boston and Melbourne
*in association with*
Kuwait University

First published in 1982
by Kegan Paul International Ltd
39 Store Street
London WC1E 7DD,
9 Park Street
Boston, Mass. 02108, USA, and
296 Beaconsfield Parade, Middle Park,
Melbourne, 3206, Australia,
Set in IBM 10 on 12pt Press Roman by
Hope Services, Abingdon, Oxon
and printed in Great Britain by
Ebenezer Baylis & Son Ltd, Worcester

Library of Congress Cataloging in Publication Data

Al-Asfour, Taiba A.
Changing sea-level along the north coast of
Kuwait Bay.

Bibliography: p.
Includes index.
1. Sea level–Kuwait–Kuwait Bay.    I. Title.
GC89.A4    551.46'735    81–14314

ISBN 0-7103-0010-7    AACR2

To my parents

# Contents

# Plates

# Figures

# Tables

# Acknowledgments

I would like to express my gratitude to the following: The University of Kuwait, which supported and financed this research project; Professor H. Bowen-Jones of the University of Durham, whose guidance was of great value and most generously given throughout the work; Dr M. J. Tooley, who provided stimulating discussion, and help and advice on numerous occasions; Mr H. E. J. Biggs of the British Museum (Natural History), who identified the fossil shells presented in this work and whose experience, especially in relation to the Arabian Gulf mollusca, has been greatly appreciated; Dr J. D. Taylor and Mr C. P. Nuttal, British Museum (Natural History), for their assistance with the fossil identification; Dr G. A. L. Johnson of the Geology Department, University of Durham, for taking an interest in this work and giving assistance with geological problems; Mr C. C. S. Davies, British Petroleum, for information and valuable discussions related to the geology of Kuwait; Dr P. J. Vincent of Lancaster University, for arranging the work on the scanning electron microscope and helpful discussion; Professor F. W. Shotton of Birmingham University, who kindly dated two of the shell samples; Dr P. Beaumont of the Geography Department, University of Wales, for assistance and advice, especially at the beginning of this research project; The Kuwait Education Office in London for their liaison; The Municipality of Kuwait, especially the surveying department, for their co-operation and assistance; the technical staff at the University of Kuwait who assisted me in the field; the technical staff of the University of Durham, Department of Geography, especially M. J. Telford, for laboratory advice; the staff at the University of Durham Science Library, particularly Mrs Jean Chisholm, for their assistance; many researchers who generously provided me with unpublished information; last of all my parents, for their continual encouragement, support and patience during the whole of my life.

# Chapter 1

# Introduction

The theme of this research is the study of the changes of sea-level along the north coast of Kuwait Bay by an investigation of the land surface in the area between Kathma and Al-Bahra (Figure 1.1). The area is characterized by the presence of three main topographic elements (Figure 1.2). First, the Jal-Az-Zor escarpment, an outstanding feature. The escarpment is composed of rocks of Miocene and Pliocene age capped with more recent deposits. It extends from west to east for a distance of about 65 kilometres, with a maximum height of about 145 metres. The escarpment follows a north-easterly direction, until near Al-Bahra where it changes its course and swings northwards in a ·gentle arc through east to the south-east. The escarpment is also dissected by several wadis which are most evident in the area between Kathma and Mudairah. Secondly, there is the slope-area at the foot of the escarpment

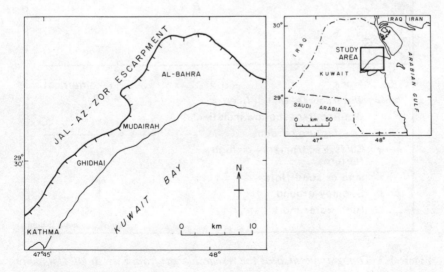

**Figure 1.1** *Location map*

1

which varies in width from Kathma to Al-Bahra with several breaks of slopes scattered throughout the area. Conspicuous terraces covered by marine and terrestrial deposits are formed at different levels. Lastly, there is the area between high- and low-water mark sometimes wide, marshy and ill-defined, sometimes with clear beach characteristics.

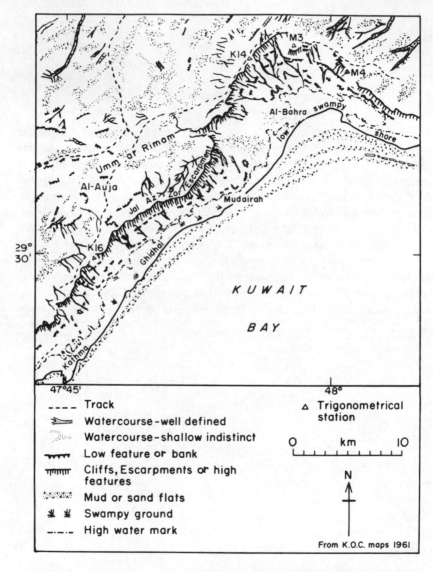

**Figure 1.2** *Topographic map of the research area (from Kuwait Oil Company maps, 1961)*

The area under investigation has been chosen for the study of sea-level changes because of the existence of the terraces and fragments of terraces above, and because this part of the Kuwait coast has not been physically disturbed by the increase in settlement and building of seaside cottages to which a large part of the southern coast is exposed. The research area is not permanently settled apart from a few wandering groups of people. However, it is worth while mentioning that Kathma used to be a town of some importance in the early Islamic period and previously extended from its present location as far west as the village of Al-Jahra. A preliminary archeological investigation by a Danish expedition has referred to the existence of some implements found in Kathma and Mudairah belonging to civilizations of the Stone Ages (Al-Kuwait Al-Youm, 1958).

Some obstacles which were met in the research included the physical conditions of the area during the fieldwork — mainly the dust storms and the high temperatures — and the fact that there had never been previous research focused on sea-level changes in Kuwait.

The basic but limited geological reports have contributed to some extent to our understanding of the geological history of the area, but, as will be seen in chapter 2, the extent and certainty of our knowledge of the historical geomorphology of the Gulf is very limited. Accordingly, all the material set out in this study is original and all possible efforts have been made to present it as a start to the study of sea-level changes on the Kuwait coast.

The first portion of this study comprises a brief summary of the relevant literature available about the Gulf and adjacent areas; the physical characteristics of the Gulf, and the structural stability of the head of the Gulf (important because of its location close to the area of research), as well as evidence of sea-level changes around the Gulf. This is followed by an introductory chapter on the geology and physical geography of Kuwait.

Chapters 4 and 5 discuss the methods which have been adopted for the investigation of this research and the raw data obtained from each method. In the fourth chapter, the methods discussed include levelling, radiocarbon dating and sediment analyses, the importance of each method in relation to the present work being fully discussed. The fifth chapter presents the results obtained independently from each method of investigation.

Chapter 6 presents the interpretation of the results obtained by the various methods of investigation; it attempts a correlation between the terraces or fragments of terraces between Kathma, Ghidhai, Mudairah and Al-Bahra. A comparison and correlation between the results of this research with worldwide changes of sea-level is also presented. Chapter 7 examines the implications of the Kuwait Bay findings and the geomorphic evolution of the Gulf is tentatively discussed. It also considers whether there is any correlation between the results obtained from Kuwait and those in other parts of the Gulf. The concluding chapter reviews the procedures followed in this work and the results obtained.

Chapter 2

# Summary of relevant literature about the Arabian Gulf and adjacent areas

Since the coast of Kuwait extends along the north-west shore of the Arabian Gulf, it is necessary first to outline our present state of knowledge as shown in related literature about the Gulf and adjacent areas.

## 2.1 The physical characteristics of the Gulf

The Arabian Gulf is a shallow sea oriented in a north-west—south-east direction with an open connection with the Indian Ocean through the Strait of Hormuz and the Gulf of Oman. In general, the Gulf is located between the north-west—south-east trend lines of the folded and thrust ranges of the Zagros mountains of Iran and the pre-Cambrian Arabian Shield. The latter, which is tilted slightly towards the north-east, is covered by palaeozoic, mesozoic and cainozoic sediments (Powers et al., 1966; Evans, 1966). The low western coast of the Gulf is broken at its southern end by the Oman mountains which resulted from the folding and crushing movements that started at the beginning of the Cretaceous Period and were completed in the Mio-Pleistocene (Pilgrim, 1908).

The Zagros mountains emerged from a geosyncline squeezed between the relatively resistant mass of Iran and the Arabian foreland (Mitchell, 1958), the ranges representing a belt of folded and faulted palaeozoic, mesozoic and cainozoic rocks. The tectonic movements started in the upper Cretaceous Period, reaching their peak in the Late Tertiary and in the Pliocene (Powers et al., 1966). This area is still active as can be witnessed in the river terraces on the Makran coast (Lees and Falcon, 1952; Falcon, 1947). The geology of the Arabian Gulf has been much discussed (see e.g. Pilgrim, 1908; Geographical Section of the Naval Intelligence Division, 1918; Lees and Richardson, 1940; Henson, 1951; Evans, 1966; Mina et al., 1967; and Kassler, 1973).

The Arabian Gulf has an area of about 24,000 square kilometres and is characterized by relative shallowness. The average depth is 31 metres, and the

4

maximum depth is about 110 metres near the Strait of Hormuz as compared with depths of 900 metres found in the Gulf of Oman.

In the Gulf basin, the greatest depths occur along the Iranian coast; here the coast differs considerably in topography from the west as it is mountainous, and the mountain ranges run parallel to the coast, in some cases close to the coastline and forming cliffs through which several rivers discharge into the Gulf.

The Arabian coasts are generally low with desert characteristics and an absence of freshwater discharging into the sea. The head of the Gulf is an area of deltaic sedimentation formed by the Euphrates, Tigris and the Karun rivers. The south-west coast is generally flat except where the Oman mountains, in the extreme south, reach the sea around Ras Musandum. The south-western parts of the Gulf, especially around Abu Dhabi and the Qatar peninsula, have been studied in further detail by Houbolt (1957), Evans *et al.* (1964), Butler (1966), Evans *et al.* (1969), Kendall and Skipwith (1969), Evans (1970) and Shinn (1973).

The Gulf is also characterized by its high temperature and high rate of evaporation, with a maximum evaporation in December and a minimum in May (Privett, 1959). These conditions, together with the absence of a large supply of freshwater except from the Tigris and Euphrates river system (and these also vary seasonably), and from the Karun and some intermittent small streams flowing from the Zagros mountains, produce a high rate of salinity (Schott, 1908; Emery, 1956; Sugden, 1963; and Evans, 1970). The replacement of the loss occurs by the broad anti-clockwise surface current which brings in new ocean water affecting the distribution of temperature and salinity in the Gulf. Water made dense by evaporation sinks to the bottom and leaves the Gulf following the deeps near the Musandum peninsula (Emery, 1956; Purser and Seibold, 1973). The tidal range in the Gulf is from 2 to 3.5 metres. Winds in the Gulf are south-easterly as well as north-westerly, but the latter, known locally as the 'Shamal' (the Arabic version of the north, implying the source of wind), predominate. The Shamal is a very dry wind which blows more continuously in summer than in winter and carries a large dust load which, as well as sometimes making visibility difficult, carries terrigenous sediments to most parts of the Gulf, especially the Arabian coasts, and causes waves and surface currents.

## 2.2 Structural stability of the head of the Gulf

The north-western part of the Gulf is an area of both structural instability and extensive deposition caused by the Tigris—Euphrates and Karun rivers. The geological history of the northern part of the Arabian Gulf has been confused by two contradictory points of view put forward by archeologists and geologists. Because the structural history of this part is closely bound up with that of the area under review it is necessary to pay special attention to the viewpoints concerned.

The general thesis of the archeologists, supported by De Morgan (1900), is that the shoreline at the head of the Gulf is advancing towards the south because of the long-continued deposition of the sediments brought down by the Tigris—Euphrates and Karun rivers. Several estimates have been put forward as to the rate of accumulation and progradation of the head of the Gulf; Beke (1835) stated that originally both the Tigris and Euphrates discharged their water by separate channels into the Gulf and that during the last 2,000 years there had been an accession of land area considerably greater than 1,000 square miles. Rawlinson (1857) estimated that during the historic period the advance of the area towards the Gulf was about a mile in 30 years. According to Loftus (1857) the growth of the Tigris and Euphrates delta was a mile in about every 70 years. Geological support was given to these ideas in 1900 by De Morgan, who attempted to demonstrate that most of the land at the head of the Gulf had appeared as a result of the silt brought down by the Tigris—Euphrates and Karun rivers. He produced maps on the basis of which the Geographical Section of the Naval Intelligence Division of the Admiralty prepared a summarized map (Figure 2.1). De Morgan brought together the

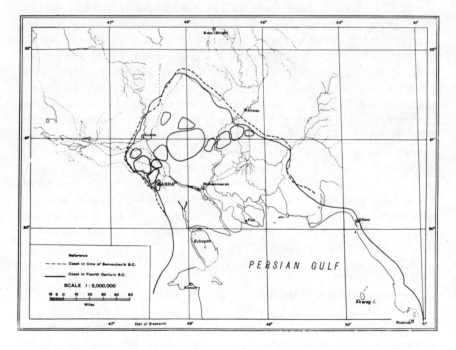

**Figure 2.1** *Advance of the Euphrates-Tigris delta since early historic times, after maps of de Morgan (from 'Geology of Mesopotamia and its borderlands', compiled by the Geographical Section of the Naval Intelligence Division, Naval Staff, Admiralty, HMSO, 1918)*

classical evidence of the changes of the shorelines since early Assyrian times. He referred to Assyrian documents which discuss the naval expedition of Sennacherib in 696 BC when he invaded Elam and he also reviewed the journey of Nearchus in 326–325 BC. Both sets of records may be interpreted as showing that the four rivers – Tigris, Euphrates, Karkeh and Karun – earlier flowed separately into the Gulf, but by the fourth century BC the sediments which were carried by the Karun and Karkeh had pushed their deltas from east to west across the Gulf and built a chain of islands which separated from the sea a lake, which later became filled by Tigris and Euphrates sediments (the lake is represented at present by marsh). As a result of the advance of the coastline, the land behind gradually dried out in places to produce the present conditions. Woolley (1938) mentioned that advancing deposition had covered many cities of older civilizations; excavation at Ur showed that there is a bed of clay which separates implements and painted pottery of an old period from the more recent remains of the Sumerian period. He attributed this deposit to the 'Deluge' which is correlated with the story of Noah in Sumerian history. Lloyd (1943), in recording the list of the kings of Sumer and Akkad, divided the chronology into two parts – before and after a great flood which occurred about 3,000 BC. He also suggested that the shoreline before 4,000 BC was about 60 miles north-west of Baghdad, while in Sumerian times it was in the neighbourhood of Ur (Figure 2.2).

Holmes (1944) and recently Sarnthein (1972) put forward a different point of view stating that the northern shoreline of the Gulf had retreated northward, and that the basin of the Gulf was a dry land during the Pleistocene Glacial Period, but after the melting of the ice sheets, the water level rose and the sea advanced northward in the Gulf depression. Lees and Falcon (1952) claimed that the picture is more complicated than the simple explanation presented by the archeologists, and that the head of the Gulf had never been north-west of its present limit since Early Pliocene. They presented a geological point of view in which they showed that the area of the head of the Gulf is structurally unstable and that the dominant vertical movement is one of crustal subsidence. They also maintained that the continued existence of the marshes and lakes at the head of the Gulf resulted from tectonic movement since otherwise they would have been silted up; they stated 'It is important that the events of the Recent history of the Mesopotamian plains should be understood, as the dominant motive is subsidence. It is not just that a static depression is being filled by river sediments; it is the long-continued subsidence which allows the sedimentation to continue. In addition to the broad and dominant downwarp there may also be local depressions caused by slight synclinal movements between anticlines which are still being gently folded. The geological evidence of the Recent history of the "Sunkland" of Iraq would seem therefore to point to continuing depression, and this is the simplest explanation of the extensive marshes.' Lees and Falcon (ibid.) also maintained that the general rise of sea-level as a result of glacial-eustatic movement had in all probability expanded prior to the time of the

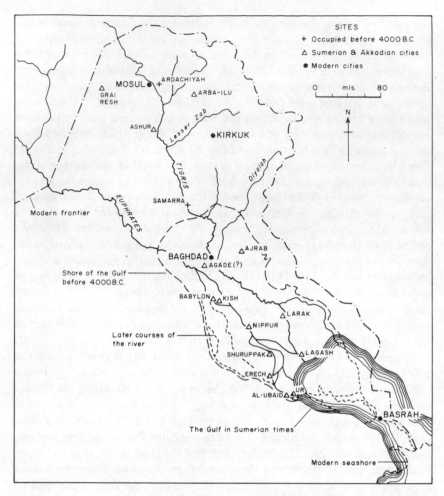

**Figure** 2.2 *Changing shorelines at the head of the Arabian Gulf (from S. Lloyd, 1943)*

earliest organized civilization in Iraq and that the marine terraces in the areas surrounding the Gulf are related to tectonic movements which are still active. The authors presented a variety of evidence to demonstrate the tectonic movements during Recent times among which is the archeological evidence from the old site at Dar-i-Khazineh dated archeologically between 4,000 and 3,000 BC and claimed that this site represents a standstill period of alluviation and occupation from 4,000 BC to 3,000 BC during which alluvium was built up. Between 3,000 BC and probably the Sassanian period, it appears that the build-up of sediments was interrupted by an erosional event. The latter was followed by deposition of coarse river gravels, sand and silt. These fluvial deposits were overlain by 2 metres of silt which was laid down into Sassanian times. According to Lees and Falcon (ibid.) the next great event occurred as a result of the rejuvenation of stream erosion which caused the exposure of the Dar-i-Khazineh site. This rejuvenation resulted from the renewed subsidence of the plain to the south-west, or from a tilting of the hill country to the north-east or from both reasons. They also recorded that Bubiyan Island of Kuwait was affected by subsidence to the north and that this is shown by the trend of the island's drainage towards the north-west and the increasing area of land in the southern part of the island. These geological points of view have been rejected by Ionides (1954) and Smith (1954). More recently, Larsen (1975) has re-examined the Lees and Falcon results in the light of more updated data about the area. He argued that the alluviation of Dar-i-Khazineh, the stream erosion and the drowned irrigation systems in the Khor Musa and Khor Zubair, do not indicate such factors but have resulted from various environmental causes. These include post-glacial sea-level movements and climatic changes as well as hydrology. Larsen (1975) mentioned that as a result of post-Pleistocene marine transgression of sea-level, stream erosion would be replaced by alluviation. Accordingly, as the sea attained its present level near 4,000–3,000 BC, the streams would tend to alluviate and hence settlements in riverine or marsh environments before 4,000–3,000 BC would at present be covered by alluvial sediments as in the case of the Dar-i-Khazineh site. The Holocene marine transgression sediments in the area are overlain by 2 to 3 metres of alluvium which, according to Larsen (ibid.), has resulted from the advance of the Mesopotamian delta by 150 to 180 kilometres during the last 5,000 years. His conclusion indicates structural stability at the head of the Gulf which disproves Lees and Falcon's results, but does not disagree with the De Morgan (1900) view although a different interpretation has been presented. Kassler (1973) has also considered the structural stability of the Tigris—Euphrates delta area in discussing an unpublished oil company report by V. S. Colter, and noted that the latter referred to the subsidence of the Kuwait part of the delta by 37 metres during the last 5,000 years. Colter used as evidence for this the occurrence of dolomitic muds in association with marine mud at −37 metres which he took to indicate shallow water conditions. The C14 dating of *Oyster* shells from the marine mud gave ages from 5,080 to 5,980 years old. However, Kassler (1973) rejected Colter's evidence and maintained that not only is dolomitization not necessarily associated with shallow marine water conditions, but there is no evidence of any occurrence of shallow-water sedimentary structures. On the contrary, he believed that the Kuwait part of the delta is relatively stable. Kassler referred to a −16/−20 fathoms (−29/−37 metres) marine platform which 'has been mapped' from offshore of Abu Dhabi to Kuwait, and held that this marine platform is similar in depth to the more or less horizontal surface identified by Colter at about −115 feet (−35 metres) on which deltaic sediments have been laid. Kassler suggested that the age of that surface is about 9,000 to 11,000 BP, and that if this corresponds to the more extensive marine platform which stretches to the south then, in general, stability characterized the Holocene with some possibility of slight subsidence.

Working in the area between Tharthar-Habbaniya and Abu Dibis in south Iraq, Mitchell (1957a) stated that there is evidence of some east–west anticlinal structural movement in the area which has blocked the continuation of an old drainage pattern. Mitchell (1958) concluded that the warping there has attained values of 25 metres during Recent times and noted that there are Recent marine fauna to be found near Najaf at heights between 40.70 and 41.30 metres above present sea-level. The possibility of Recent movements within the delta as well as the effect of changes in sea-level is strengthened by such evidence (Mitchell, 1958).

### 2.3 Morphological studies of changing sea-level in the Gulf

Very little has been written about geomorphological research into marine transgression in the Gulf, especially during the Pleistocene Period. Most of the research has been concerned with Holocene sedimentation in the Gulf, and, even then, there are large areas of the coast which have not yet been investigated. However, there are scattered studies of marine terraces and raised beaches along the Gulf coast and submarine platforms in the Gulf itself. Lees (1928), writing about the physical geography of south-eastern Arabia, mentioned that he discovered 'sub-Recent' marine shells on the west side of the Oman mountains at a height of 375 metres which have been uplifted by recent movements in the Oman mountain zone. He also found fragments of sub-Recent marine shells scattered on the surface of Wadi Hatta; the shells were in a similar state of preservation to those of the low sub-Recent raised beaches along the coast. The shells were at a height of 1,045 feet (318.5 metres) and contained *Venus* sp., *Turritella* sp., *Cerithium* sp. and *Dentalium* sp. Archeological excavation in Hasa (Saudi Arabia) by Cornwall (1946) uncovered the remains of ruined and abandoned settlements such as Uqair; this was deserted for several reasons, according to Cornwall, among which was the recession of water level by 1.5 to 3 metres. South of Al-Khobar he found remnants of elongated heaps of shells which contain *Pinctada margaritifera*. According to the evidence produced from these sites and from the pearling activity of the people living there, he came to the conclusion that the sites must represent old pearling camps, and the reason for the exposure of these heaps of shells is the recession of the sea-level of the Gulf. About 12 kilometres north of Umm ar-Ruus, there are two parallel strips of habitation sites, one an old 'medieval' field which has been partly buried by sand-dunes, and a more recent settlement on the Gulf side. The distance between the two settlements is about 2.8 kilometres, the change of the settlement location (Cornwall, 1946) resulting from a gradual retreat of the shorelines which made the settlement's inhabitants move towards the new shoreline.

From the Makran coast of Iran, Harrison (1941), Falcon (1947) as well as Vita Finzi (1975) referred to the river terraces and beaches which attain various levels as a result of uplift. Falcon mentioned that the uplifted raised beaches are at altitudes of 80–90, 30 and 15 metres above sea-level. However, Butzer (1958) suggested that the previous raised beaches were also affected by eustatic changes of sea-level; Butzer added a 60-metres level and suggested that the whole sequence then agrees with the altimetric sequence from Sicilian to Monastirian. The same sequence occurs on Kharag Island, while the shore-lines of 30 and 15 metres are found on Qishm Island and Bushire.

The result of dating two shells of the material from Makran coast gave ages of 23,390 ± 400 BP and 25,610 ± 640 BP. The samples were collected from the beach at Jask and were at a height of about 8 metres above high water, but the result is believed to be contaminated by younger carbon (Vita Finzi, op. cit.).

In 1872, Blanford indicated that the Persian coast of the Strait of Hormuz was rising, while that of Arabia was sinking. The scientific expedition carried out in the Musandam peninsula by the Royal Geographical Society (Cornelius *et al.*, 1973; Falcon, 1973; and Robinson and May, 1974) as well as the expedition by the Royal Geographical Society/Imperial College of Science and Technology on the Makran coast (Falcon, 1975); and Vita Finzi (1975) have confirmed the result obtained by Blanford (1872) and revealed new information about the Quaternary history of the areas. The Musandam expedition data, which were collected from offshore hydrographic and geo-logical work as well as from the alluvial stratigraphy, point out that the penin-sula is tilting towards the north-east. The drowned valleys of the Musandam peninsula indicate that the area is sinking towards the north-east, although the Oman mountains have been uplifted. According to Vita Finzi (1973), the vertical displacement appears to have exceeded 60 metres during the last 10,000 years. No raised beaches have been noticed in the peninsula, but there are alluvial deposits which are well exposed and called the Makhus Formation. These deposits were formed about 35,000 years ago equating with the last marine regression. The Makhus deposits have been traced inside the Gulf as cemented wadi gravels which have been covered by the Flandrian trans-gression. It seems also that the Makhus alluvial deposits were deposited at the same time as Tehran alluvium of northern and western Iran dated archeo-logically between 36,000 and 7,000 years ago (Vita Finzi, 1969).

The steps which sea-level followed to reach its present level since the beginning of the Flandrian transgression have left their marks as submarine platforms cut by still-stands of rising sea-levels. Houbolt (1957) recognized four submarine terrace-like levels around the north and east of Qatar peninsula. He called them: (1) the near-shore terrace at a depth of 3–9 fathoms (5.5–16.5 metres); (2) the first offshore terrace at a depth of 11–17 fathoms (20–31 metres); (3) the second offshore terrace at a depth of 17–28 fathoms (31–51 metres); and (4) the central Persian Gulf, which is the deepest terrace at about 30–40 fathoms (55–73 metres). All the terraces have slight dips towards the axis of the Gulf deeps and are separated from each other by clear zones of steep gradient towards the offset Gulf axis. According to Houbolt (ibid.) these four terraces or levels represent five stages of post-glacial rise of sea-level. By comparing the values of the deepest terrace (40 fathoms or 73 metres) with estimates which have been made of the amount of recession of sea-level during the Pleistocene, he came to the conclusion that the area round Qatar peninsula and most parts of the Arabian Gulf were above sea-level during periods of maximum glaciation and he assumed that these terraces resulted from eustatic changes of sea-level during the post-glacial period. Radiocarbon dating of an age of 9,910 ± 100 BP has come from Fao in Iraq and it is represented in a graph (Figure 2.3) showing the eustatic rise

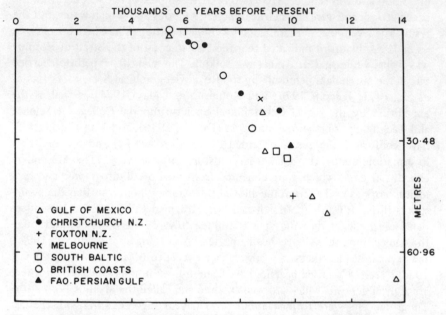

**Figure 2.3** *Eustatic rise of ocean levels (from Godwin* et al., *1958)*

of sea-level during the last 14,000 years (Godwin *et al.*, 1958). The sample is a freshwater detrital mud which represents an organic layer at a depth of about 32 metres below sea-level (Godwin and Willis, 1959),

Possibilities of high stands of the sea in the Arabian Gulf in Pleistocene times were noticed by Holm (1960). The highest sea-level implied a marine transgression at the base of present east-facing cliffs and wave-cut benches at an elevation of 150 metres. Sabkhahs at the same height were found inland, which indicates that they may have been early embayments of the Gulf at that height. Glennie (1970) has also suggested that the inland Sabkha of Umm as-Samim in Oman, which stands at an elevation of less than 70 metres, may represent a relict arm of the sea. Holm (1960) mentioned that there is evidence of a low-level shell bed at a height of 1.5 to 2 metres above sea-level along the coast between Ras al-Misha'ab and Salwah, and along the Trucial Coast. Powers *et al.* (1966) referred to marine transgression of Pleistocene age and maintained that there are marine terraces which extend along the coast of Saudi Arabia from north of Al-Jubayl to southern Dawhat Salwah. These terraces are of sand and coquina and are found at heights of 1-2 metres above mean high-tide. Along Dawhat Salwah there are well-preserved marine fossils existing in soft pebbly sandstone and coquina of maximum thickness of about 3 metres. Other Quaternary marine fossils are found about 3 metres below mean high-tide of Sabkhat Sawda Nahil. The possibility of a higher Pleistocene sea-level was suggested by Kapel (1967) who referred to C14 dating of shells which gave an age of > 39,800 years. The sample was collected from current bedded formation of calcareous sandstone which occurs as raised beaches at a height of about 25 to + 30 metres. Voute (1957) mentioned the occurrence of recent marine fauna on raised beaches of the Abu Dibbis depression in Iraq. A high sea-level of about +25 metres would be required to connect Abu Dibbis with the sea (Larsen, 1975). Radiocarbon dating of Sabkhah sediments in Abu Dhabi revealed that the Sabkhah was formed during the past 7,000 years when a marine transgression inundated the coastal area of Abu Dhabi where it reworked the coastal sandstone and reached the level of about 1 metre above present sea-level sometime before 4,000 BP (Evans *et al.*, 1969). Taylor and Illing (1969) mentioned that there are old strandlines in Qatar represented by cemented sands which stand at heights between 1.5 and 2.5 metres above sea-level. The ages of the dated samples are 3,930 ± 130, 4,200 ± 200 and 4,340 ± 180 BP. In 1972 Sarnthein presented a study of the Late Pleistocene–Early Holocene transgression in the Gulf; he maintained that during the last glacial period, the Shatt-al-Arab reached the shelf margin in the Gulf of Oman which today stands at −110 metres. Holding that throughout the Holocene the Gulf was not affected severely by tectonic movements, he supported his claim by referring to the several level surfaces at different depths which he believed to represent still-stand transgressions. The depth of these surfaces are −64/−61 metres, −53/−40 metres and about −30 metres. Kassler (1973), quoting an unpublished oil company report written by W. A. C. Russell, mentioned that Quaternary raised beaches are found on many islands of the Gulf. They are at a height of + 60 metres on Das Island, at +45 metres on Zirko and at + 18 metres on Ardhana and Qarnain Islands. He also referred to six submarine platforms of post-glacial age which occurred as a result of still-stands of rising sea-level. These platforms are mainly found in the Arabian parts of the Gulf: (1) −62 fathoms (−120 metres); (2) −55 fathoms (−100 metres); (3) −36/−44 fathoms (−66/−80 metres); (4) −16/−20 fathoms (−29/−37 metres); (5) −10 fathoms (−18 metres); (6) −5 fathoms (−9 metres). Kassler (ibid.) indicated that at present, both the north-east of the Gulf of Oman and the Arabian Gulf are tectonically stable. He built his suggestion on the occurrence and constancy of two submarine platforms at depths of −62 fathoms (−120 metres) and −55 fathoms (−100 metres). The first platform occurs in both the Gulf of Oman and the Strait of Hormuz, while the other occurs in the Gulf of Oman and the Arabian Gulf.

The picture which appears from these studies is one of continued disagreement concerning the relative importance of the dominant processes affecting the physiography. However, it is possible to conclude that during different periods of the Pleistocene and Holocene the two main forces, eustatic sea-level changes and structural instability, including isostatic changes, were variously balanced in different areas of the Gulf. One is therefore faced with a regionally varied and complex geomorphological history which can only be further elucidated by detailed studies.

# Chapter 3

# Geology and physical geography of Kuwait

Kuwait is situated at the north-western part of the Arabian Gulf and lies between latitudes 28°30' and 30°5' north and between longitudes 46°30' and 48°30' east. Kuwait is bordered on the north and west by Iraq, by Saudi Arabia in the south-west and south and by the Arabian Gulf in the east. There are several islands belonging to Kuwait, the largest of which is Bubiyan Island in the north. Summer in Kuwait is very hot with an absolute maximum temperature of 49°C and cold in winter with an absolute minimum temperature of −3°C. The mean temperature in July is 37°C and 13°C in January. The prevailing wind is NNW by west followed by SSE by east. Dust storms laden with very fine sand often occur, frequently in spring and summer. Rain is generally variable, falling between November and April. Meteorological reports covering the period 1955–67 (Directorate General of Civil Aviation), show that the annual rainfall never exceeded 195.8 millimetres.

## 3.1 Geology

Kuwait is situated at the border of the Tigris–Euphrates sedimentary basin and at the edge of the Arabian foreland, precisely the most unstable part of the Arabian Shelf (Mitchell, 1957b; Powers *et al.*, 1966). The Arabian Shelf represents the north-eastern part of the Shield which has been slightly tilted north-east towards the Tethys trough, allowing marine transgressions across the tilted area which buried the crystalline rocks beneath with relatively horizontal sediments. This region has gentle deformations but according to Milton (1967) the general dip in Kuwait towards the north-east is about 3 metres per 2 kilometres. Higginbottom (1954) indicated that there is a slight northerly dip along the Jal-Az-Zor escarpment which accords with the evidence of subsidence at Zubair and the north end of Bubiyan Island. He also mentioned that there is indication of an uplift of the whole northern shore of the Bay as there are recent marine shells on the surface of terrace-like features at the foot of the escarpment, although aerial photographs which have been taken at intervals over a number of years showed that the tendency of the uplift is at present reversed and the sea is slowly advancing. A local structure of note is the Bahra Anticline, which Cox and Rhoades (1935) describe as a symmetrical, plunging anticline exposed only in its northern parts (Figure 3.1).

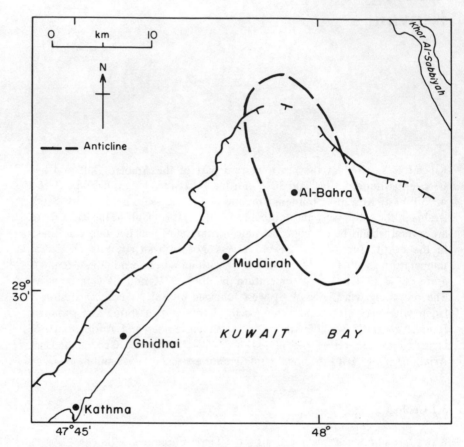

**Figure 3.1** *Approximate location of Bahra anticline (after Cox and Rhoades, 1935; and Moody, 1947)*

The tectonic history of Kuwait shows that from the Cambrian to Middle Cretaceous times it was exposed to a steady downwarping which gave way to the accumulation of sediments. That was followed by uplift movement, then renewed general subsidence during the Upper Cretaceous and the Eocene with the main structures steadily rising relative to their surroundings (Fox, 1959). The Zagros orogeny in Iran had small-scale effects on Kuwait, limited to gentle folds superimposed upon earlier uplifts occurring since Upper Cretaceous time.

Local interruptions of the general north-eastern gradient of the sediments are not obvious except along the coastline zone. The features in that zone can be attributed not only to structural movements of Tertiary–Quaternary origin, but also to the rejuvenation of the older structural elements probably of the Mesozoic Era. Evidence from seismic, aeromagnetic and gravity surveys has served to identify a fundamental lineation in basement rocks below Kuwait. The structure termed the 'Kuwait Arch' has a north–south orientation and extends from the Wafra area in the south of Kuwait to at least as far north as the Zubair area in southern Iraq. It has exerted the predominant influence upon Mesozoic folding and upon contemporaneous and subsequent sedimentation patterns in the area. Isopach maps of post-Cenomanian stratigraphic units show the evidence of continental growth beyond the Mesozoic and possibly throughout the Cainozoic (Davies, C. C. S., personal communication). Several features are found related to the 'Kuwait Arch' as in the gentle arching within the Jal-Az-Zor escarpment and the remnant surface heights of the Burgan hills and the elevated areas of Magwa field. Moody (1947) noted that it is possible that the Kuwait Arch continues into Saudi Arabia and that in the Kuwait area at least it is still undergoing uplift at the present time.

According to Milton (1967), the Ahmadi Ridge is related to the Zagros orogeny of post-Eocene times and appears to have resulted from horizontal compression, while the growth of structures such as Umm Gadir, Manageesh and Raudhatain is the result of vertical movement which has been growing since at least the Middle Cretaceous and are possibly as old as the Late Jurassic. It is also possible that the axis of the Ahmadi fold continues under the Bay of Kuwait and is responsible for the change of the direction of the Jal-Az-Zor escarpment behind Al-Bahra and for the elevated area at Al-Rakham (Higginbottom, 1954). Fox (1959) mentioned that the Burgan and Magwa elevations are uplift features of salt intrusion. This phenomenon of salt purges is common in the surrounding areas, the nearest being Jabal Sanam, south of Iraq. The origin of the Jal-Az-Zor escarpment has not been definitely determined. However, Owen and Nasr (1958) and Fuchs *et al.* (1968) related it to faulting origin with some kind of relationship with the Wadi Al-Musannat in the south-west of the country, disagreeing with Milton (1967) who described the escarpment as being possibly an erosional feature because no indication of a tectonic origin has been discovered in oil wells in the Al-Bahra area.

The phenomenon of the raised beaches which appears in Mina Sa'ud and Ras Al-Jlay'ah in the south but dies away towards Salimiyah, and similarly occurs between the Sabbiyah promontory and the head of the Khor Al-Sabbiyah has been interpreted by C. C. S. Davies (personal communication) to have resulted from the progressive tilting of the surface towards the north, with the southern sector acting independently from the northern, and separated by an ENE–WSW line of discontinuity in Kuwait Bay (Figure 3.2). The line of separation between the two blocks is believed to be a right-lateral transcurrent fault in the pre-Cambrian, striking NE–SW and generated at the time of the Zagros folding as a result of the arcuate drift of Arabia away from

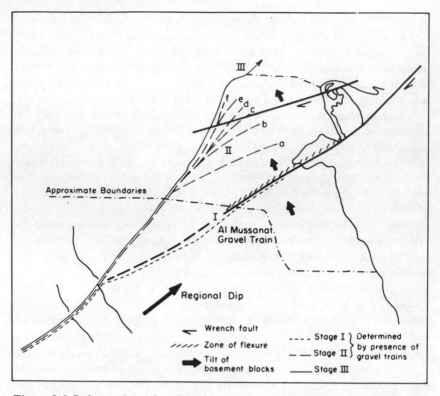

**Figure 3.2** *Relationship of surface drainage to tertiary tectonics (after C. C. S. Davies, personal communication)*

the African continent. However, he mentioned that there is no confirmation of its existence in the geophysical survey results and the only indirect evidence for its position can be offered from consideration of possible surface effects. Accordingly, Davies thinks that the Jal-Az-Zor escarpment originated as a flexure in cover rocks overlying the basement fault which has subsequently been cut by the joint action of fluviatile and the marine erosions with the latter postdating the former and becoming the main influence agent. River channels extended in an almost straight line along this flexure over a distance of several hundred kilometres and flowed north–eastward from the Arabian highlands in the direction of southern Kuwait. The previous characteristics indicate control by a fundamental structure lineation with surface expression and a flexure which has provided the appropriate control. The distribution of the gravel trains west of Kuwait suggests that they represent several stages in stream migration from an original Musannat–Kuwait Bay flow to the more recently developed channel of the Wadi Al-Batin (C. C. S. Davies, personal communication).

*Stratigraphy of surface deposits*

The surface of Kuwait is formed of sedimentary rocks of Middle Eocene to present age (Fuchs *et al.*, 1968). The very slight dip and the lithological similarity of most of the sedimentary strata, together with the lack of fossil evidence, make correlation of formations difficult. It is only along some parts of the Jal-Az-Zor escarpment that three formations can be distinguished because of the presence of the fossiliferous Lower Fars Formation (Figures 3.3 and 3.4).

Fuchs *et al.* (1968) have provided the most recent classification of the surface rocks in Kuwait, a classification which is largely followed in this study.

### Dammam Formation (Middle Eocene)

This is the oldest sedimentary rock exposed in Kuwait. Parsons (1963), quoted by Fuchs *et al.* (1968), recorded that the highest point of the top of this formation was encountered at a depth of about 80 metres southwest of Kuwait. The formation has a gradual dip towards the north and north–east except for the slight interruption by local structures. It appears at a depth of about 400 metres at Raudhatain. The approximate thickness of the Dammam Formation is 200 metres. Parsons (1963) divided this formation into three parts according to lithological criteria, from bottom to top as follows:

1 Lower Dammam (Group 3)
   Shelly, chalky-to-granular porous limestone with hard siliceous cherty limestone on top
2 Middle Dammam (Group 2)
   Composed of chalky, locally shelly limestone with thin siliceous cherty limestone at the top and siliceous limestone with sand-beds at base.
3 Upper Dammam (Group 1)
   Dense dolomitic limestone, with a lower fossiliferous dolomitic limestone, thin and green shale beds at base.

According to Fuchs *et al.* (1968), this subdivision of the formation makes it possible to recognize the intensity of erosion which took place from Late Eocene to probably Early Oligocene times.

### Ghar and Lower Fars Formation (Oligocene? to Lower Miocene)

*Ghar Formation II* This formation is easy to identify especially in the Jal-Az-Zor escarpment because of the overlying fossiliferous Lower Fars Formation. The Ghar Formation is composed of coarse-grained, pebbly, current sandstones with intercalation of sandy limestone and marls.

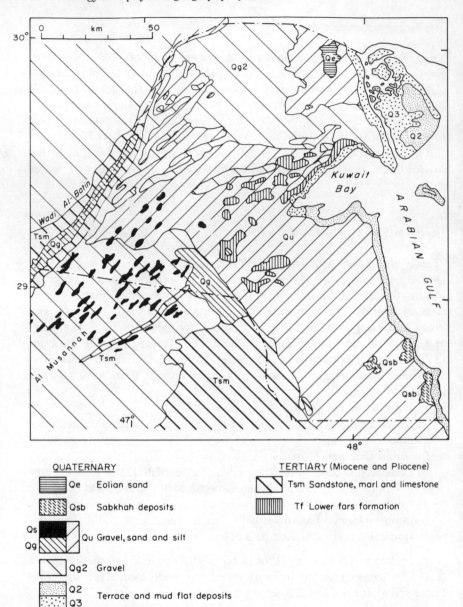

**Figure 3.3** *Geology of Kuwait (from geologic map of Arabian peninsula, US Geological Survey, 1963)*

According to Owen and Nasr (1958), there is a close similarity between this clastic formation and the overlying clastic Dibdibba Formation. In case of the absence of the middle fossiliferous bed of Lower Fars Formation, reference to all three formations is included in the so-called 'Kuwait Group'.

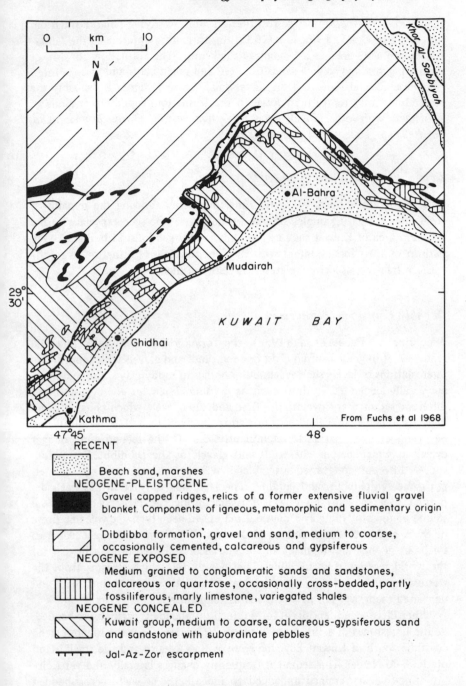

RECENT

Beach sand, marshes

NEOGENE-PLEISTOCENE

Gravel capped ridges, relics of a former extensive fluvial gravel blanket. Components of igneous, metamorphic and sedimentary origin

'Dibdibba formation', gravel and sand, medium to coarse, occasionally cemented, calcareous and gypsiferous

NEOGENE EXPOSED

Medium grained to conglomeratic sands and sandstones, calcareous or quartzose, occasionally cross-bedded, partly fossiliferous, marly limestone, variegated shales

NEOGENE CONCEALED

'Kuwait group', medium to coarse, calcareous-gypsiferous sand and sandstone with subordinate pebbles

Jal-Az-Zor escarpment

**Figure 3.4** *Geology of the research and adjacent areas (from Fuchs et al., 1968)*

*Lower Fars Formation I*    A fossiliferous unit overlying Ghar Formation. According to Cox and Rhoades (1935) this formation outcrops in the Jal-Az-Zor escarpment area as a 38-metres thick unit. The formation consists of alternating red and yellow sandstone, red and green clays and various inter-mediate clay sandstones and silt clays. Small *Lamellibranchs* is probably the most abundantly represented fossil in the formation, found either alone or associated with other fossils such as *Ostrea vestita*, *Ostrea latimarginata*, *Turritella* sp., *Lucina* sp. and *Balanus* sp.

## Zahra Formation (Miocene-Pliocene)

This formation consists of sandy limestone often showing the remains of freshwater fossils. Examples of this formation can be seen especially in the southern area of Kuwait such as Wara hill and Burgan hills. Lithological com-parison of their fossil content with those of the Zahra Formation in south-western Iraq reveals a close relationship between them.

## Dibdibba Formation (Pleistocene)

According to Fuchs *et al*. (1968), the formation consists of a fluviatile sequence of ungraded, often cross-bedded sands and gravels with subordinate intercalations of layers such as lenticular bodies of sandy clays. The sediments are locally cemented by lime such as gypsum. Fuchs *et al*. suggested two different sedimentary cycles: the first and older cycle which consists of all deposits older than Dibdibba Formation is characterized by a uniformly heavy–mineral association (predominantly zircon); the second and younger cycle, to which belong the sands and gravels of the Dibdibba Formation, shows different and varied assemblage of heavy minerals such as garnet, pyroxene, amphiboles and epidote. The Dibdibba Formation has been de-posited over the area by powerful rivers during the Pleistocene, and the source of most of the gravel material may have been the large volcanic flows of Syria and northern Arabia of Pliocene and Pleistocene age, according to Fuchs *et al*. Also during many of the glacial periods of Europe, this part of the world was experiencing pluvial periods during which streams from the western mountains, fed by considerable precipitation, carried their loads and deposited them over this part of the Arabian peninsula.

Other Pleistocene deposits of fine-grained thin-bedded, partly cross-bedded, oolitic limestones of a thickness of up to 10 metres, form the low but steep coastline south of Kuwait Bay, the spur of Ras Ashairij and the small island of Umm Al-Nemel. This sediment frequently changes laterally and vertically into fine-to-coarse-grained unbedded to indistinctly or well-to-cross-bedded local firmly cemented quartz sandstone with a varying content of oolitic grains and of sporadically reworked reddish-brown clay balls (Fuchs *et al*.). They commonly contain relics of molluscs which correspond to recent shells.

*Recent deposits*

These are composed of deltaic and tidal mudflats, and are found around the north shore of Kuwait Bay and along the north-east coast of Kuwait and Bubiyan Island. According to Milton (1967), these deposits are composed of plastic clay and silt having a high saline content. The material is considered to be of deltaic origin from the Tigris–Euphrates river system.

'Coral rocks', which are composed of stratified, porous, often poorly consolidated calcareous sandstones with a varying content of fossils, are found in the tidal zone of the southern edge of the Bay of Kuwait and around the isles. Reworked reef material, comprised of organic debris and high-quartz sand, firmly cemented, surrounds the small isles of Kubbar and Umm Al-Maradim (Fuchs *et al.*, 1968). Playas, represented by a thin sheet of silty clays, cover the bottom of small shallow basins in the interior of Kuwait. Windblown deposits are found covering wide areas of the state. Salty marshlands (sabkha) extend along the southern coast and the northern shore of Kuwait Bay.

## 3.2 Topography

Apart from the Wadi Al-Batin, Jal-Az-Zor escarpment and the Ahmadi ridge, Kuwait generally has a gentle surface and the altitude arises from sea-level in the east to about 300 metres in the south-western part of the country (Figure 3.5). The greater part of Kuwait and especially the north and west part of the country is covered by sand and gravels. According to Fuchs *et al.* (1968) northern and south-western Kuwait represent parts of a wide pediment formed during Pleistocene times by rivers or sheet floods. Holm (1960) stated that the Rimah–Batin Wadi system was one of active surface-water action during the pluvial periods of the Pleistocene. It carried its debris, which was composed of igneous, metamorphic and sedimentary rocks eroded from the crystalline uplands and sedimentary steppes of north Najd, and spread towards the north-east of the Arabian peninsula as a coastal plain called Ad-Dibdibba. The Wadi Al-Batin forms a conspicuous negative feature extending along the west border of Kuwait. It has a SSW to NNE direction of about 150 kilometres in length. According to Cox and Rhoades (1935), the Wadi Al-Batin feature is the result of stream erosion, the course of which was no doubt controlled by a tectonic line of unknown character. Owen and Nasr (1958) mentioned that it may be due to subsidence recurring along a north-east–south-west, deep-seated line of faulting. Al-Batin and Al-Musannat wadis are both thought by Fuchs *et al.* (1968) to represent old tectonic lines. The width of Wadi Al-Batin varies from 6.4 kilometres at Hafar to about 3.2 kilometres at Riqat (ar-Ruqi) but it is very broad and shallow at Ratk near its end. However, Higginbottom (1954) suggested that Wadi Al-Batin is con-

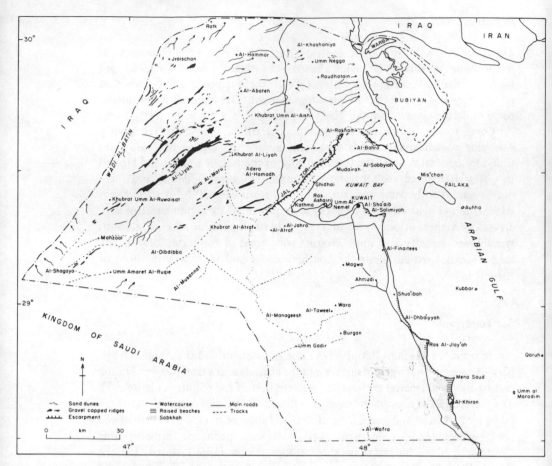

**Figure 3.5** *Topography of Kuwait (based on several sources)*

structed near its downstream end at Jraischan and widens towards its up-
stream. Also the numerous depressions around there tend to converge and
meet at Mahzool. He came to the conclusion that the former drainage of
Wadi Al-Batin was of south-western direction towards the Arabian interior,
but as a result of the geosynclinal subsidence around the Zubair area, the
drainage pattern had become reversed. West of Kuwait the plain is dissected
by north-eastern, parallel, elongated depressions, separated by gravel-capped
ridges and holding some vegetation for some parts of the year. The northern
and north-western parts of the country are covered by drainage systems of
different sizes and patterns. Khalaf (1969) mentioned that their patterns
range from long wadis as in the Raudhatain–Al-Abateh and Al-Hammar–Liyah
areas to those small in size as in Al-Sabbiyah area. There are dendritic drainage patterns in the gravelly areas such as in Raudhatain–Al-Abateh and Al-
Shagaya areas. Parallel and sub-parallel drainage patterns are found in the

Hammar-Liyah area, and pinnate drainage in Sabbiyah towards Khor Al-Sabbiyah. There are no true sand-dunes in Kuwait except in the area between Al-Khashaniya and Umm Negga in the north. The height of these crescent dunes is about 25 metres.

One of the most conspicuous features in Kuwait is the Jal-Az-Zor escarpment which extends north of Kuwait Bay for a distance of about 65 kilometres with a maximum height of about 145 metres. From Al-Atraf the escarpment follows a north-eastern direction until near Al-Bahra where it changes its course and swings to the south-east. According to Fuchs *et al.* (1968), there are several terraces developed at the foot of the escarpment reflecting the sea-level changes during the Pleistocene Period. Behind the escarpment the surface slopes gently towards the north. West of Jal-Az-Zor there are several gentle ridges such as Kura Al-Maru and Al-Liyah. They tend to take a north-eastern direction and are usually dissected by depressions. Numerous depressions which are usually called 'Khubrah' or 'Themaila' are distributed over Kuwait, e.g. Umm Gadir, Umm Al-Aish, Umm Amaret Al-Ruqie, Al-Atraf, Umm Al-Ruwaisat.

The southern part of the country is generally featureless except for some depressions or hills. The only conspicuous feature is the Ahmadi ridge which has an elevation of about 137 metres. It lies about 8 kilometres inland, with both the east and west slopes being very gentle. The ridge separates the coastal plain from the plain of Burgan and it is related to the Zagros orogeny of post-Eocene times. Apart from the Ahmadi ridge there are the conical hills of Wara with a local relief of about 30 metres and the Burgan with a height of about 46 metres.

### 3.3 General remarks on the coastal geomorphology

The coast of Kuwait is generally of lowland type with conspicuous features of low character which are partly covered during tidal flow, e.g. the north coast of Kuwait Bay especially around Al-Bahra. It is also characterized by the presence of numerous coves extending along the southern coast of Kuwait Bay. Parallel to the coast there are several islands extending from Warba in the extreme north to Bubiyan, Mis'chan, Failaka, Auha, Umm Al-Nemel, Kubbar, Qaruh and Umm Al-Maradim. The first two islands are greatly affected by the sediments brought down by the Tigris–Euphrates river system. The north part of Bubiyan Island has a northern dip towards the north and accords with the general subsidence at Zubair area (Lees and Falcon, 1952), while the southern part of the island is characterized by a system of strandlines which may represent a storm beach. Extensive deltaic mudflats of sandy and silty clay deposits spread across the north-east coast. Perry and Al-Refai (1958) mentioned that the 6 metres of uplifted cliffs at Ras Al-Jlay'ah on the south-east coast of Kuwait are formed of oolitic sandstone; they also claim that this deposit, as well as containing fossils of Recent age, is similar to the deposits which extend along the Saudi Arabian coast in the south, suggesting eustatic lowering of the shoreline. Fuchs *et al.* (1968) referred to the Pleistocene deposit which consists of fine-grained, thin-bedded, partly cross-bedded oolitic limestone of a thickness of up to 10 metres; it spreads south of Kuwait Bay, the spur of Ras Ashairij and Umm Al-Nemel Island. The deposit often changes laterally and vertically into fine-to-coarse-grained unbedded to indistinctly or well-to-cross-bedded firmly cemented quartz sandstones with varying amounts of oolitic grains. According to Milton (1967), these sediments are of recent deposition. Examples of these formations have been noted by the author on the southern coast near Al-Dhba'iyyah and around Al-Jlay'ah at a height of about 5 metres above Kuwait Land Chart Datum. The deposit often contains relics of recent shells. Higginbottom (1954) mentioned that there are recent marine deposits which include shelly sands and other deposits, often with calcareous cementing agent. The deposits extend along the southern coast of Kuwait Bay and continue south of Kuwait territory along the coast of the Arabian Gulf. More recently, Khalaf (1969) mentioned that the calcareous sandstone has a thickness which varies from a few centimetres at Al-Sabbiyah to about 4 metres at Ras-Ashairij, and merely consists of oolitic limestone with some shell fragments at Al-Khiran. According to Khalaf these rocks contain fragments of shells which are similar to those in recent beach sediments and hence he considered them to be Recent marine 'terrace' deposits. An extension of this marine terrace has been noticed during the fieldwork in Al-Sha'aib area, although it has no lateral continuation with that mentioned by Khalaf in Al-Salimiyah because most of the sands of this part of the coast have been used for building purposes.

Little else is factually available concerning the geomorphology and terrain characteristics of Kuwait. It is in the context of the data which are available and which have been presented in Chapters 2 and 3 that we shall consider the specific research work carried out in Kuwait.

# Chapter 4

# Methods

Three methods were used to carry out the present work:

1 The survey of morphological features including levelling.
2 The radiocarbon dating of shells.
3 The analysis of sediments by particle-size analysis and scanning electron microscope.

It was decided to apply these methods in order to help in correlating the field data. The reasons for the choice of methods are examined below. Besides these methods, topographic maps (scales 250,000 and 100,000) and aerial photographs were consulted.

## 4.1 Levelling

Surveying is an important technique in the study of raised beaches and the present survey was carried out for the following purposes:

1 To trace and determine the number of the terraces around the north coast of Kuwait Bay, between Kathma in the west and Al-Bahra in the east.
2 To measure their height above Kuwait Land Chart Datum.
3 To elucidate the tectonic history of the area and to find out whether or not these terraces are horizontally warped, and if so, how much and in which direction.
4 To reveal any relationships, if they exist, between the present area of research and the Mesopotamia area.

First, the choice had to be made of the position and alignment of the transect lines. A reconnaissance was made of the Kuwait coastline in order to identify significant stretches of coastal zone in which, as noted in Chapter 1, there was little or no human disturbance of materials and slopes. The research area was the only such zone existing, and it also had the positive advantage of possessing the largest height amplitude over relatively short distances – up to about 145 metres amplitude over 3 to 5 kilometres. In this area, four trigonometrical stations had been established before 1961 by the Kuwait Oil Company with reference to the Admiralty chart datum and located on the top of the escarpment.

At the request of the author and the Botany Department of the University of Kuwait, the Kuwait Municipality established two temporary bench-marks by reference to a KOC trigonometric station or bench-mark. The temporary bench-mark at Mudairah was surveyed from trigonometric station K16, and that at Kathma from bench-mark 1491 (Table 4.1).

**Table 4.1** *List of the stations which have been used for levelling*

| Station | Location | Height | Source |
| --- | --- | --- | --- |
| *TBM | Kathma | 3.37 m | Municipality of Kuwait |
| K16 | Ghidhai | 110.12 m | Kuwait Oil Company |
| TBM | Mudairah | 83.13 m | Municipality of Kuwait |
| K14 | Al-Bahra | 94.21 m | Kuwait Oil Company |
| M3 | Al-Bahra | 80.61 m | Kuwait Oil Company |
| M4 | Al-Bahra | 60.38 m | Kuwait Oil Company |

*Temporary bench-mark.

The number of levelling transects which could be surveyed was in part determined by the maximum number of accurate bench-marks and trigono-metrical stations which were established or could be provided since errors could be minimized by working from such points. During the first field season between April and August 1971, during which it was necessary to complete the levelling programme, the time available was limited considerably by the weather, in particular by dust storms. It was finally decided to choose seven transect lines, each of which could be based on a fixed bench-mark, or on a surveyed point which could be established from such a bench-mark. Each transect was also chosen, following reconnaissance on the ground, so as to cross the longest and best-defined terrace fragments. The location is shown in Figure 4.1.

The procedure adopted in each case was to open the traverse at a height point established as described above. A line of constant direction was first marked by ranging poles aligned by prismatic compass from the starting point. The sequence of each traverse is described individually below.

The survey was carried out using a Kern automatic level GKI-A. The readings were taken to the nearest millimetre, by estimation; all distances were measured optically which increased the speed of taking the measurements. In all the cases, a metric staff was used and foresights and backsights taken on each station; the sightings were taken in full daylight. The actual distance between stations was determined very largely by the detailed ground topography. Surfaces in most cases were extremely uneven and changes in

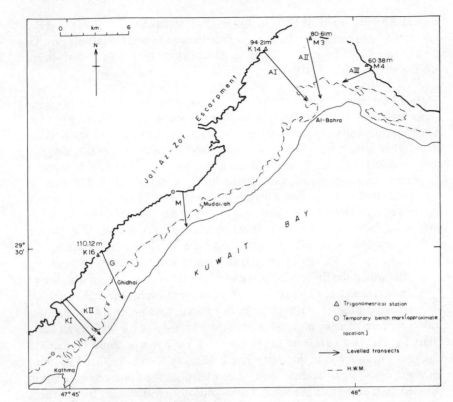

**Figure 4.1** *Location of the profiles*

gradient often extreme over short distances, particularly on the higher terraces; therefore some levelled distances had to be as short as 2 metres.

Given the very small number of trigonometrical stations and bench-marks to which reference could be made, together with the fact that all but one of these were located on the Jal-Az-Zor, it was impossible to close each traverse. Checking adjustment traverses made before levelling commenced indicated that, over an open traverse of up to 5 kilometres, height measurement was accurate within ± 1 metre. Thus, while the detailed measurements of heights are presented in Table 5.1, the values obtained from the survey indicate differences between terrace heights all of which are significantly greater than the possible levelling error. There is no statistical invalidation of later analysis or of the preservation of terrace correlations in Figure 6.1 or Table 8.1, arising from this element of survey error. This question is further examined in Chapter 6.

*Procedure*

A series of seven lines of levelling were run along the Jal-Az-Zor escarpment towards the present coast north of Kuwait Bay (Figure 4.1), starting from the west in Kathma, towards the east in Ghidhai, Mudairah and Al-Bahra areas. The profiles are coded as follows according to their location: Kathma profiles are KI and KII, Ghidhai profile is G, Mudairah profile is M and Al-Bahra profiles are AI, AII and AIII.

*Kathma I* Owing to the lack of trigonometric stations and bench-marks on the upper surface of the escarpment in Kathma, it was necessary to carry out the survey starting from a temporary bench-mark in the lower part of the Kathma coast. This temporary bench-mark was fixed by Kuwait Municipality by running a line of levelling from bench-mark No. 1,491 west of Kathma to its present location, which was chosen by Kuwait University. However, it was found that the temporary bench-mark was, first of all, not very accessible in distance from the present area of research. Secondly, the point was covered by the sea for most of the time. Accordingly, it was decided to choose a third levelled point inland which was at a height of 3.37 metres and at a distance of 100 metres from the first point which was often covered by water. Regarding the first obstacle, a line of levels which covered a distance of 3,852.2 metres was run from a point 3.37 metres towards the east to a point of suitable position at a height of 6.53 metres. A value of 0.47 metre was added in order to establish heights which would match with the Kuwait Land Chart Datum. (Kuwait Land Chart Datum is 0.47 metre above Kuwait Oil Company measurement, the latter is the same as Admiralty Chart Datum.) This would also make it easier to find out whether there was any correlation between the features of the present area and other features on the southern coast which elevation data depended on the Kuwait Land Chart Datum. From the last point which has a height of 7.0 metres (6.53 + 0.47) above Kuwait Datum a line of levels was run towards the escarpment. During the levelling it was possible to pick up several breaks of slopes which tended to become more distinguishable as one progressed towards the escarpment. The surveying ended on the upper surface of the escarpment behind which the surface slopes gently towards the north. The line covered a distance of 4,523.2 metres.

*Kathma II* The starting point for this line was established by levelling from the last point in line with Kathma I to a point of elevation at 93.37 metres. From this point a series of levels were run down the escarpment towards the coastline. When completing the survey several breaks of slopes were also noted. The line covered a distance of 4,333.4 metres.

*Ghidhai* Trigonometric station No. K16 at an elevation of 110.12 metres was used to run a series of levels. According to the Kuwait Oil Company, the height of the trigonometric station refers to the top of the concrete pillar. As the levelling was carried out while the metric staff was on the ground, 0.61 metre, representing the height of the concrete pillar, was deducted from 110.12 metres. A value of 0.47 metre was added and, according to the previous procedure, the height of the starting point was 109.98 metres. From trigonometric station No. K16 the survey was run towards a suitable position at a height of 108.921 metres. Then the levelling was carried out from the top of the escarpment towards the present shoreline. During the working of this line it was noticed that some of the terraces were strewn with shells, and also that there was a greater number of terraces along this line than in the Kathma lines. The distance of the surveyed line was 4,500 metres.

*Mudairah* A temporary bench-mark was established in Mudairah by Kuwait Municipality for the purpose of the present research. The elevation of the point was decided by running a series of levels from trigonometric station No. K16.

The height was given as 83.13 metres. A difference of 0.47 metre was added which gave a fixed height of 83.60 metres. As was previously done with the other lines, the levelling was carried out from the temporary bench-mark to a suitable position at a height of 82.25 metres. The survey then continued down the escarpment for a distance of 3,057 metres during which several terraces were noticed. Until Mudairah, the Jal-Az-Zor escarpment runs more or less parallel to the coast.

*Al-Bahra I* In Al-Bahra, the surveying was carried out in three areas. The escarpment here tends to follow a north-east direction. The first line is located west of Al-Bahra and a trigonometric station was used. The concrete pillar of the trigonometric station No. K14 has a height of 94.21 metres. The metric staff was on the ground and hence 0.61 metre was deducted, then 0.47 metre was added, giving a fixed height of 94.07 metres. From this point, which is located on the upper surface of the escarpment, the levelling was carried on down the escarpment for a distance of 5,724.6 metres.

*Al-Bahra II* Surveying for this line was carried out from trigonometric station No. M3 at a height of 80.61 metres. The first reading was taken while the metric staff was on the concrete pillar, so it was only necessary to add 0.47 metre. The elevation of the trigonometric station was 81.08 metres. A series of levels was first run to the west of the pillar to a point 76.65 metres in height. The levelled line covered a distance of 5,301.7 metres.

*Al-Bahra III* The last line of levelling is in the east portion of Al-Bahra area, where the survey started from a trigonometric station No. M4 which, according to the Kuwait Oil Company (see Table 4.1), has an elevation of 60.38 metres. The station is situated on the upper surface of the escarpment. The metric staff was placed on the concrete pillar and hence a value of 0.47 metre was added which gave an ultimate height of 60.85 metres. From that point, a series of levels was carried out first towards the east to a temporary point established at an elevation of 55.27 metres. The surveyed line towards the coast covered a distance of 2,744 metres. The results of the levelling are given in the following chapter.

## 4.2 Radiocarbon dating technique

In order to obtain some absolute chronology for the terraces it became necessary to select material from the terrace surfaces which would be associated
with their formation and also was suitable for one of the dating techniques.

One such type of technique commonly used is radiometric and, specific-
ally, radiocarbon dating. Radiometric analysis would have to be carried out in
specialized laboratories and, of these, a greater number are able to carry out
contract work for radiocarbon dating than for any other method. Moreover,
the radiocarbon dating method is now a well-established process which has
been used in the great majority of studies in changing sea-levels. The degree
of precision of dating by using this method has been reasonably well-established and most of these technical problems are identified by specialists in
this field.

This is a method used effectively in determining geological and prehistoric
chronology. The specific prognosis of the occurrence of radioactive carbon
(C14) in the atmosphere was made by Libby in 1946. In 1947 Anderson *et al.*
pointed out the potentiality of using C14 for the age determination of
organic matter. Subsequently Libby *et al.* (1949) made first world-wide
measurements of C14 residual from specimens of wood, peat, charcoal and
other organic matter. The method was later given a somewhat surer founda-
tion in archeology by comparing the age obtained by the C14 method with
archeological objects whose ages were already known within narrow limits
from other evidence; early Egyptian materials were particularly useful. The
results were generally found to be satisfactory (Arnold and Libby, 1949),
but since then, further research has been carried out and has led to extra
refinements in the technique.

The radiocarbon dating technique itself was described by Libby in 1955.
The fundamental assumption of the theory can be summarized as follows:
C14 is formed in the upper atmosphere under the influence of cosmic rays.
This C14 mixes freely with atmospheric carbon dioxide and achieves a
theoretically uniform global distribution; for this reason, taken with carbon
dioxide into all living organisms, radioactive carbon is present in the structure of all creatures, plants or animals. As soon as the organism dies, there
will be no further uptake or exchange of radiocarbon. On the contrary, the
radioactive carbon present in the dead organism will disintegrate at a rate
corresponding to a half life of 5,730 years and therefore the proportion of
radiocarbon found in a fossil can be used to give the age of the sample.

The span of dating enabled by present techniques reaches back to a
maximum of 70,000 years and the objects acceptable for this technique
include all organic material such as wood, charcoal, shells, hair and leaves.
However, although this method has been accepted universally and has helped
in answering many questions, the results of the dating ought to be accepted
with care as there are errors which may affect the value of the technique.
Butzer (1964) and Shotton (1967) have considered the possible sources of

errors relating to this technique. These include the temporal and spatial variations of carbon 14 in the atmosphere, the contamination of old carbon-aceous matter, contamination by modern organic matter, the contamination of the samples during or after collection, as well as statistical errors concerned with the technique.

Since part of the problem of elucidating the recent geomorphological history of the Kuwaiti littoral is one of chronology of sedimentation, an attempt was made to use the radiocarbon dating technique to date suitable material in the area studied.

In the field, reconnaissance observation showed the presence on the terraces in some localities of fossil or fossil-casts of molluscs. This was the only material found and suitable for radiocarbon analysis. It was not possible in Kuwait to carry out any sampling below sea-level. The presence of molluscs fossil material was noted during the reconnaissance and levelling. The shells were found either loose on the surface or cemented onto the terrace surfaces by carbonate deposits. The origin of the uncemented shells is generally doubtful since they could have been transported by many agencies long after a first hypothetical deposition. However, where they were found in large clusters – always more than 50 and usually more than 100 contiguously – whether cemented or uncemented, it was assumed that the probability was high that they were in their original position or had been mass transported at a later date by some geomorphological process. This latter possibility would have to be taken into account after dating and during correlation.

The shells which could be validly sampled, therefore, had to be taken from those few clusters which lay within a narrow zone centred on each levelled transverse. Whenever a sample was taken from a point more than 3 metres from the traverse line, the height was calculated as accurately as possible. Such non-levelled heights were recorded and are shown in Table 5.3. Each sample contained up to ten shells selected for their contiguity regardless of species. In all, over twenty-five samples were collected from those sites which, on the basis of clustering and lack of disturbance, appeared most suitable. A constraint on sampling resulted from the need to transport all the samples to Durham and from the limitation of identification and analysis facilities.

Shell samples for radiocarbon dating were collected in polythene bags and no further treatment was given to them before submitting for analysis. The minimum weight of each shell sample sent to the laboratories was 20 grams. The amount of material actually analysed by each laboratory had to be at their discretion. The shell assemblages have been obtained from different parts of the research area (see Chapter 5.1). They occur either in shell beds covering parts of the terraces, as in Kathma and Ghidhai areas, or scattered on the surfaces of the terraces. The locations of the dated samples are plotted in Figures 5.4, 5.8, 5.10, 5.14 and 5.16.

Eighteen samples have been submitted for dating of which seventeen came from the research area between Kathma and Al-Bahra. The other came from Al-Dhba'iyyah area which is located on the southern coast of Kuwait, the sample coming from a terrace at a height of about 5 metres above Kuwait Datum.

The limit on the number of individual shell samples which could be dated was imposed by several factors. First, some of the group samples were contaminated during air-freight by damage to the containers. Second, there was a question of cost – that dating which was carried out cost £600. Third, most of the radiocarbon dating laboratories are heavily loaded with samples for analysis and ultimately five different laboratories had to be used to get the samples analysed. It was recognized that the results would have been more accurately comparable had they been produced in one laboratory. Other points concerning sources of errors are examined in Chapter 6. In Table 5.3 the laboratory reference, as well as sample reference, is given in each case so that the error element can be assessed. Some of the samples have been submitted to the Radiological Dating Laboratory, Trondheim, Norway. Professor F. W. Shotton has dated two samples at Birmingham and others have been dated at Sydney University Radiological Laboratory. In addition, Dr M. A. Geyh of Hannover dated one sample, and two samples have been submitted to Teledyne Isotopes of New Jersey.

## 4.3 Sediment analyses

The purpose of the analysis of the sediment is to deduce their depositional environments, which will assist in understanding the processes involved in the development of the coastal terraces as well as other physiographic features in the research area.

Two methods of investigation have been applied: (1) particle size analysis, as a main method and (2) the investigation of the sediment by scanning electron microscopy as a subsidiary technique.

### 4.3.1 *Particle size analysis*

*Introduction* Particle size analysis or mechanical analysis is an important sedimentological technique which has been greatly used for the interpretation of sedimentary particles. It may give information about the agent or environment responsible for the origin of the sediment. This includes the distinction between marine, lacustrine, fluviatile, aeolian and other deposits as well as possible knowledge about the physical properties of the transporting agent, e.g. capacity, current velocity and wave action. Investigators have become able to assume that the nature and structure of a deposit is a reflection of the sorting agent (running water, wind-wave action, etc.) which deposited sedimentary particles of different sizes, densities and shapes.

As early as 1898 and 1914 Udden used this technique as a correlative and discriminative method and noticed that there is a relationship between the type of sediment involved and the results obtained from the analysis of particle size. Since then many workers have contributed to advances in the application of this technique, some concerning themselves especially with the interpretation of results of particle size analysis, e.g. Krumbein (1934) and Otto (1938). Keller (1945) was the first to discriminate between beach and dune sands.

Identification of ancient environments on the basis of grain size has been discussed also by Moss (1962, 1963); Visher (1965); Shepard and Young (1961); and Solohub and Klovan (1970). Others have attempted to relate statistical parameters from grain-size distributions to different environments of deposition, namely Otto (1939); Inman (1952); Folk and Ward (1957); Mason and Folk (1958); Friedman (1961, 1962, 1967); McCammon (1962) and Chappell (1967).

Folk and Ward (1957) studied the grain size parameters of a bar on the Brazos River, Texas. By plotting skewness against kurtosis, they were able to interpret the genesis of the sediments. The very high or low values of kurtosis suggest that part of the sediment was sorted in a high energy region, and was then transported without change of character to another environment, possibly of low energy, where it was mixed with another type of material. This mixed type of sediment will be strongly bimodal.

Mason and Folk (1958) showed that the grain size analysis was successful in distinguishing three environments of beach, dune and aeolian flat on Mustang Island, Texas. Skewness and kurtosis are the best parameters to identify the environments because these properties reflect the changes in the 'tails' of the distribution. Beach sands had nearly normal curves, dune sands had nearly normal kurtosis but were positively skewed, while those samples of aeolian flats were positively skewed and had high kurtosis.

Friedman (1961) identified the environment of deposition and the processes involved. He analysed 267 sand samples derived from dunes, rivers, ocean beaches and lake beaches. These samples were collected from a widely distributed geographical location including Canada, the United States, Mexico, the Bahamas, Bermuda, North Africa and Hawaii. The parameters used for analyses were the mean, skewness and kurtosis. An almost complete separation of the fields of dunes and beach sand is made when the mean grain size is plotted against skewness. When plotting skewness against kurtosis for river and beach sands most of the river samples showed positive skewness as did the dune sands. However, some of the beach samples also exhibited positive skewness; these came from southern Padre Island, Texas, opposite the Rio Grande delta from which they have inherited the positive skewness. The wind and river transportation resulting from indirect flow is believed to explain the positive skewness of dune and river sands. Samples of beach origin have generally negative skewness, because sands on a marine beach are exposed to two unequal forces – the incoming waves and outgoing wash which act in opposite directions and bring the removal of the fine particles. Friedman plotted the skewness against standard deviation for beach and river sands; this method showed that sorting is helpful in distinguishing beach from river sands. Beach sands of positive skewness have a low value for standard deviation (better sorted), while the negatively skewed river sands can be distinguished from beach on the basis of their high numerical values of their standard deviation. Three fields of environments have been noticed by Friedman when standard deviation is plotted against mean size, river, dune and overlapping fields.

Khalaf (1969) investigated the grain size distribution of the beach sediments of Kuwait. The results showed that samples located in the Kuwait Bay area and near the Shatt-al-Arab area are of the clay sand type, while those collected from the south are generally of the sandy type.

Many workers tend to encourage the use of the statistical parameters as a good discriminative measurement between environments, while others have dealt with interpretation of the shape of the grain size distribution curves and relate them to specific environment of deposition.

The researches have indicated that there are three modes of transport: suspension, saltation and surface creep or rolling. These modes give the final shape of the grain size distribution of any sediment and hence information about the genesis of the sediment investigated. Reineck and Singh (1973) summarized the characteristics of the three modes:

1 *Suspension transport* The maximum grain size of sediment which may be held in suspension varies in different environments and also depends upon the hydrodynamic conditions at the time of sedimentation and their transporting medium. In general the grain size is usually less than 0.1 millimetre.

2 *Saltation transport* Reineck and Singh (1973) quoting data of the US Waterways Experiment Station (1939) showed that grains up to 1.0 millimetre in diameter were sampled 60 centimetres above the bottom. The maximum size transported by saltation depends upon different factors, e.g. the current velocity and water depth.

3 *Rolling transport* The coarsest grains in the sediment are transported by rolling, but in some fluvial sediments it is not possible to differentiate completely between rolling and saltation subpopulations. Fuller (1961) made a detailed mechanical analysis of shallow marine sediment from the coasts of the Cape of Good Hope. He suggested that in many cases the value near 2 phi represents the break between saltation and rolling subpopulations.

Doeglas (1946) attempted to recognize the genesis of deposits from visual inspection of the shape of curves plotted on arithmetic size scale. The main points of Doeglas's work on texture can be summarized in two parts: (1) the grain size distribution of a sediment is a mixture of several component distributions or populations; (2) these distributions have resulted from different transport conditions.

In 1949, Inman published a significant paper in which he related the sedimentation dynamics to textures. He pointed out that there are three fundamental modes of transport, surface creep, saltation and suspension. Sindowski (1957) classified size distribution curves and provided a careful study of the relation of sediment textures from known depositional environments to the shape of grain size curves. Spencer (1963) mentioned that all clastic sediments are a mixture of three or less log-normally distributed populations (gravel, sand and clay). He recognized sorted and truncated deposits by the shapes of the graphs. The three processes (rolling, saltation and suspension) are important in characterizing the textural parameters of river and beach sands, but while in the deposition of river sands, saltation and suspension are usually active, and commonly rolling as well, beach sands show a straight line indicating deposition by saltation only (Friedman, 1967). The size of the grains affected by each of the three modes varies, rolling or sliding affecting the grain size between 0.25 millimetres and larger than 0.50 millimetres ($+2.0 \phi$ to $< 1.0 \phi$), saltation from a finer point of about 0.14 millimetres (about $2.80 \phi$) to 0.062 millimetres ($4.0 \phi$), while suspension affects grains of less than 0.14 millimetres (about $2.80 \phi$) and especially those in the $< 62$ micron range ($4.0 \phi$).

Visher (1969) studied log-probability grain size distribution curves of modern as well as ancient environments and recognized the subpopulation within each individual grain size distribution which is related to a mode of transport (suspension, saltation, rolling), e.g. beach samples have two saltation populations which are related to swash and backwash in the foreshore zone. The truncation point differs from 1.0 to 2.0 phi. Dune sands adjacent to the beach have one saltation population which represents about 98 per cent of the distribution. The sorting of this population is the best and is indicated by a better graph slope than with the beach samples. The truncation of the coarse traction (rolling) is also between 1.0 and 2.0 phi. Marine sands, from the lower tidal flat to a water depth of about 17 feet, have three characteristics: (1) a poorly sorted, coarse, sliding or a rolling population; (2) a very well-sorted saltation population of a size range of between about 2.0 and 3.5 phi, and (3) a variable percentage of suspension population which depends upon the location of the depositional site from the source of fine clastics. The marine sand samples from the zone of breaking waves are characterized by having relatively high percentages of material of rolling population and range from a few to 80 per cent of the grain-size distribution. The saltation population is truncated at its fine end and this percentage of the suspension population is small. Last, the modern fluvial samples are characterized by a well-developed suspension population of about 20 per cent of the distribution. A truncation between suspension and saltation is between 2.75 and 3.5 phi with a saltation population range in size from 1.75 to 2.5 phi. For the present research, mechanical analysis has been carried out to investigate the grain size distribution of the sediments, from which their sedimentary origin can be deduced.

*Method* Numerous sediments have a range of size from coarse to fine particles; for such sediments, a composite method of analysis is required so that the coarse material may be sieved and the fine material then analysed by a sedimentation method. Details of these techniques have been described by several investigators, e.g. Krumbein and Pettijohn (1938); Milner (1962); Irani and Callis (1963); British Standards Institution (1967); and Griffiths (1967). More recently, Iriondo (1972) has introduced a rapid method for size of coarse sediments by using a photographic method which aims to avoid the problem of carrying heavy samples. For the present work, the British Standards Institution (BS 1377) method has been adopted.

Methods of coarse analysis involve dry and wet sieving through a nest of sieves beginning with the largest aperture sieve. The sieves are placed on an automatic shaker and the sample retained on each sieve is weighed and recorded after a finite time. For silt and clay analysis, two methods are available, the pipette and hydrometer. Both involve a gradual settling in water of a sample suspension maintained at a constant temperature. For the present work the pipette method has been applied.

The grain size analysis was carried out on 65 samples collected from different parts of the research area and along the levelled profiles (Chapter 5.1). Several authors have dealt with the sampling procedure, e.g. Thompson (1937); Apfel (1938); Emery and Stevenson (1950); Krumbein (1953 and 1954); Krumbein and Slack (1956); and Griffiths (1967).

On this basis, the samples were collected selectively rather than randomly and all the samples (except for three) were collected along the transect lines during the levelling procedure. The only three samples which were collected offset from the transect lines came from Kathma and Ghidhai, two of the samples came from the Fourth terrace west of the first levelled transect in Kathma (where a shell sample was also collected for C14 dating). The third soil sample came from the Fourth terrace in Ghidhai; it was collected from west of the levelled line and near a shell sample submitted for C14 dating.

All the samples were collected from the deposits covering the base of the terrace in order to find out the origin of the deposits laid down on the terrace base itself. Material covering the slopes was avoided because the slopes are often covered by recent windblown sands. The range of the collected samples along the transect lines covers the area from the top of the escarpment to the present beach. The purpose – as well as to distinguish the origin of the sediment on those particular sites – was also to find out the differences as well as the similarities in the historical depositional environments under which materials on the top of the escarpment, the terraces and the present beach, were laid down.

From each locality four samples were collected from a standardized depth of about 50 centimetres. This was sufficiently deep to avoid the collection of superficial and possibly recently transported material while greater depths could not have been sampled in all localities without major excavation into hard concreted masses. The four samples were combined together so as to produce a composite sample. They were collected in polythene bags fitted inside cloth bags in order to prevent the loss of the fine material in the samples and breakage during their shipment.

The question of the weight of the sample collected was decided according to several considerations, one of which was that the sample should be representative for the purpose of analysis, but small enough to be manageable for transportation (as the analyses were carried out at Durham University). Accordingly, a sample weight of about 2 kilograms was collected from each locality.

In the laboratory, the wet samples were broken by hand and put in the drying cupboard, maintaining a temperature of $105-10°C$, while the dry consolidated deposits were crushed gently in a mortar using a rubber-tipped pestle. Each sample was passed through a ¾ inch British Standard sieve, and a representative sample of 500 grams for coarse particle size analysis was obtained by a riffle. The representative sample largely depends upon the size ranges being sampled, e.g. whether a wide or small range of particles. There is no general agreement about the size of the analysed samples, as different sizes have been suggested by various authors, e.g. Krumbein (1953); Cochran *et al.* (1954); McIntyre (1959); and Gees (1969). However, a large sample will give better results than a smaller one, but one also has to remember not to overload the sieves as this will help in increasing the error of analysis. A total range from coarse sand to fine sand was mechanically analysed by automatic shaker using wet and dry sieving methods. There is no fixed time for which the sample should be shaken; Wentworth (1927) examined the question of sieving quantitatively and found that separation of particles, especially among smaller size, can never be complete. He concluded that shaking in an automatic shaker for five or ten minutes is usually sufficient. It has also been found by King (1967) and Griffiths (1967) that shaking for 15 to 25 minutes is sufficient, this being based on a compromise aimed at avoiding the wear of sieve mesh and particles which tends to take place after 20 minutes. Accordingly, it was decided that sieving the sample for 15 minutes was sufficient to produce a reliable separation of the particles.

The total amount of time involved in the analysis by coarse analysis and pipette was considerable as each sample took about 3 days from start to finish.

A further 500 grams were passed through sieve No. 8 BS for pipette and for scanning electron microscope.

The particle size categories are dependent on the type of equipment available. The present writer has used a nest of sieves which has been recommended by the British Standards Institution (BS 1377, 1967). Their grade scale is as follows:

|              | *Diameter in millimetres* |   |       |
|--------------|---------------------------|---|-------|
| Cobbles      | 200.0                     | — | 60.0  |
| Coarse gravel| 60.0                      | — | 20.0  |
| Medium gravel| 20.0                      | — | 6.0   |
| Fine gravel  | 6.0                       | — | 2.0   |
| Coarse sand  | 2.0                       | — | 0.6   |
| Medium sand  | 0.6                       | — | 0.2   |
| Fine sand    | 0.2                       | — | 0.06  |
| Coarse silt  | 0.06                      | — | 0.02  |
| Medium silt  | 0.02                      | — | 0.006 |
| Fine silt    | 0.006                     | — | 0.002 |
| Clay         | Smaller than 0.002        |   |       |

Other scales exist, as the Wentworth scale (1922), and the phi scale by Krumbein (1934). They are more convenient for presenting the data than if the values are presented in millimetres.

The advantage of this method is that small fractions are not required for the smaller particles and that for many of the common sediment sizes the results in phi units are positive (Table 4.2). The phi units are found by conversion from the millimetre scale, where phi is $-\log_2$ of the diameter in millimetres. Conversion from millimetres to phi units means that one division on the Wentworth grade scale, a commonly used scale, is equivalent to one unit on the phi scale. For every unit on the phi scale, the value on the Wentworth scale in millimetres is either doubled or halved. Negative values of phi units are the values coarser than 1 millimetre, and as the phi units increase,

**Table 4.2**  *Conversion of millimetres to phi units     Source: Page, 1955*

| Millimetres | phi units |
|-------------|-----------|
| 12.5        | − 3.64    |
| 6.0         | − 2.58    |
| 2.0         | − 1.00    |
| 1.2         | − 0.26    |
| 0.600       | 0.74      |
| 0.420       | 1.25      |
| 0.300       | 1.74      |
| 0.210       | 2.25      |
| 0.150       | 2.74      |
| 0.100       | 3.25      |
| 0.075       | 3.74      |
| 0.063       | 4.0       |
| 0.020       | 5.64      |
| 0.006       | 7.39      |
| 0.002       | 9         |

the size of the particle decreases. Nomograms for conversion from millimetres to phi units have been presented by several authors (Krumbein, 1936;
Folk, 1959), and numerical conversion tables have been made by Page
(1955) and Griffiths and McIntyre (1958). For the present work Page's
(1955) conversion table has been followed.

The results of the particle size analysis (Chapter 5.3) have been plotted as
cumulative percentage curves against phi diameter on arithmetic probability
paper. This type of paper has the advantage that the normal distribution
curve would plot on this paper as a straight line. Deviations from a normal
distribution are indicated by deflections from the straight line. Also the tail
of the curve can be of considerable importance in studying the characteristics
of the sediment.

### 4.3.2 *Sediment investigation by scanning electron microscope*

The application of the scanning electron microscope (SEM) for the investigation of sediments has been widely used in recent years for solving problems
of Quaternary geology, geomorphology and paleoclimatology. Investigators
have shown that depositional sedimentary environments can be identified
by examining the surface textures which are developed on sand grains. The
agent of deposition can be identified by studying the surface features, particularly on the quartz grains, because each agent imposes characteristic surface
features. The first results of examining the surface textures of sand grains
using the transmission electron microscope were obtained in 1962, when
valuable information about the surface textures of quartz grains was provided by Krinsley and Takahashi (1962a, 1962b, 1962c), Biederman (1962),
Porter (1962), and Kuenen and Perdok (1962). These authors concluded
that the mechanisms of transport and the conditions of the environments
of deposition characterize the nature of the quartz grain surface textures.
The surface features of the quartz grains can be observed at magnification by
using either a transmission electron microscope (TEM) or a scanning electron
microscope (SEM). In this study the SEM was used. Schneider (1970) and
Krinsley and Doornkamp (1973) noticed the advantages of using the latter
rather than the transmission electron microscope for the following reasons.
With the use of the SEM, the grain surfaces can be observed directly without
duplication which means the avoidance of artifacts and distortions. More
details can be observed by using the SEM than with TEM because when
using the TEM several small features are obliterated or distorted with the
replica method. With the SEM more than forty sand grains can be mounted
together in one single specimen stub without the need to change the specimen, while the specimen stub can also be tilted, rotated or raised and lowered
so that more than half of the surface of the grains can be directly examined.
Another advantage of the SEM is that it gives a simulated three-dimensional
view of the objects which help in the interpretation of the features.

Numerous papers have dealt with this subject and some examples will be reviewed. Krinsley and Funnel (1965) examined the surface textures of quartz sand grains of the Lower and Middle Pleistocene deposits of Norfolk, England and their results agreed with the previous investigations based on the fauna and general sedimentary character of these deposits. They also recognized several surface textures associated with glacial, littoral, and aeolian environments and with chemical etching. Soutendam (1967), quoting Cailleux (1942), mentioned that the amount of well-rounded frosted grains in a sediment increases proportionally with the intensity of wind action the sand has undergone. For instance, in desert sands about 98 per cent of the grains are well-rounded and frosted; sands from coastal dunes next to a sandy beach contain an average of 81 per cent of these grains, but the amount decreases to 0 per cent when the dunes are thin and deposited on a rocky coast. The surface textures of more than 4,000 quartz grains were examined by Krinsley and Donahue (1968) and they concluded that the characteristics of surface textures created in different environments are sufficiently distinct and uniform for these characteristics to be used as standard reference indicators for environmental identification. Hodgson and Scott (1970) applied the combined methods of size analysis as well as the electron microscope to find out whether beach sediments are present within the Lower Carboniferous Fell Sandstone of south-east Scotland and north England. The results of both confirmed the presence of beach sediments. Surface textures of the quartz sand can be affected both by mechanical and chemical weathering depending on the environments involved. Doornkamp and Krinsley (1971) have demonstrated these features from a tropical environment (Uganda).

Accordingly, and on the basis of the surface texture of quartz grains, electron microscopy has made it possible to discriminate between several different sedimentary environments.

*Method* Eighteen samples from the total of sixty-five field samples have been investigated by scanning electron microscope; the samples were taken from the same bags as the mechanically analysed samples.

Samples were prepared for the scanning electron microscope first in the laboratory by boiling in concentrated HCl to remove $CaCO_3$ and any iron staining. The samples were then washed by distilled water, dried and sieved to obtain the fine sand fraction, after which they were placed in bromoform to separate off the light grains from the heavy grains. The separated quartz grains were washed with acetone to remove the heavy liquid.

Approximately 100 grains for each sample were available for preparation for scanning electron microscope analysis. The samples were then prepared at the physics Department, Salford University, where a random sample of the prepared grains was sprinkled on the face of a small metal stub. The grains were then covered with gold palladium under vacuum. The specimen was then placed in a Cambridge Mark II scanning electron microscope and was ready for viewing.

# Chapter 5

# Presentation of data

In Chapters 1 to 3 the geological and geomorphological background of Kuwait and the area chosen for field study has been examined. The methods adopted for investigation have been outlined in Chapter 4. Here, the research data obtained in the field area are reviewed. This chapter is divided into three sections.

The first is concerned with examining the field data concerning the levelling results and description of the terraces, including the general topography of the area where the levellings were carried out. The lithology of the bedrock of the terraces is described wherever it is possible to distinguish their vertical succession. Also, the morphology of the terraces is examined, together with their heights, their superficial deposits, the location of the soil samples collected for analysis and the location of the shells which were collected for radiocarbon dating.

The second section is devoted to the marine fossils found in the area and to the results of radiocarbon dating of the shells collected during field investigation.

The last section is concerned with the results of sediment analyses, these results contributing to confirmation or rejection of hypotheses of marine action in the research area.

## 5.1 Field data, levelling results and description

The transects located in Figure 4.1 were levelled using the technique described in Chapter 4.1, and the results are plotted in Figures 5.1 and 5.2. Each profile is later presented in three forms or divisions. The first represents the complete altitudinal transect from the upper surface of the escarpment to the present shoreline; thus, in Figures 5.1 and 5.2 all the complete profiles may be compared. Second, the most significant part of the profiles has been divided into two main sections: the upper section profile and the lower

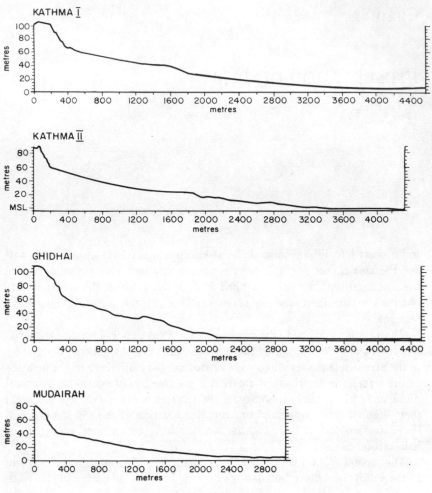

**Figure 5.1** *Complete profiles of Kathma, Ghidhai and Mudairah*

section profile. The extreme seaward parts of the profiles (except for one tran-sect in the Al-Bahra area) have not been enlarged as they are all characterized by a gentle slope and are partly covered by water at high tide. The scale of the complete profiles is uniform for all the transects, but has been modified when the profiles are enlarged into two sections. Both the upper and the lower profiles have the same vertical scale, but differ in the horizontal scale. The reason is that the terraces, especially those of the lower sections, do not appear clearly in the complete profiles, and in order to show the terraces in a manner similar to their existence in nature, either their horizontal or verti-cal scales had to be changed. At the same time, to present the profiles in a reasonably compact form, it proved better to change the horizontal rather than the vertical scale. Each profile has been further subdivided for reference

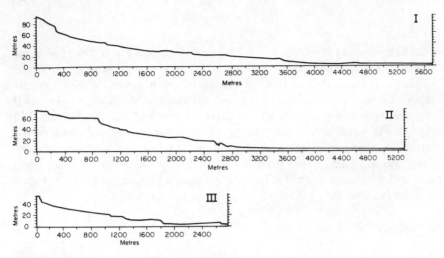

**Figure 5.2** *Complete profiles of Al-Bahra*

to individual slope elements so that the higher elements have the lowest numerical value. For example, Kathma I is further divided into KI.1 to KI.7 progressively from west to east. The lithological descriptions are given for identifiable beds in the lithological succession. The measurements given in metres are of depth below the surface of the escarpment.

*Kathma*

Two lines of levelling were surveyed in Kathma, the first area to be investigated. In general, it does not differ in its geomorphological features from the neighbouring areas to the east and west. Here, the coastal plain is covered by both marine and terrestrial deposits and can be divided into two parts, a lower and upper part according to the cover of the superficial material. The lower part is composed of a low-angle spread of beach sands and marshes and is partly covered by the sea at high tide. The upper part of the coastal plain is characterized by its 'staircase' topography. Several terraces extend along the escarpment and between the lower section of the coastal plain and the escarpment. This upper part of the coastal plain is dry throughout the year except in the rainy season. It is largely covered by terrestrial deposits and scattered with rocks and debris brought down from the escarpment. Large blocks of detrital rocks have accumulated, especially along the margin of the escarpment. The plant communities in Kathma are typically *halophytic*, becoming less so as one progresses inland away from the coast.

*Kathma I*

*Lithology and stratigraphy of the bedrocks* The bedrock is described along
the surveyed profiles. Along Kathma I (KI) it was possible to identify four
separate terraces at heights ranging from a mean height of 50.76 metres
above Kuwait Datum (KD) for the lowest terrace to 90.60 metres above KD
for the highest. The stratigraphy of these terraces was examined in the field
and it was possible in many areas to identify the vertical succession of terraces along the escarpment where erosion has exposed sections in the terraces.
This was especially so on the steep section of the escarpment where wadis
are well developed (Plate 1). The stratigraphic sequences illustrated in Figure
5.3 are as follows:

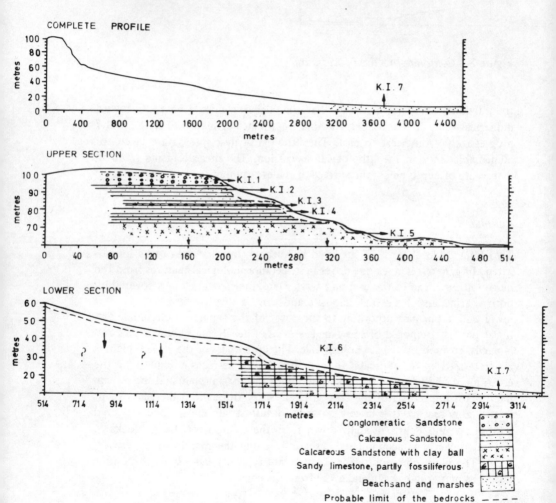

**Figure 5.3** *Profile sections of Kathma I, showing the lithology of the bedrocks*

0–0.5 metres The upper surface of the escarpment at the profile Kathma I (KI) is covered by lag gravels and windblown sands.

(KI.1) 0.5–6.5 metres below the surface, there is a horizon of fine conglomeritic sandstone cemented by carbonate.

(KI.2) 6.5–15.5 metres, a calcareous sandstone.

(KI.3) 15.5–16.5 metres. Conglomerate.

(KI.4) 16.5–27.5 metres. Calcareous sandstone of medium hardness.

(KI.5) 27.5–? metres. Calcareous sandstone with clayballs rich in gypsum. Depth unknown. (Stratigraphy at this depth uncertain.)

(KI.6) Medium-grained to conglomeratic sands and sandstone, calcareous or quartzose. Occasionally cross-bedded, partly fossiliferous, mainly limestone; variegated shales. This deposit could not be observed in studying the area, and the former description is based on the geologic map of Kuwait (Fuchs *et al.*, 1968).

(KI.7) Beach sand and marshes of Recent age.

*Morphology of the terraces* Four clear terraces have been identified along this profile (Figure 5.4). The terraces are characterized by their lack of marine deposits, apart from a few shells strewn on the lower terrace. (These are probably not *in situ*.) The superficial deposits are of terrestrial origin, and the upper surface of the escarpment is covered by lag gravels and sands of which a soil sample was collected (Figure 5.4).

The escarpment gravels have been interpreted by Cox and Rhoades (1935), Milton (1967), and Fuchs *et al.* (1968) to be of Pleistocene age; this layer has a thickness of about 50 centimetres and is strongly calcareous.

The surface of the escarpment slopes gently towards the north approximately accordant with the general dip. On its seaward face it displays a fine staircase topography. The slope of the First terrace is covered mainly by locally derived weathered material and windblown sands. The First terrace has a width of 70.80 metres and a mean height of 90.60 metres above KD. (The height of the terraces has been established by averaging the height of the relatively clearly identifiable edge of the terrace and the height of the terrace surface at its junction with the back slope; for example the height of First terrace is the mean height of 94.75 + 86.43 metres.

The reason for taking the mean height arises from the difficulties resulting from the accumulation of deposits which cover the junction between the landward point of the terrace and its slope.)

In the field it was noticed that this terrace continues laterally for some distance on either side of the chosen transect line. No positive traces either of marine erosional or depositional features have been found on this terrace and both the terrace flat and the slope above are covered with the same material. A soil sample was collected for laboratory analysis (Figure 5.4).

The Second terrace, in descending order, also has a similar character, the terrace base of this conglomerate bed joining the upper calcareous sandstone. Neither bed is exposed except in the wadi sides which trench the terraces, as its surface is veneered by fine sands and weathered conglomeratic rocks. The width of the terrace is 56.4 metres and its mean height is 77.92 metres above KD. The material covering the terrace is the same as that covering the back slope and a sample was collected from there. This terrace, too, can be followed laterally for some distance.

The Third terrace is at a mean height of 67.38 metres above KD. The surface is eroded in parts and gives rise to what looks like, in sections, another terrace, but this feature was only found on the line of levelling and is assumed to be due to aeolian erosion. A soil sample was also collected from this terrace. Sands and fine gravels also cover this terrace which has a width of 120 metres, after which it slopes gently towards the Fourth terrace. The slope is dissected by several stream beds.

The lowest terrace in this sequence (Terrace 4) is at a mean height of 50.76 metres above KD. It takes the form of an elongated hill of about 1,091 metres in width and is composed of cemented sands covered with gravels from which several samples were collected.

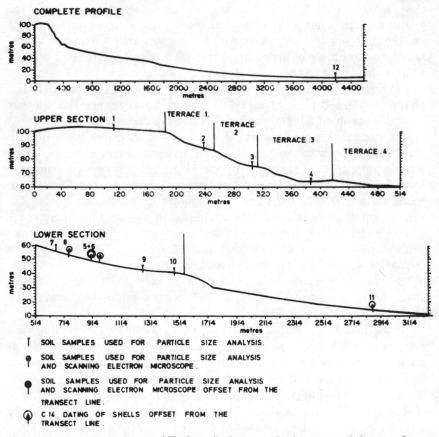

Figure 5.4 *Profile sections of Kathma I, showing the location of the samples*

1 An example of the wadis dissecting the Jal-Az-Zor escarpment

2a  A fragment of the Fourth terrace in Kathma, looking west towards the village of Al-
Jahra

2b  The fossiliferous limestone which covers the fragment of the Fourth terrace in Kathma

3   A cluster of *Ostrea* shells in Kathma

4   The cross-bedded fossiliferous superficial deposits which overlie the Lower Fars Formation

5  General view of the terraces in Ghidhai, looking from the top of the escarpment towards the south

6  General view of the terraces in Mudairah, looking east towards Al-Bahra area. Note the low topography of the terraces

7 Profile of the upper three terraces in Mudairah, view looking west

8a  An exposure of the fossiliferous bed at the edge of the Second terrace. Hammer is
resting against the bed

8b  A close-up photograph of the fossiliferous bed

9   Fossiliferous deposits at Al-Bahra

10  The lowest terrace along AII transect, showing the embayment-like feature. The dotted
    line represents the direction followed by the levelling line

11 Beach rock overlying the bedrock and forming a cliff. Note the small cave which is blocked by fallen rocks and sand

12 The superficial deposits covering the top of the escarpment. Gravels of different sizes can be noted

13  *Ostrea* sp.

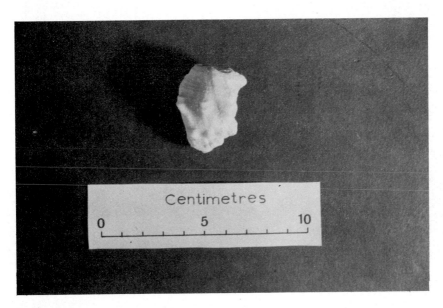

14  *Thais cainifera* (Lamarck)

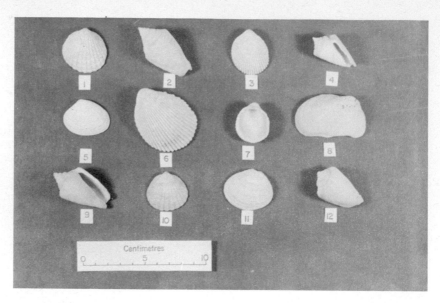

15  1, 10 *Glycymeris pectunculus* (Linné); 2, 4, 9, 12, *Strombus persicus*; 3, 6,
*Trachycardium lacunosum* (Reeve); 5, *Gafrarium arabicum* (Lamarck); 7, possibly
*Trachycardium maculosum* (Wood); 8, *Barbatia laccrata* (Linné); 11, *Circe
(parmulophora) corrugata* (Dillwyn)

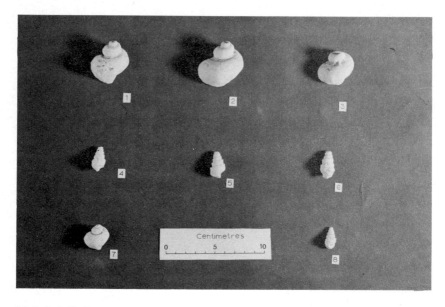

16  1, 2, 3, 7, *Turbo coronatus*; 4, 5, 6, 8, *Cerithium*

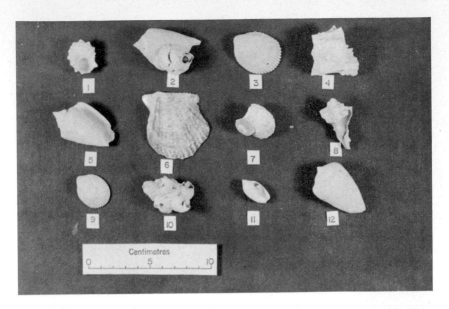

17  1, 7, *Turbo coronatus* (Gmelin); 2, *Strombus persicus* and *Veremetus sulcatus (?)*; 3, *Trachycardium lacunosum* (Reeve); 4, 8, *Murex küsterianus*; 5, 12, *Strombus persicus*; 6, *Pinctada radiata* (Leach); 9, *Trachycardium maculosum* (Wood); 10, *Vermetus sulcatus*; 11, *Ancillaria cinammomea* (Lamarck)

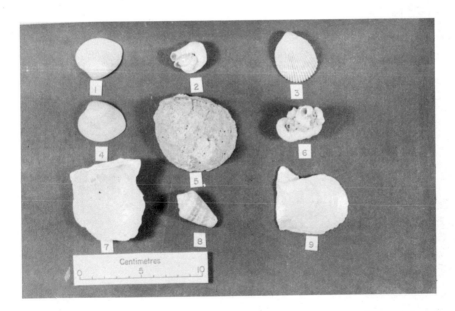

18  1, 4, *Gafrarium arabicum* (Lamarck); 2, 6, *Vermetus* sp.; 3, *Trachycardium maculosum* (Wood); 5, *Spondylus exillis* (Sowerby); 7, *Pinctada* sp. most probably *radiata* (Leach); 8, *Strombus persicus*

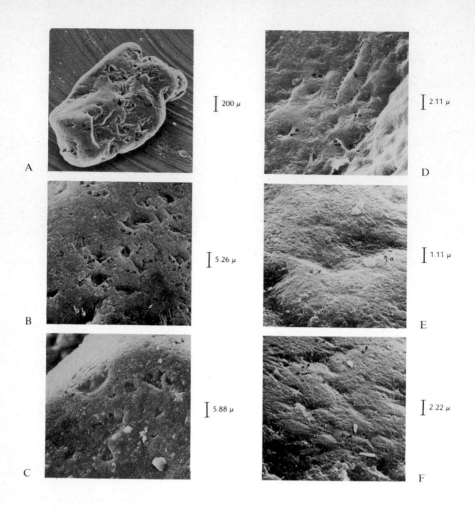

19 Quartz sand grains associated with subaqueous environment: (A) a, V-shaped patterns;
b, straight or slightly curved grooves; c, V-shaped patterns along axis of some grooves;
(B) a, V-shaped patterns; b, grooves; c, grooves with V-shaped patterns along their axis;
(C) a, V-shaped patterns; b, grooves; c, curved depression; (D) a, V-shaped patterns
with high relief; b, blocky breakage patterns; (E) a, V-shaped patterns, with adhering
particles; (F) a, V-shaped patterns; b, grooves

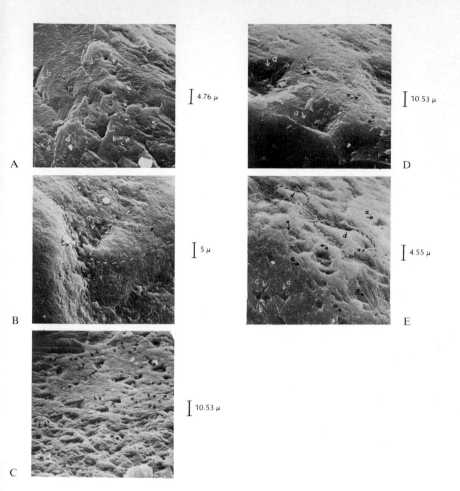

20 Quartz sand grains associated with subaqueous environment: (A) a, V-shaped patterns; b, grooves; c, V-shaped patterns along axes of grooves; d, blocky conchoidal breakage patterns; (B) a, V-shaped patterns; b, deep depression; c, blocky conchoidal breakage patterns; (C) a, V-shaped patterns; b, grooves; c, V-shaped patterns along axes of grooves; (D) a, V-shaped patterns with adhering particles; (E) a, V-shaped patterns; b, grooves; c, V-shaped pattern along some axes of grooves; d, blocky conchoidal breakage pattern; e, chatter marks

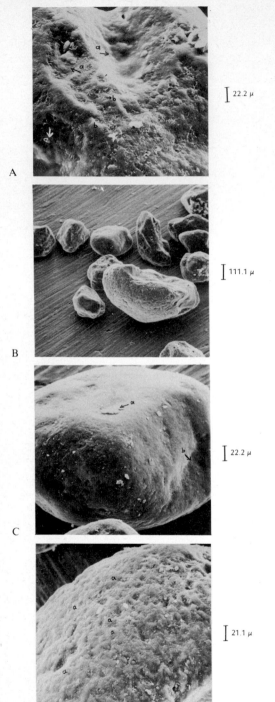

21 Quartz sand grains associated with aeolian environment: (A) a, irregular depressions; b, upturned plates; (B) general view of aeolian sand grains at different stages of development; (C) smooth rounded aeolian grain; a, adhering particles; b, irregular depression; (D) another example of aeolian grain; a, upturned plate

A

22.2 μ

B

111.1 μ

C

22.2 μ

D

21.1 μ

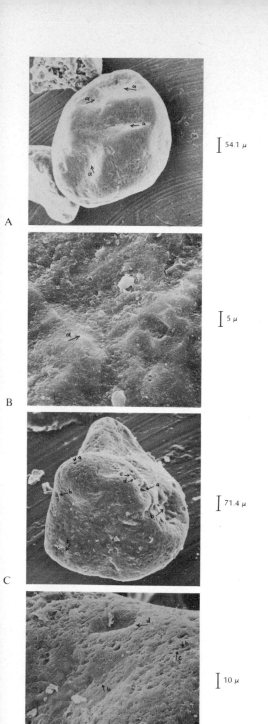

22 Quartz sand grains associated with superimposed environment: (A) a, aeolian grain with smooth surface and dish-shaped depression; (B) a, surface of another grain with faint V-shaped patterns; (C) a, V-shaped patterns; b, depressions; c, groove; d, V-shaped along groove axis; (D) a, V-shaped patterns; b, grooves; c, dish-shaped feature

A

54.1 μ

B

5 μ

C

71.4 μ

D

10 μ

23 Quartz sand grains associated with superimposed environment: (A) a, aeolian grain with rounded smooth surface and irregular depressions; (B) a, V-shaped patterns; b, grooves; c, grooves with V-shaped patterns; (C) a, V-shaped pattern; b, grooves and adhering particles cover the surface; (D) a, faint V-shaped pattern; b, adhering particles cover most of the surface

66.7 μ

10 μ

11.11 μ

2.16 μ

Approximately 1 kilometre west of this transect line, there is a small terrace (Plate 2a), which appears to be a fragment of the Fourth terrace. The surface of this fragment terrace is covered by a fossiliferous bed composed of shelly limestone (Plate 2b). The shells of molluscs were removed by solution leaving internal and external moulds. The mollusca fossils have been identified by Dr J. Taylor and C. Nuttal to be bivalves, *Paphia, Davaricella* and indeterminate gastropods sp. Beneath this fossiliferous bed, there is a consolidated calcareous soil containing traces of shell remains; the thickness of this bed is about 1.50 metres.

To determine the origin of the sediment involved, soil samples were collected for further investigations by particle size and scanning electron microscope. With regard to the fossiliferous bed on the surface, fragments of indeterminate shells were collected in a polythene bag for radiocarbon dating (Figure 5.4).

Behind this terrace, there is a fragment of a higher terrace of a similar height to terrace No. 3 in profile KI. Also, there are small clusters of *Ostrea* shells of different sizes (Plate 3). The origin of these shells is not certain; they may represent marine deposits left by higher sea-levels, or they may have been carried down to this level by another agent of transportation; they may also belong to the fossiliferous Fars Formation which is exposed in some part of the research area.

The Fourth terrace slopes gently towards the coast with no traces of more terraces. *Xerophytic* vegetation covers the coastal plain from which soil samples were collected for particle size and scanning electron microscope analysis. The vegetation increases in density near the coastline.

## Kathma II

The location of this profile is about 1 kilometre east of profile KI (see Figure 4.1). The terraces along this line are more or less a continuation of those in profile KI. Apart from the coastal plain which can be considered as a recent terrace in process of formation, there are four terraces cut by the transect.

*Lithology and stratigraphy of the bedrocks* Apart from the thin superficial deposits which do not exceed 1 metre on the top of the escarpment, the following is the stratigraphic sequence from the top of the escarpment to the present coastline (Figure 5.5).

(KII.1) 1-5 metres, conglomeratic sandstone, the clastic grains about 2-4 millimetres in diameter. According to Fuchs *et al.* (1968) these gravels and sands belong to the Dibdibba Formation of Pleistocene age. The thickness identified in the field is about 3-4 metres.

(KII.2) 5-15 metres. Calcareous sandstone; with calcareous patches.

(KII.3) 15-5.75 metres. Conglomeratic bed.

(KII.4) 15.75-23.75 metres. Calcareous sandstone of medium hardness.

(KII.5) 23.75-31.25 metres. Calcareous sandstone with clay balls rich in

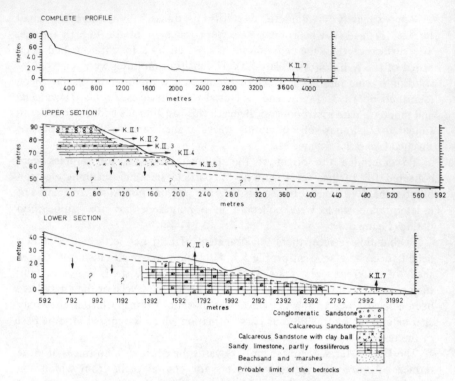

**Figure 5.5** *Profile sections of Kathma II, showing the lithology of the bedrocks*

gypsum. The thickness identified is about 7.5 metres. It is not possible to follow the depth of this formation nor to establish whether it extends in depth to join (KII.6) or whether there are other formations between them. (KII.6) Medium-grained to conglomeratic sands and sandstones, calcareous or quartzose, occasionally cross-bedded, partly fossiliferous; mainly limestone, variegated shales (Fuchs *et al.*, 1968). This unit is exposed in the lower section of the profile below the more recent marine deposits. (KII.7) Beach sand and marshes of Recent age.

*Morphology of the terraces* Similarities have been noticed in the field between the terraces along this line of levelling and those identified in KI. The terraces in KI extend laterally into KII and give some indication that they might have had the same history.

In general, the terrace surfaces are covered by superficial deposits which have been laid down either by wind, as is usually the case, or by marine agents; the latter have been noticed on the lower terraces. The escarpment is covered by large gravels which are usually of fine and medium sizes, varying from a few centimetres to about 1 metre; from this material a soil sample for particle size analysis and scanning electron microscopy was collected (Figure 5.6).

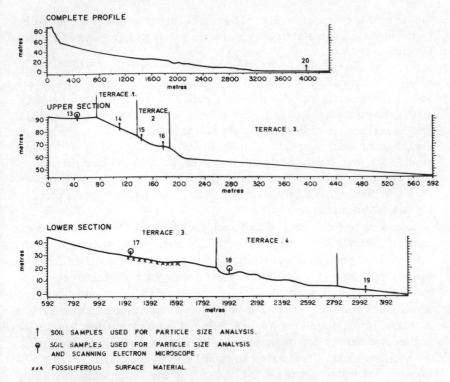

**Figure 5.6** *Profile sections of Kathma II, showing the location of the samples*

The surface of the escarpment slopes steeply into the First terrace, which appears to be less in width than the First terrace in KI. The width of this terrace is 60.8 metres, both the terrace and its slope being covered with the same deposits as KI, except that the base of the terrace has thinner deposits than its back slope. There were no traces of notches or caves at the back of this terrace. The existence of a thick deposit of detritus covering the slope causes the terrace base to be very narrow in width, and made it very difficult to find the real width of the terrace base (Figure 5.5). An arbitrary line was traced below the deposits covering the slope in order to establish the approximate height of the landward edge of the terrace.

The deposits covering the slope and the terrace are composed of weathered material from the surface sediments and from the bedrock together with fine partly cemented sands and gravels. A sample was collected for analysis. The mean height of this terrace is 81.53 metres above KD.

The Second terrace has a mean altitude of 69.65 metres above KD and a width of 49 metres. In the field, it was also possible to follow this feature laterally to terrace No. 2 in KI, and it was possible to establish the lithology of this terrace and its slope as they are partly eroded. There were pieces of rocks from the bedrock broken and settling at the sides of the slope. A soil sample was collected from the material covering the slope which seems to be similar to that covering the First terrace, but the terrace itself is covered by recent desert deposits and fragments of small-sized rocks, from which another sample was collected.

From the Second, the profile slopes to the Third terrace at a mean height of 40.55 metres above KD. As Figure 5.6 shows, the Third terrace is very wide in comparison with the first two as it occupies a distance of 1,708.6 metres. Material covering this terrace is both of terrestrial and marine origin. The upper part is covered by terrestrial deposits, and the lower part is composed of partly decalcified shelly limestone, bioclastic, and the shell of molluscs were removed by solution leaving internal and external moulds. The limestone matrix contains sand grains. Shells include small indeterminate bivalves, an internal mould of a buccinid gastropod sp. and a part of a high-spired cerithiid gastropod.

According to Dr Taylor and C. Nuttal, the molluscan fossils of this deposit contain *Turritella?*, *Crassatella*, venerid bivalves. This material is cross-bedded and spreads over a considerable area (Plate 4). About 1 to 2 metres beneath this deposit, there is a white fossiliferous bed. According to the geological map of Kuwait, this formation represents the exposed Neogene which is described in KII.6. Patches of this deposit are exposed on the surface in several places. A soil sample was collected from the marine deposits for further investigation and its location is illustrated in Figure 5.6. The surface of the Third terrace slopes gently towards the Fourth and last terrace. A distinct concave feature appears at the beginning of the terrace which is possibly related to the role of erosion in the area and a soil sample was also collected for both particle size analysis and scanning electron microscopy. The terrace has a mean height of 10.7 metres above KD and a width of 985.8 metres. No traces of marine action have been discovered on this terrace apart from a few shells which could have been transported by the wind. After this terrace the land has a gentle slope and the superficial deposits change from dry sandy terrestrial soils into soft wet soil near the present shoreline with an increase of vegetation near the sea.

*Ghidhai*

The third profile is in the Ghidhai area, about 6 kilometres north-east of Kathma. Investigation of the area between Kathma and Ghidhai shows that the landscape does not change considerably. The terraces appear consistently along the escarpment, and the fossiliferous bed which was found on the terraces at the foot of the escarpment in Kathma appears occasionally in the area. However, Ghidhai itself is an area of more interesting geomorphological features than Kathma (Plate 5). Here, there are six separate terraces, their height ranging from a mean of about 13 metres for the lowest terrace to 92.62 metres above KD for the highest. Plant communities in this area are similar to that of Kathma area.

*Lithology and stratigraphy of the bedrocks* As in the previous two areas, the upper crest of the escarpment is covered by lag gravels and sands of Recent and of Pleistocene age with a thickness of about 1 metre. Beneath this deposit the following beds are found in descending order (Figure 5.7):

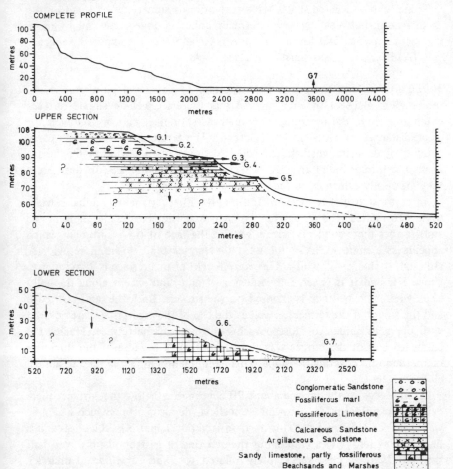

**Figure 5.7** *Profile sections of Ghidhai, showing the lithology of the bedrocks*

(G.1) 1-4 metres. Conglomeratic sandstone similar to that of KI.1 and KII.1 in Kathma area.

(G.2) 4-17 metres. At a depth of about 4 metres from the surface, there is a fossiliferous white marl, more or less friable, and containing indeterminate shell fragments.

(G.3) 17-18 metres. A highly fossiliferous limestone, extremely rich in fossil shells.

(G.4) 18-24 metres. Calcareous sandstone, medium hard with a thickness of about 5 to 6 metres.

(G.5) 24-? metres. A calcareous sandstone with clay balls, rich in gypsum. Its thickness is not known.

(G.6) Medium-grained to conglomeratic sands and sandstone, calcareous or quartzose, occasionally cross-bedded, partly fossiliferous, marly lime-stone with variegated shales. This formation is sometimes exposed on the surface in between the lower terraces but it is largely covered by more recent deposits. This formation appears to belong to the exposed Neogene.

(G.7) Beach sand and marshes of Recent age.

*Morphology of the terraces* A field examination of aerial photographs and topographic maps of the area showed that there are well-developed terraces extending along the escarpment. Numerous shorelines can be followed for great distances by visual means (Plate 5). The terraces were found to carry patches of deposits which have been laid down by the wind or by the sea itself, the former hiding the bedrock and the marine deposits. In some areas they are firmly cemented to the surface of the bedrock.

In contrast to the terraces in Kathma, the First terrace in Ghidhai is wide, some 110 metres. The terrace has no clear extension east of the transect line and finishes there suddenly, giving way to the face of the escarpment which appears as a sharp cliff. To the west the terrace tends to be more evident, although it changes in width. The mean height of this terrace is 92.62 metres above KD and it is covered by fine gravel and sand except along the gully sides where the bedrock is exposed on the surface. Both the landward edge and the slopes of the terrace, as well as the top of the escarpment, are covered with deposits similar to those covering the base of the terrace. Tracing the landward end of the terrace was almost impossible because of the thickness of the deposits covering the slope. This phenomenon in fact applies to almost all the terraces.

At the edge of the terrace about 20 centimetres below the surface, there exists a fossiliferous bed carrying superficial deposits from which a sample was collected (Figure 5.8). This horizon is about 1 metre in thickness and is highly fossiliferous and containing the remains of gastropods, bivalves, half shell of *Thais* species, very closely related to *Thais carinifera* (Lamarck). This horizon can be easily observed as it is exposed along the slope and faces the sea (Figure 5.8).

The slope of the Second terrace is steeper than that of the First. Fragments of the fossiliferous bed mixed with the terrestrial deposits hide the slope and a large part of the back of the Second terrace. The mean elevation of the terrace is 79.27 metres above KD and has a width of only 58.4 metres as well as a very limited horizontal extension; it may represent a fragment of a larger terrace. The bedrock of the Second terrace is largely exposed on the surface with a very thin superficial deposit mainly composed of windblown sands, and consolidated sands and fine gravel, from which a soil sample was collected.

The Third is at mean height of 65.0 metres above KD. It has a width of

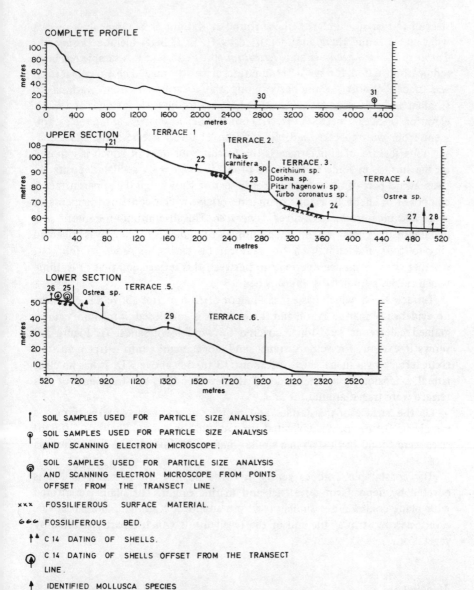

**Figure** 5.8 *Profile sections of Ghidhai, showing the location of the samples*

about 107.2 metres and is dissected by small wadis. The slope of the terrace is covered by partly consolidated sands and fragments of white limestone, from which a sample was collected for analysis.

A large part of the terrace is covered by fossiliferous deposits (Figure 5.8) consisting of bioclastic limestone and sand grains with casts of gastropods and cerithiids which have been weathered out of limestone by solution and mechanical weathering. The terrace is also strewn with shells of different sizes of *Ostrea* sp. similar to those found at Kathma area. Other shell species which were found there and identified by H. E. J. Biggs include *Dosina* sp., *Turbo* sp., *Pitar hagenowi* and *Cerithium* sp. (Figure 5.8). A sample has been radiocarbon dated for age determination of this terrace. The Fourth terrace was traced almost continuously along the escarpment from Kathma to Ghidhai and almost as far as the Al-Bahra area to the east. It stands at a mean elevation of 52.94 metres above KD but this height changes along the escarpment from west to east, and has a width of 250.2 metres. The most conspicuous feature of this terrace is the fossiliferous deposit which is exposed on the surface in some areas but in others is covered by aeolian deposits. At the seaward part of the terrace a profile section shows that the upper surface is composed of shelly limestone of marine origin, which contains fragments of shells and indeterminate bivalves, *veneracea*. This discontinuous deposit has a maximum thickness of 1 metre; a sample of fragments of shells was collected (Figure 5.8) and submitted for radiocarbon dating in order to find out whether there is an age relationship between this terrace and that of Kathma which carries a similar fossiliferous bed.

Terrace No. 5, which has a mean height of 33.6 metres above KD possesses no evidence of marine action and the bedrock is composed of medium coarse-grained calcareous sandstone, covered by windblown sands. As Figure 5.8 shows it extends for some distance and slopes gently into a fragment of a sixth terrace of a mean height of about 13 metres above KD. It has no clear lateral extension along each side of the levelling line, but fragments of this terrace were traced around the area.

On the surface of this terrace and on the landward parts of the terrace, a sample of *Ostrea* sp. was collected for radiocarbon dating. Shells of different sizes were found in clusters in a similar manner to those found in the Kathma area.

The coastal plain slopes gently towards the present shoreline and it is covered by deposits of terrestrial and marine origin. The plain is scattered with plant communities similar to those found at Kathma. Sabkhah covers a very narrow strip at the end of the levelled line which is partly covered by vegetation.

### Mudairah

This area is situated in the middle of the coastal zone north of the bay of Kuwait before the escarpment changes its direction in the Al-Bahra area.

The landscape here is characterized by being more gentle than Ghidhai, but there are a few scattered hills which are built up of sands and sandstones.

At the edge of this area salty sabkhah appears. The sabkhah is bare of vegetation and can be observed as a white plain extending east of Mudairah. In general, there is a similarity between the plant community of this area and those of Ghidhai and Kathma. Investigation of the area between Kathma,

Ghidhai and Mudairah showed that the terraces appear more or less consistently along the escarpment, especially the upper three terraces. Patches of the white fossiliferous bed, which was found at the foot of the escarpment in the previous two areas appear between Ghidhai and Mudairah. The same was also noted in connection with the thin fossiliferous bed (G.3) in line G of Ghidhai. This was found also between Ghidhai and Mudairah, although it is more clearly visible in some places than others and the thickness varies from about 1 metre to a maximum of about 2 metres.

*Stratigraphy and lithology of the bedrocks* Collecting rock samples to draw the stratigraphic sequence of this line (M) was more difficult than in the previous areas, as the bedrocks here are not often exposed along the gully sides. The stratigraphy of this profile (Figure 5.9) has been drawn from field observations and from information provided by the cross-sections drawn by Fuchs *et al.* (1968).

Five terraces were traced along the levelling line, their heights ranging between a mean height of 11.60 metres for the lowest terrace to a mean

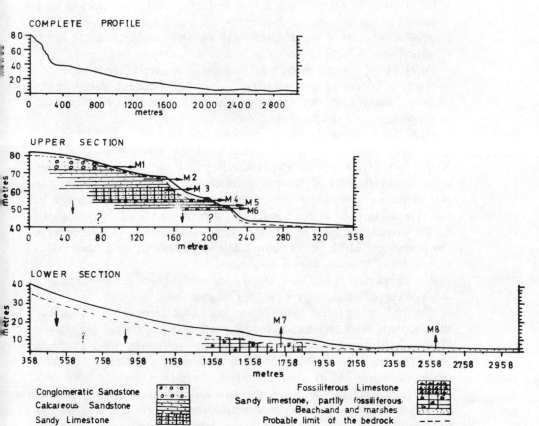

**Figure 5.9** *Profile sections of Mudairah, showing the lithology of the bedrocks*

height of 71.12 metres above KD for the highest. The terraces here appear generally to lie at a lower height than in the previous areas.

As in the last three profiles, the top of the escarpment is covered by lag gravels mixed with windblown sands. The thickness of this deposit varies from place to place, so near the seaward side of the escarpment it has a thickness of about 1 metre.

The stratigraphic sequence from top to bottom is as follows:

(M.1) 1–9 metres. Conglomeratic sandstone of a medium hardness is 1 metre below the surface of the topmost level of the escarpment and was traced to a depth of 8 metres.

(M.2) 9–19 metres. This horizon is harder than (M.1). It is composed of calcareous sandstone and covers the First terrace.

(M.3) 19–26 metres, of soft limestone with many well-rounded sand grains.

(M.4) 26–27 metres. Highly fossiliferous limestone, extremely rich in fossil shells (Plates 8a and 8b).

(M.5) 27–30 metres. Calcareous sandstone of medium hardness.

(M.6) 30–31.0 metres. Fossiliferous bed of a maximum thickness of 1 metre. It was difficult to decide whether this horizon is superficial or whether it is part of the stratigraphy of the terraces, due to the difficulty of finding a contact surface.

(M.7) 31.0–? metres, medium-grained to conglomerate sands and sandstone, calcareous or quartzose, occasionally cross-bedded, partly fossiliferous, mainly limestone; variegated shales. This formation belongs to the exposed Neogene (Fuchs *et al.*, 1968).

(M.8) Beach sands and marshes of Recent age.

*Morphology of the terraces* The landscape below the escarpment is rather gentle, with remnants of terraces scattered in the area (Plate 6). On this part of the escarpment five terraces have been identified. Marine action in this area is expressed in the fossiliferous deposits and fossil shells scattered on the terraces. The mean height of the terraces ranges from 11.61 metres for the lowest and 71.12 metres above KD for the highest, while their width varies from a few metres to over 1 kilometre.

The upper surface of the escarpment is artificially pitted by holes, as a result of the collection of gravels for building purposes.

The thickness of this deposit reaches to about 2 metres in some areas, but this decreases when one descends, and a sample was collected for analysis (Figure 5.10). From the upper surface of the escarpment, the land slopes gently into the First terrace which has a width of 76.8 metres; this is a well-developed terrace and its lateral continuation can be followed visually for a considerable distance. Both the terrace base and its slope are entirely covered by terrestrial deposits from which a sample was obtained. It is only towards its seaward end (Plate 7) that the bedrock is exposed, at which point the mean measured height of the terrace is 71.12 metres above KD.

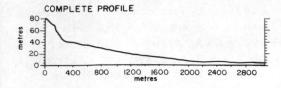

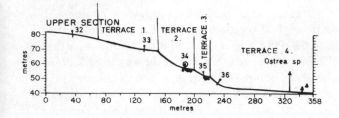

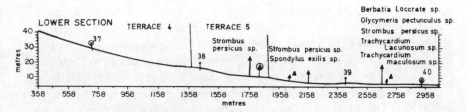

| | |
|---|---|
| ⏐ | SOIL SAMPLES USED FOR PARTICLE SIZE ANALYSIS. |
| ⌀ | SOIL SAMPLES USED FOR PARTICLE SIZE ANALYSIS AND SCANNING ELECTRON MICROSCOPE. |
| ⊖⊖⊖ | FOSSILIFEROUS BED. |
| ⏐▲ | C 14 DATING OF SHELLS. |
| ⊕ | C 14 DATING OF SHELLS OFFSET FROM THE TRANSECT LINE. |
| ⏐ | IDENTIFIED MOLLUSCA SPECIES. |

**Figure 5.10** *Profile sections of Mudairah, showing the location of the samples*

Descending to the Second terrace it was found difficult to trace the junction between the base and its slope, because, as the photograph illustrates (Plate 7), more recent deposits especially fine windblown sand as well as fragments of the bed of the First terrace cover the landward part of the terrace, where the soil sample was collected. The bedrock is exposed in some parts, especially near its slope, but towards the seaward end of the terrace the limestone bed tends to be thinner and gives way to the fossiliferous bed to appear on the surface and along both sides of the terrace (Figures 5.9 and 5.10 and Plates 8a and 8b). This horizon is similar to that found in Ghidhai and it may have the same origin. It is composed of shelly limestone which contains casts of bivalves and small gastropods. This terrace has a mean elevation of 59.57 metres above KD and a width of 49.2 metres.

The Third terrace is small in size and has very limited lateral extension on both sides of the levelling line. Its width does not exceed 20.2 metres. A fossiliferous bed resembling that found on the Second terrace is found on the base of this terrace (Figure 5.10) although its thickness here does not exceed ½ metre. The mean height of the terrace is 52.30 metres above KD and a soil sample was collected from there. The slopes of this terrace and the one below are covered by windblown sand.

The Fourth and Fifth terraces have a width of 1,149.2 and 521.4 metres. Their mean heights range from 31.23 metres for the former and 11.61 metres above KD for the latter. Aerial photographs and field investigation show that there are fragments of the Fourth terrace extending all the way from Kathma to Mudairah. Here, the terrace is covered by terrestrial and marine deposits. The latter being found on the upper part of the terrace. The marine deposit is composed of sand with millet seed grains and quartz pebbles. Fragments of partly decalcified bioclastic shelly limestone contain casts of large buccinid gastropods. Fossil shells of *Ostrea* sp. were found scattered around and a sample submitted for radiocarbon dating. It was found at a height of about 40–42 metres above KD. The slope of the terrace is covered by terrestrial deposits as well as some parts of the middle, and the seaward part is formed of red sandstone with a thickness varying from a few centimetres to about 50 centimetres. The last terrace along this profile (M) is represented here by a fragment of an older, more extensive surface; the mean height is 11.61 metres above KD. The superficial deposits covering its base are similar to those covering the previous terrace, but they are of non-marine origin. This terrace has no obvious lateral extension, but from observations in the area, fragments of similar height and composition are scattered around Mudairah. Shells (*Strombus persicus*) are strewn on the terrace here and a sample was collected for dating, Soil samples for analysis were collected from this terrace and from the lower coastal plain (Figure 5.10).

South-east of the Fifth terrace, the land slopes gently to the coastline where deposits are composed of saline soil covering parent material of shelly sand. The drainage in this area is poor and the vegetation is richer, especially near the coastline. Marine shells are scattered in this zone (Figure 5.10) and have been identified by H. Biggs as: *Strombus persicus*, (Swains), valves of *Trachycardium lacunosum* (Reeve), valve possibly *T. maculosum* (Wood), valves of *Glycymeris pectunculus* (Linné), valve *Barbatia laccrata* (Linné), (*Parmulophora*) *corrugata* (Dillwyn), besides fragments of *Spondylus*, ? *exillis* (Sowerby).

Two samples of shells at a height of about 7.23 and 5.11 metres above KD were also submitted for age determination by radiocarbon dating method.

*Al-Bahra I*

Immediately north of Mudairah, the escarpment gradually retreats further inland, allowing the coastal plain to expand to where it reaches its maximum width in central Al-Bahra (see Figure 1.2). From Al-Bahra the scarp swings in a broad arc through east to a south-east direction until it meets the present shoreline as a cliff face.

The escarpment also has a more gentle gradient within this part of the area than in Kathma, Ghidhai and Mudairah and its crest declines gradually towards the east. Deep wadis do not appear to have a role in this area. Here again, the terraces have a lower elevation than in the previous areas and some of the terraces are only represented by short discontinuous fragments. Another general characteristic of Al-Bahra is the width of the terraces. In general, they have the greatest width, but they are less well preserved.

As far as the plant community is concerned, a large part of the Al-Bahra is covered by its coastal sand association of vegetation, chiefly *Panicum turgidum* and *Rhanterium epappossum*, which covers almost all the area.

Profile number (AI) in Al-Bahra is situated west of the Al-Bahra area (see Figure 4.1). Along that profile six terraces and fragments were located. One of the difficulties met in this region was to trace rock outcrops along the profiles because, as has been mentioned before, the low topography of the area and the poor state of preservation of the terraces together with the lack of valleys cutting across the terraces made it almost impossible to draw clear stratigraphic lines. However, the following stratigraphic description along the profile (Figure 5.11) is tentatively presented, drawn almost entirely from field investigation.

Three main horizons have been identified on the upper section profile (Figure 5.11):

0–1 metre. The upper surface is covered by the lag gravels similar to those covering the topmost surface of the escarpment in Kathma, Ghidhai and Mudairah. The thickness of this deposit varies from a few centimetres to 1 metre.

(AI.1) 1–12 metres. White conglomeratic sandstone (Figure 5.11).

(AI.2) 12–24 metres. Calcareous sandstone of medium hardness.

(AI.3) 24–? metres. White limestone containing sand grains; probably this horizon extends into the Second terrace. Its thickness cannot be decided because of the long gentle slope of the terrace. Neither was it possible to recognize whether there are other formations between this horizon and unit No. AI.4.

(AI.4) –? metres. According to the geological map of Kuwait the area between the Jal-Az-Zor escarpment and the beach material is part of the exposed Neogene. However, this rock unit was not identified along this line except on the landward slope of the last terrace. It is composed of medium-grained conglomeratic sands and sandstone, calcareous or quartzose; occasionally cross-bedded, partly fossiliferous, mainly limestone, variegated shales.

(AI.5) Beach sands and marshes of Recent age.

**Figure 5.11** *Profile sections of Al-Bahra I, showing the lithology of the bedrocks*

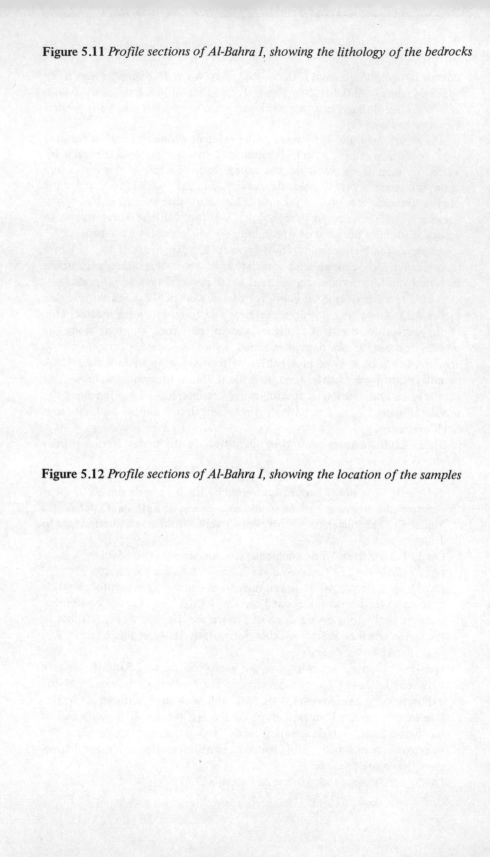

**Figure 5.12** *Profile sections of Al-Bahra I, showing the location of the samples*

*Morphology of the terraces* More terraces have been identified in this part of Al-Bahra than in previous areas, as it was possible to trace and level the remains of six terraces (Figure 5.12). Almost all the terraces slope gently towards the sea and most of their surfaces are covered by solid rocks. Marine and terrestrial deposits cover the terraces. The latter are mainly concentrated on the upper sections of the profiles on the highest terraces along the escarpment, while those of marine origin are found mainly on the lower terraces. A few shells found very close to the coastline were collected and are similar to those of the Mudairah area with a predominance of *Strombus persicus.*

The topmost surface of the escarpment which is covered by lag gravels and sands slopes gently into the First terrace which has a mean height of 79.85 metres above KD. Both the slope and the terrace, which extends in width to 165.4 metres, are covered with fine gravels and sands partly consolidated and mixed with weathered material of the bedrock. Soil samples which were collected along this line are located in Figure 5.12. The bedrock of conglomeratic material is exposed along some parts of the terrace sides and no signs of marine action are imprinted in any way on that terrace.

From this terrace, the surface drops more or less vertically into the Second terrace. Neither the landward end of this terrace nor its slope possesses marine deposits, notches, or even holes which might suggest any biological action. The superficial deposits covering this part of the terrace are merely of terrestrial origin and the slope has been largely covered by windblown sands. It was noticed also that the back of this terrace is dissected by several small shallow wadis filled with fine windblown sands. These wadis are the remains of an old drainage system which was once fed by water descending from the upper surface of the escarpment. The terrace has a mean elevation of 56.10 metres above KD and a width of 741.8 metres.

The Third terrace has a mean height of 40.39 metres KD. There is no linear extension of this terrace and it is represented by fragments of terrace surfaces which can be followed towards the east and west. The terrace has a width of 183 metres and is only covered by fragments of red sandstone and thin terrestrial deposits. It grades into the next terrace with a very gentle slope.

The Fourth terrace has a similar character in that it is composed of fragments of terrace surface. The slope of this terrace is covered mainly by weathered material from terrace No. 3 and windblown deposits. The terrestrial deposit which is mainly of sand and fine pebbles, has a thickness of about 1 metre. Reddened sandstone appears more clearly towards the seaward end of the terrace. It does not extend as one unit sheet of hard rock, but is often broken into small pieces. The terrace stands at a mean height of 31.79 metres above KD. The dome feature which stands near the edge of the terrace is merely an accumulation of medium and fine gravels consolidated with sands covered with some vegetation. The width of this terrace was found to differ from place to place in the area, and the distance measured here on the transect is 1,030.2 metres.

The last two terraces in this area (Plate 9) were clearly identified as following each other in downward sequence. Their lateral extensions are also well developed in the area. The surfaces of both terraces are covered by red sandstone, veneered with sands and fine gravels. The first of them (terrace No. 5) has a mean elevation of 22.32 metres above KD and a width of 482.2 metres. The lower part (Figure 5.12 and Plate 9) of the terrace is covered by rose-coloured granular, porous limestone containing many fragments of fossils which have been identified by Dr Taylor of the British Museum as being the remains of Crab. When the thickness of this deposit was measured, it was also found to vary from place to place, but here it has a maximum thickness of about 1 metre.

The lowest terrace (No. 6) has a gentle slope covered by weathered material of the bedrock of terrace No. 5 and terrestrial deposit. The terrace mean elevation is 16.10 metres above KD and most of its surface is covered by red sandstone with very small amounts of sands. Vegetation is almost absent on this terrace which extends to 779.8 metres in width. Only the rocks at the outer edge (Figure 5.12) contain fossil fragments, the red fossiliferous rock having indeterminate *crustacean* fragments (Dr Taylor, personal communication).

This deposit overlies hard rocks composed of off-white compact limestone, yellow and red stained in places, which may belong to the exposed Neogene in the area. These two formations form a cliff in some parts at the edge of the terrace. It was not possible to see the lower part of the cliff as it was covered by fine windblown sand. In other parts of the terrace, this form of cliff disappears and the terrace seems to converge very smoothly into the present coastal zone. Immediately after the descent into the coastal plain vegetation of *halophytic* type grows in density and holds the sand, behind which small hills are sometimes formed, as the one illustrated at the end of the present profile. The vegetation then decreases in size and quantity until the area is composed merely of sabkhah deposits.

### Al-Bahra II

The second line of levelling (A.II) is situated in the north-east of the Al-Bahra area and just before the Jal-Az-Zor escarpment changes its direction towards the south (see Figure 4.1). The escarpment here follows an irregular shape and the terraces in this area are obscured and do not have a clear areal extension. Most of the terraces, apart from the lowest one, are represented by fragments, which can be followed around the coast and usually end in a cliff. Marine deposits are confined to the lower terraces, especially on their seaward margins. The upper terraces are entirely covered by terrestrial deposits, hiding their bedrock as well as their slopes. The thickness of these deposits ranges from a few centimetres to more than 1 metre.

*Lithology and stratigraphy of the bedrocks* The difficulties in following the stratigraphy of the terraces in some of the previous areas have also been met along this profile. The main reason being the low amplitude of the terraces, the disappearance of the deep wadis which were pronounced between Kathma and Mudairah, and the widespread terrestrial deposits which, as has been mentioned before, cover large parts of the bedrock. Information entirely depending on the rock samples collected during investigating the area gives the following results (Figure 5.13):

The surface of the escarpment is covered to a depth of 1.0 to 1.5 metres by superficial deposits of sand and gravels of fine and medium size.

(AII.1) 1.5–4.5 metres. Conglomeratic sandstone containing many sand grains and sand pebbles of fluviatile or deltaic origin

(AII.2) 4.5–10.5 metres. Calcareous sandstone with small pebbles, of a thickness of about 6 metres.

(AII.3) 10.5–28.5 metres. Soft bedded limestone containing many sand grains. The thickness of this terrace is not certain, but the next bed was found 18 metres below this deposit on the Second terrace. The terrestrial deposit which covers parts of the terrace base and its slope obscures the situation.

(AII.4) 28.5–29.5 metres. Has been traced at the landward side of the Second terrace. It is composed of stratified pebbly sandstone with calcareous cement.

(AII.5) 29.5–32.5 metres. Calcereous sandstone with large sand grains and small pebbles. As the base of the slope of the following terrace is not largely covered by terrestrial deposits, it is easy to trace this horizon into the next terrace.

(AII.6) 30.5–?metres. Variegated orange-to-yellow fine-grained sandstone with calcareous cement, partly fossiliferous; thickness is not known. It is more probable that the bed is a continuation of the exposed Neogene.

(AII.7) Beach sand and marshes of Recent age.

*Morphology of the terraces* The upper surface of the escarpment slopes into the First terrace, the slope being dissected by dry small wadis filled with sands. The First terrace along this line is remarkably wide, being 724.1 metres. It has a mean elevation of 63.72 metres above KD. This terrace can be followed horizontally east and west of the levelled line. The superficial deposit is of windblown sands and gravels and small broken material of a conglomeratic deposit. The soil samples which were collected are located in Figure 5.14. Towards the seaward part of the terrace, the deposit tends to be thinner and allows the bedrock to appear in some places.

The Second terrace in descending order has a mean height of 47.82 metres above KD. It is dissected by two distinct dry wadis, with some scattered

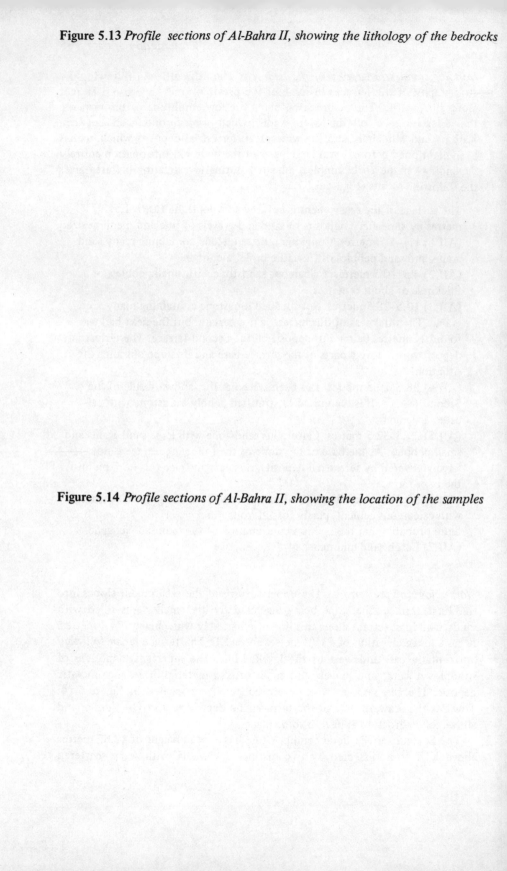

**Figure 5.13** *Profile  sections of Al-Bahra II, showing the lithology of the bedrocks*

**Figure 5.14** *Profile sections of Al-Bahra II, showing the location of the samples*

shrubs. The wadis meet at the lower part of the terrace. Although this terrace appears clearly to descend into another small and lower terrace, its lateral continuation is not very evident, but fragments of this terrace were noticed scattered in the area. The width here is 282 metres but this width varies and even with the help of the aerial photographs, it was difficult to follow the right remnants. The slope of this terrace is also covered by terrestrial deposits which become thinner towards the sea and the bedrock of red sandstone is exposed on the surface in several places.

Although the superficial deposits indicate a non-marine origin, a soil sample was collected for further laboratory examination (Figure 5.14). From this terrace, the land slopes gently into a Third narrow terrace which has a mean height of 39.45 metres above KD and extends a short distance in width to 118.6 metres. The slope of this terrace is partly hidden by windblown sands, while the terrace base is veneered with fragments of red rock and very thin terrestrial deposits.

The lower, or seaward part of the terrace is covered by fossiliferous deposits (Figure 5.14) which contain gastropod fragments. This deposit was found scattered in the area in small patches.

Terrace No. 4 is also characterized by being composed of several fragments. Sands and fine gravels are accumulated on the surface and beneath them there is a fine-grained, stratified red sandstone of medium hardness. The mean height of this terrace is 29.86 metres above KD and extends in width to 864.4 metres. There is no trace of the Third terrace fossiliferous bed on this terrace, nor of any other marine action, except that in some places, about a metre below the surface, a hardrock appears to be of the fossiliferous Neogene.

The terrace fragments slope into the lowest and Fifth terrace which has a mean elevation of 14.43 metres above KD. In the field it was clear that this terrace does not stretch parallel to the present coastline, but has an undulating face. Around the levelled profile, the terrace to the west extends more or less parallel to the coastline, then it retreats towards the interior in a zig-zag fashion, forming an embayment-like feature (Plate 10). This has an effect on the recorded transect profile (Figure 5.14), because the levelling line, following a straight direction from the upper part of the escarpment to the present coastline, crossed twice over the same Fifth terrace. The last concavity in the lower section profile represents the base level of the lowland in between the terrace. The dotted line represents the original slope of the terrace, while the two small concave shapes beneath the supposed original base of the terraces are also related to the levelling procedure. Material eroded from the terrace surface and redeposited in a depression forms a small rise (Plate 10). The terrace width average along the transect line is 616.6 metres and its slope is covered by weathered material from the upper terrace as well as by fine windblown sands. The upper part of the terrace is veneered by broken red sandstone of a thickness which does not exceed 50 centimetres.

Beneath it is the variegated orange-to-yellow, medium-to-fine-grained sandstone, calcareous and partly fossiliferous. (AII.6)

Towards the seaward end of the terraces the bedrock is covered by consolidated beachrock, yellow to red in colour. It is mainly composed of indeterminate shell fragments and sand grains cemented together by calcite. This marine deposit has a thickness varying from a few centimetres to a maximum of 1.5 metres. It rests on a cliff of sandy limestone (Plate 11) which has traces of fossils which may, according to Dr Taylor and C. Nuttal, be *Hydrobia.* The cliff stands almost vertical and at its base there is a cave, the exact height of which is not known because of the thick sands and rock fragments from the superficial marine deposit which covers large parts of the floor (Plate 11). Large blocks of the overhanging parts of the marine deposit have collapsed, and been covered by aeolian sands, hiding the bedrock in this area; as part of the topography they form the convex shape just below the main part of the terrace noted on Figure 5.14.

Several broken and complete fossil shells have been scattered or cemented onto the surface of the beachrock and in the lowland in between the area, at different heights. Some of these shells have been dated by radiocarbon dating method and they have been identified as *Strombus persicus* and *Thais carinifera* (Lamarck) (Figure 5.14).

Downslope of this terrace the land slopes evenly into the coastal plain with scattered vegetation. The superficial deposits here are composed of marine sands and terrestrial deposits with a higher percentage of clay content.

### Al-Bahra III

This is the last levelled line in Al-Bahra area, located about 5 kilometres south-east of line AII (see Figure 4.1). The height of the terraces in this area conforms with the general tendency of a decrease from west to east. The escarpment changes its direction towards south-east and east, progressing towards the sea leaving a very narrow coastal plain. Consequently, the lowest terrace ends in a cliff in a similar way to that of AII but with a lower height.

Between the AII and AIII profiles, fragments of terraces are numerous (see Figure 1.2). Some of these terraces have been traced all the way between the two transects and often carry similar deposits. Here also marine deposits which were found to be confined to the lower terraces in all the previous areas from KI in Kathma to AII in Al-Bahra, were recorded. The upper terraces are covered with terrestrial deposits and have no particular geomorphological features related to sea-level changes, except that of the wide monotonous physiographic terrace surfaces which are dissected in the upper part by the old, now dry, drainage systems.

*Lithology and stratigraphy of the bedrocks* Samples for elucidating the lithology of the bedrock were collected from the few outcrop rocks along the levelled line. As the superficial deposits covering the slope of the First terrace were not of great thickness, it was possible to remove them and cut a vertical section from which samples representing each horizon were collected. Concerning the other parts of the profile, holes were made through the unconsolidated superficial deposits between the discontinuous hard superficial deposits until boring was met by a hard base. From that part the samples for the bedrock were collected. The samples were examined in the field and in the laboratory and compared with the geological map of Kuwait.

The result is summarized as shown in Figure 5.15.

(AIII.1) 1–6 metres. Conglomeratic sandstone of the same composition as AII.1.

(AIII.2) 6–12 metres. Calcareous sandstone with small pebbles.

(AIII.3) 12–? metres. Coarse-grained sandy limestone with bands of small pebbles. It was not possible to trace the thickness of this bed, nor ascertain whether there are other horizons beneath it. Samples of this bed were traced to approximately the middle of the First terrace.

(AIII.4) Red mottled medium-grained calcareous sandstone. This bed is similar to the exposed Neogene which extends from the escarpment to the lower part of the coastal plain. According to Fuchs *et al.* (op. cit.) the exposed Neogene is composed of medium-grained to conglomerate sands, sandstone, calcareous or quartzose. It is occasionally cross-bedded, partly fossiliferous, mainly limestone, variegated shales.

(AIII.5) Beach sands and marshes of Recent age.


*Morphology and superficial deposits of the terraces* Four separate terraces have been levelled in this area (Figure 5.16), their mean height ranging from 33.11 metres above KD for the highest to 5.99 metres for the lowest. Three of them, including terraces 1, 2 and 4, have been traced horizontally for a considerable distance, some of them being extensions of those identified in the previous areas. If one describes their morphological features with their superficial deposits from which soil samples were collected for analysis (Figure 5.16), it will appear that they in fact do not vary significantly. The superficial material covering the topmost surface of the escarpment is composed of windblown deposits cemented together with fine and medium-size gravels by calcite. The surface is also covered in some places with large-size gravels (Plate 12). Cox and Rhoades (1935), Higginbottom (1954), Milton (1967) and Fuchs *et al.* (1968), have all related this gravel to a fluviatile origin of Pleistocene age. This deposit covers the top of the escarpment as well as the slope of the First terrace.

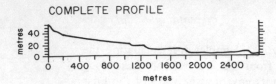

COMPLETE PROFILE

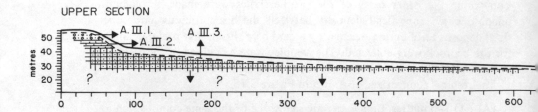

UPPER SECTION

A.III.1.
A.III.2.
A.III.3.

?          ?          ?

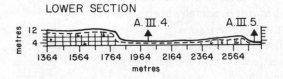

LOWER SECTION

A.III.4.          A.III.5.

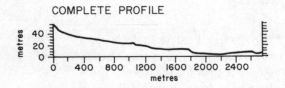

COMPLETE PROFILE

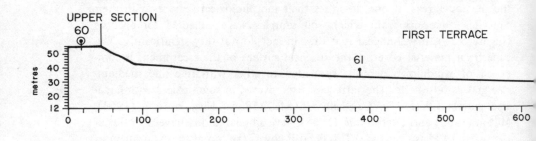

UPPER SECTION

60

FIRST TERRACE

61

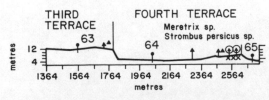

LOWER SECTION

THIRD
TERRACE          FOURTH TERRACE

Meretrix sp.
Strombus persicus sp.

63          64          65

**Figure 5.15** *Profile sections of Al-Bahra III, showing the lithology of the bedrocks*

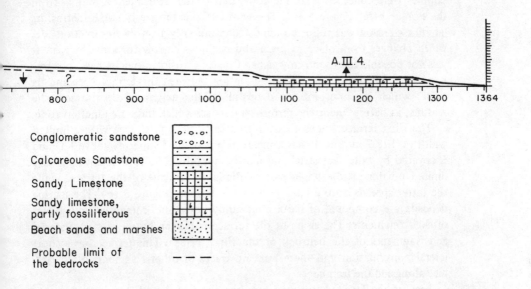

Conglomeratic sandstone

Calcareous Sandstone

Sandy Limestone

Sandy limestone,
partly fossiliferous

Beach sands and marshes

Probable limit of
the bedrocks

**Figure 5.16** *Profile sections of Al-Bahra III, showing the location of the samples*

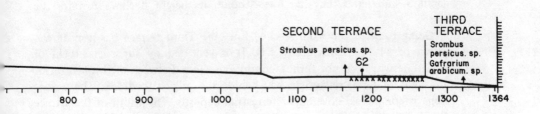

↑ Soil samples used for particle analysis

⦿ Soil samples used for particle analysis
and scanning electron microscope

↑ Identified mollusca species

xxx Fossilliferous surface material

↑▲ C 14 dating of shells

⦿ C 14 dating of shells offset
from the transect line

This, which stands at a mean elevation of 33.11 metres above KD, is dissected on its landward part and slopes by shallow dry wadis, these wadis now filled with fine windblown sands. To about the middle of the terrace, the superficial deposits are mainly of windblown sands mixed with fragments of the conglomeratic rocks from the upper part of the escarpment. Soil samples were collected from the upper part of the escarpment as well as from the terrace base (Figure 5.16). The width of this terrace is 1,018 metres. Its lateral extension was followed almost continuously from both directions. Its width changes from place to place and becomes narrow towards the east. It was not possible to observe any signs of marine erosion along its base, nor was it possible to locate the probable junction between the terrace base and its slope, which is important for determining the height of the terrace: the reasons, as before, being the terrestrial deposits which hide the junction zone.

The First terrace slopes gently into a small Second terrace with a limited width of 195.7 metres. It has a mean height of 18.58 metres above KD and is covered by both terrestrial and marine deposits. The former covers a very limited portion of the upper part of the landward side of the terrace, while the latter spreads onto a large part of the terrace (Figure 5.16). The marine deposits are composed of hard, pink sandy limestone, cemented with traces of shell fragments. The slope of the terrace is hidden by weathered material and fragments of the bedrock of the First terrace. This terrace has a short lateral continuation and there were no traces of other fragments of the terrace alongside the transect.

East of the levelled line and between terraces 1 and 2, there is another clear terrace extending parallel to the sea and facing the narrow coastal plain with a vertical cliff. The morphological feature of this terrace is very similar to the last terrace found in the second profile in the Al-Bahra area (AII). The cliff carries rocks of consolidated beach material composed of sands, fine pebbles as well as the remains of bivalves and indeterminate shells; the deposit is cemented together with calcite. This deposit covers a large part of the terrace, especially the seaward part. The slope of the cliff is largely hidden by broken pieces of the superficial deposits but the exposed height of the cliff is about 3.76 metres. This terrace extends linearly for about 3 kilometres, but like the Second, its height declines towards the east.

Going back to the main levelled line, the Third terrace has a mean elevation of 11.72 metres above KD. It is veneered by superficial rocks of sandstone which do not form a continuous sheet. Between the broken rocks, are sands of terrestrial origin which hide the original bedrock. The terrace slope is completely covered by terrestrial deposits. The width of the terrace is 551.2 metres and it was possible to trace its extension in the surrounding area.

Shells in complete shape and in fragments are scattered extensively on this terrace. They include *Strombus persicus* which represents the majority species as well as *Gafrarium arabicum* (Lamarck); one sample at a height of about 12.5 metres was submitted for dating.

The lowest terrace (No. 4) extends in width to a distance of 826.6 metres. It decreases in height from west to east, so it has a mean height of 5.99 metres above KD at the levelling line, while it declines to a vanishing point towards the east. The seaward part of the terrace ends in a cliff, the latter with a height of about 2 metres; it is composed of sandy limestone with iron stains and fragments and traces of shells; this bed is similar to the exposed Neogene.

The superficial deposit covering the terrace and its cliff is composed of red sandy limestone with shell fragments, it has a thickness of less than a metre which also becomes thinner and discontinuous towards the land. Other superficial deposits include the windblown sands which change in colour and texture from the surface to the bedrock, e.g. the upper 30 or 50 centimetres are of pale-brown sandy soil, after that it becomes softer and the colour changes into yellow-to-brown soil. This last deposit overlies the original bedrock, and in order to examine the composition and sources of these deposits, samples were collected for laboratory examination. The material covering the slope of this terrace is of windblown sands.

Investigation along this terrace showed that towards the west, it meets the lowest terrace of profile AII in Al-Bahra. The superficial deposit is similar in many ways, but the terrace becomes higher towards the west. Also the marine shells of similar species have been strewn on the terrace between the two areas. The shells are not confined to the seaward end of the terraces because they have also been found near the slopes. They contain *Meretrix* sp. as well as *Strombus persicus*, and four samples of shells from which two along the levelled line and two offset the line were submitted for C14 dating (Figure 5.16).

The coastal plain in front of this terrace is very narrow and largely covered by the sea at high-water mark, but it does not reach the base of the present cliff. Between the cliff and the present coastline the coastal plain does not have a gentle slope; it is rather steep and covered by fine sands at the foot of the escarpment, while downslope it contains a higher percentage of clay.

Finally, the results of the levelling which show the numbers and mean heights of the terraces are illustrated in Table 5.1. In Table 5.1 the terraces are numbered along each transect solely on the basis of the sequence in which they were visually identifiable in the field from the escarpment downward. At this stage, deliberately, no correlation between transects was made.

## 5.2 Marine fossils and dating results

A total of twenty species of mollusca have been identified in the survey's fossil collection, of which sixteen come from the research area between Kathma and Al-Bahra. The rest are from Al-Dhba'iyyah. The shells have been identified by H. E. J. Biggs as being of marine origin (Table 5.2 and

**Table 5.1** *Showing the mean heights of the terraces above Kuwait Datum (in metres)**

| Terrace number | Kathma I | Kathma II | Ghidhai | Mudairah | Al-Bahra I | Al-Bahra II | Al-Bahra III |
|---|---|---|---|---|---|---|---|
| 1 | 90.60 | 81.53 | 92.62 | 71.12 | 79.85 | 63.72 | 33.11 |
| 2 | 77.92 | 69.65 | 79.27 | 59.57 | 56.10 | 47.82 | 18.58 |
| 3 | 67.38 | 40.55 | 65 | 52.30 | 40.39 | 39.45 | 11.72 |
| 4 | 50.76 | 10.70 | 52.94 | 31.23 | 31.79 | 29.86 | 5.99 |
| 5 | | | 33.60 | 11.61 | 22.32 | 14.43 | |
| 6 | | | 13 | | 16.10 | | |

* Although heights are given to two places of decimals of a metre, their accuracy is subject to an error of ± 1 metre (see p. 132).

Plates 13–18). A suspicion that freshwater mollusca were present among the samples arose for two reasons. The first is that the present area of research is close to the Tigris and Euphrates river system discharge area. Khalaf (1969) found that the Tigris and Euphrates river system is the main transporting agent of the detrital grain deposits found especially along the northern coasts of Kuwait. The other possibility of freshwater effect might have occurred during the Pleistocene Period, especially since the superficial sheet of gravels which covers the north and north-east of Kuwait territory has been deposited by river action. Nevertheless, in the expert judgment of H. E. J. Biggs, all the samples identified are of marine origin.

In general, the state of preservation of the shells differs in correspondence with the heights above Kuwait Datum at which they were found; shells which come from near the present coastline are better preserved than those collected further inland. The only example from a height of 90 metres above KD was collected from Ghidhai area and is represented in one shell, *Thais carinifera* Lamarck (Plate 14 and Figure 5.8). No other examples have been collected at similar heights in any other area. At heights between 69 and 60 metres above KD, the dominant species were *Turbo coronatus* and *Cerithium* sp. The first have been found to be completely dissolved and represented only by their casts (Plate 16), while the *Cerithium* sp. are partly preserved. Hence it was possible to submit the latter for C14 dating.

The shell samples collected from Kathma shell bed are composed of fragments of, and whole, small shells, mainly bivalves and *Ostrea* sp. The shell assemblages from Al-Dhba'iyyah area are better preserved (Plates 17 and 18).

Literature on the molluscs of the Arabian/Persian Gulf has recorded the known distribution of the same and similar species to those which were found in Kuwait. They have been discovered on the islands and the coastal areas of the Gulf as well as along the coasts of the Indian Ocean (Melvill, 1897; Newton, 1905; Lees, 1928; Cornwall, 1946; Haas, 1954; Biggs, 1958; Biggs and Grantier, 1960). There is, however, no adequate reference work concerning the mollusca of Kuwait. Steininger (1968) indicated that mollusca collected from the coastal area of Kuwait corresponded very well in type to known assemblages of living mollusca of the Red Sea and the Indian Ocean. However, Cox and Rhoades (1935) have referred to the fossil assemblages found in the Middle Zor Formation (corresponding to Lower Fars Formation) which outcrops in the Jal-Az-Zor escarpment. They also referred to other Recent and post-Kuwait series fossils found north of Kuwait Bay. The first is represented by *Dendritina cf. rangii*, *Ostrea vestita*, *Ostrea latimarginata*, *Turritella* sp., *Lucina* sp. and *Balanus* sp. Some of these species were found at the foot of the Jal-Az-Zor escarpment during the fieldwork in the area. As to the Recent fossils found, Cox and Rhoades mentioned that they are still flourishing on the present-day beaches and include *Conus* sp., *Solen* sp. and *Turbo* sp.

From the coastal area of Al-Jlay'ah, Perry and Al-Refai (1958) recorded fossil assemblages which also match with present species on the shore. They

**Table 5.2** *List of species*

| Name of species | Locality |
| --- | --- |
| Pelecypoda | |
| *Barbatia laccrata* (Linné) | Mudairah |
| *Circe (Parmulophora) corrugata* (Dillwyn) | Mudairah |
| *Dosina* sp. | Ghidhai |
| *Gafrarium arabicum* (Lamarck) | Al-Bahra |
| *Glycymeris pectunculus* (Linné) | Mudairah |
| *Meretrix* sp. | Al-Bahra |
| *Ostrea* sp. | Kathma, Ghidhai, Mudairah and Al-Bahra |
| Large and small bivalves indet | Kathma to Al-Bahra |
| *Pitar hagenowi* (Dunker) | Ghidhai |
| *Plicatula* sp. almost certainly  p. *imbricata* (Menke) | Kathma |
| *Spondylus exillis* (Sowerby) | Mudairah |
| *Trachycardium lacunosum* (Reeve) | Mudairah |
| *Trachycardium maculosum* (Wood) | Mudairah |
| | |
| Gastropoda | |
| *Cerithium* sp. | Kathma, Ghidhai and Mudairah |
| *Strombus persicus* | Kathma |
| ,,        ,, | Ghidhai |
| ,,     ,, | Mudairah |
| ,,        ,, | Al-Bahra |
| *Thais carinifera* | Ghidhai & Al-Bahra |
| *Turbo coronatus* | Ghidhai & Al-Bahra |
| Small gastropods indet | Kathma to Al-Bahra |
| | |
| Pelecypoda | |
| *Gafrarium arabicum* (Lamarck) | |
| *Glycymeris* (Linné) | |
| *Pinctada radiata* (Leach) | |
| *Spondylus exillis* (Sowerby) | |
| *Trachicardium maculosum* (Wood) | |
| | Al-Dhba'iyyah area |
| Gastropoda | |
| *Ancillaria cinammomea* (Lamarck) | |
| *Murex küsterianus* | |
| *Strombus persicus* (Swains) | |
| *Turbo coronatus* (Gmelin) | |
| *Vermetus sulcatus* | |

contain *Conus* sp., *Calliostoma* sp., *Cardium* sp., *Mactra* sp., *Pinctada* sp., *Arca* sp. and *Astarte*.

Sieber (1968) identified the following fossils of Fars Group (Miocene to Pliocene) in the area between Kathma and Al-Bahra: *Chlamys* div. sp., *Ostrea latimarginata*, *Clausinell* sp., *Spondylus* sp., div. *Veneridae*, *Natica* sp., large and small bivalves indet, *Turritella* sp., *Turbo* sp., as well as small gastropods.

The most recent reference about the mollusca of Kuwait was published in 1968 when Steininger gave a list of the fossil assemblages in Kuwait territory and its islands.

A list of the dated samples with their respective laboratory codes is given in Table 5.3.


## 5.3 Results of the sediment analyses

### 5.3.1 *Interpretation of the results of the particle size analysis*

Our purpose in studying the mechanical analysis of the sediments is to recognize their depositional environments and accordingly the origin of the terraces existing in the area. The characteristics of each individual sample have been analysed (Table 5.4); the information resulting from the different samples made it difficult to follow these in the area. Hence, it was decided that samples belonging to each individual terrace from Kathma I, Ghidhai, Mudairah and Al-Bahra I to Bahra III were best grouped together; the characteristic of these samples together would reveal the origin of the terrace concerned. The hypothesis implied by this treatment, i.e. that each terrace whatever its location has a similar sedimentation history, was assumed for purposes of further testing on the basis of the conclusions reached in earlier chapters.

Several methods have been applied to investigate the origin of the samples; (a) Student's *t* test (b) interpretation of the four size parameters and (c) correlation and comparison between the grain size distribution curves.

*Statistical measures used for analysis* Statistical analyses of cumulative frequency curves were calculated because they furnish a means of summarizing large amounts of information in a convenient manner, as visual comparison of more than a few curves is difficult. Also, it is an important key to the investigation of the sedimentary environments. The properties of the cumulative curves can be obtained either mathematically by method of moments or graphically by reading selected percentiles of the cumulative curves. Both methods are summarized by Krumbein and Pettijohn (1938).

For the present study, the latter has been applied because it is quicker and almost as accurate as the former.

Four size parameters were measured, namely, mean, standard deviation, skewness and kurtosis. These statistics have been discussed in a series of

**Table 5.3** *The results of radiocarbon dating of shells*

| Laboratory ref | Sample ref | Location | Height above Kuwait Datum | Years BP |
|---|---|---|---|---|
| T-1054 | E38 ZB | Al-Bahra | 15.18m | 4510±80 |
| HV.4770 | E39-40ZB | Al-Bahra | 8.42m | 3875±60 |
| T-1055 | E40 ZB | Al-Bahra | 7.69m | Outer fraction 4050±90 |
| | | | | Inner fraction 4110±70 |
| T-1056 | E42 ZB | Al-Bahra | 9.77m | Outer fraction 4910±70 |
| | | | | Inner fraction 4570±70 |
| T-1057 | F16-17ZB | Al-Bahra | 12.5m | 4170±170 |
| T-1058 | F18 ZB | Al-Bahra | 8.27m | Outer fraction 4030±70 |
| | | | | Inner fraction 4180±70 |
| T-1059 | F20 ZB | Al-Bahra | 8.87m | Outer fraction 3650±90 |
| | | | | Inner fraction 3560±60 |
| T-1060 | F24 ZB | Al-Bahra | 7.44m | Outer fraction 4050±90 |
| | | | | Inner fraction 3560±90 |
| T-1061 | F27-28ZB | Al-Bahra | 4.60m | Outer fraction 3350±90 |
| | | | | Inner fraction 3810±90 |
| Birm. 285 | G15-16ZM | Mudairah | 40-42m | Outer fraction 32,000± $^{2300}_{1800}$ |
| | | | | Middle fraction > 31,500 |
| | | | | Inner fraction  > 34,500 |
| T-1062 | G32-33ZB | Mudairah | 7.23m | Outer fraction 3270±80 |
| | | | | Inner fraction 3250±80 |
| T-1063 | G33-34ZB | Mudairah | about 11m | Outer fraction 3170±110 |
| | | | | Inner fraction 3750±90 |
| T-1064 | G35 ZB | Mudairah | 5.11m | Outer fraction 4130±90 |
| | | | | Inner fraction 4050±70 |
| SUA-86 | C15/Z | Ghidhai | 63.30m | 28350±1150 |
| Birm. 283 | C5/1 | Ghidhai | 46.51m | Outer fraction 35,000±1000 |
| | | | | 35,050 BC |
| | | | | Inner fraction > 41,000 BC |
| | | | | > 42,950 BP |
| 1-7610 | C6/Z | Ghidhai | about 52m | 31,900±1300 BP |
| 1-7609 | A.1/Z | Kathma | about 48m | 23,300±600 |
| SUA.85 | E7-8D | Al-Dhba'-iyyah | 5m | 940±80 |

articles by Trask (1932), Krumbein (1936), Otto (1939), Inman (1952), Folk and Ward (1957), Friedman (1961, 1967), McCammon (1962) and Chappell (1967).

**Table 5.4** Results of particle size analysis

| Particle size in millimetres | | | | | | | | | | | | | | |
|---|---|---|---|---|---|---|---|---|---|---|---|---|---|---|
| 12.5 | 6.0 | 2.0 | 1.2 | 0.6 | 0.42 | 0.30 | 0.21 | 0.15 | 0.10 | 0.075 | 0.063 | 0.02 | 0.006 | 0.002 |
| Equivalent phi values | | | | | | | | | | | | | | |
| −3.64 | −2.58 | −1.00 | −0.26 | 0.74 | 1.25 | 1.74 | 2.25 | 2.74 | 3.25 | 3.74 | 4.00 | 5.64 | 7.39 | 9.00 |

Sample nos

| 12.5 | 6.0 | 2.0 | 1.2 | 0.6 | 0.42 | 0.30 | 0.21 | 0.15 | 0.10 | 0.075 | 0.063 | 0.02 | 0.006 | 0.002 |
|---|---|---|---|---|---|---|---|---|---|---|---|---|---|---|
| 98.92 | 94.82 | 73.17 | 65.51 | 57.70 | 51.84 | 46.59 | 39.94 | 32.83 | 25.49 | 20.07 | 18.59 | 4.63 | 2.07 | 1.74 |
| 99.27 | 93.20 | 74.42 | 61.94 | 45.09 | 32.34 | 24.06 | 18.45 | 15.56 | 11.65 | 8.36 | 7.81 | 6.12 | 5.15 | 1.17 |
| 94.97 | 77.84 | 62.10 | 53.64 | 44.28 | 37.94 | 32.26 | 25.88 | 13.45 | 10.21 | 5.84 | 5.42 | 5.22 | 3.92 | 2.15 |
| 99.20 | 97.29 | 91.07 | 87.36 | 67.40 | 49.97 | 46.07 | 34.54 | 27.15 | 13.07 | 7.90 | 7.49 | 3.84 | 2.56 | 1.84 |
| — | — | 99.16 | 98.06 | 96.52 | 91.48 | 77.44 | 49.69 | 32.55 | 25.51 | 22.81 | 22.41 | 10.83 | 7.16 | 5.00 |
| — | — | 99.77 | 99.49 | 97.64 | 89.60 | 71.56 | 41.52 | 23.66 | 18.20 | 16.58 | 16.36 | 5.21 | 4.20 | 3.76 |
| — | — | 99.90 | 99.74 | 95.68 | 71.05 | 48.53 | 27.99 | 17.97 | 14.89 | 13.25 | 12.76 | 5.66 | 3.89 | 3.21 |
| — | — | 99.92 | 99.23 | 92.23 | 67.37 | 33.30 | 16.64 | 12.98 | 12.01 | 11.45 | 11.25 | 3.79 | 3.29 | 1.51 |
| — | — | 94.06 | 91.74 | 88.32 | 84.70 | 78.90 | 72.79 | 67.42 | 64.40 | 62.80 | 62.56 | 48.51 | 30.65 | 1.87 |
| — | — | 99.54 | 98.11 | 83.79 | 60.88 | 31.98 | 13.47 | 7.62 | 5.92 | 5.09 | 4.95 | 3.68 | 3.53 | 3.03 |
| 98.94 | 96.68 | 93.25 | 91.82 | 83.47 | 67.34 | 47.99 | 32.54 | 23.68 | 16.54 | 12.04 | 11.38 | 4.61 | 3.86 | 2.91 |
| — | — | 99.99 | 99.35 | 79.62 | 61.19 | 49.09 | 39.76 | 31.43 | 22.00 | 14.09 | 12.86 | 7.58 | 4.82 | 3.27 |
| 98.62 | 89.46 | 73.59 | 63.24 | 48.50 | 40.60 | 28.63 | 22.76 | 19.57 | 15.03 | 10.67 | 9.93 | 2.30 | 1.28 | 0.52 |
| 99.11 | 73.22 | 38.53 | 31.85 | 25.45 | 21.93 | 19.21 | 17.15 | 14.95 | 12.05 | 9.56 | 9.14 | 8.00 | 6.40 | 3.86 |
| 99.02 | 96.62 | 84.69 | 72.83 | 57.93 | 49.62 | 43.59 | 36.08 | 25.85 | 13.50 | 9.37 | 8.84 | 6.50 | 5.98 | 4.51 |
| 94.7 | 82.16 | 63.82 | 56.44 | 46.78 | 41.58 | 34.80 | 27.56 | 20.14 | 14.06 | 10.80 | 10.08 | 5.95 | 5.75 | 4.81 |
| — | 98.86 | 91.46 | 87.20 | 79.49 | 73.46 | 66.16 | 54.83 | 44.17 | 35.93 | 30.61 | 29.59 | 5.55 | 2.80 | 0.72 |
| — | — | 99.80 | 98.89 | 92.85 | 81.02 | 47.58 | 24.82 | 16.45 | 13.11 | 11.56 | 11.28 | 7.81 | 4.34 | 2.81 |
| — | — | — | 99.70 | 85.78 | 66.92 | 54.75 | 42.75 | 31.35 | 19.82 | 12.32 | 11.12 | 3.73 | 2.78 | 0.51 |

Table 5.4 (cont.)

| Particle size in millimetres | | | | | | | | | | | | | | |
| 12.5 | 6.0 | 2.0 | 1.2 | 0.6 | 0.42 | 0.30 | 0.21 | 0.15 | 0.10 | 0.075 | 0.063 | 0.02 | 0.006 | 0.002 |
| *Equivalent phi values* | | | | | | | | | | | | | | |
| −3.64 | −2.58 | −1.00 | −0.26 | 0.74 | 1.25 | 1.74 | 2.25 | 2.74 | 3.25 | 3.74 | 4.00 | 5.64 | 7.39 | 9.00 |

*Sample nos*

| | 12.5 | 6.0 | 2.0 | 1.2 | 0.6 | 0.42 | 0.30 | 0.21 | 0.15 | 0.10 | 0.075 | 0.063 | 0.02 | 0.006 | 0.002 |
|---|---|---|---|---|---|---|---|---|---|---|---|---|---|---|---|
| 20 | — | — | 99.84 | 98.94 | 89.34 | 78.38 | 66.01 | 56.97 | 46.83 | 34.05 | 22.19 | 20.03 | 4.77 | 3.10 | 2.20 |
| 21 | — | 95.50 | 70.50 | 54.74 | 35.38 | 23.58 | 17.26 | 12.66 | 9.82 | 7.92 | 6.88 | 6.61 | 4.84 | 4.28 | 3.37 |
| 22 | — | 97.52 | 92.84 | 89.25 | 63.55 | 44.32 | 31.47 | 24.75 | 19.24 | 15.66 | 13.61 | 13.36 | 3.08 | 2.31 | 1.54 |
| 23 | — | 96.76 | 93.42 | 90.24 | 85.18 | 74.90 | 62.63 | 42.23 | 26.41 | 22.51 | 12.27 | 12.17 | 4.95 | 3.36 | 2.84 |
| 24 | — | — | 98.98 | 95.59 | 59.28 | 29.38 | 20.20 | 12.20 | 9.57 | 7.95 | 7.41 | 7.33 | 5.71 | 5.14 | 2.06 |
| 25 | — | — | 99.83 | 99.02 | 87.70 | 56.29 | 23.81 | 9.61 | 6.51 | 5.35 | 5.01 | 4.97 | 5.34 | 4.50 | 3.71 |
| 26 | — | — | 99.90 | 99.56 | 98.34 | 95.78 | 90.34 | 76.20 | 48.78 | 27.82 | 21.88 | 21.30 | 7.29 | 3.39 | 0.17 |
| 27 | — | — | 96.50 | 89.68 | 79.42 | 70.82 | 61.34 | 49.77 | 37.54 | 29.04 | 24.64 | 24.10 | 16.53 | 3.53 | 2.17 |
| 28 | — | 99.78 | 97.72 | 94.33 | 85.67 | 77.55 | 64.94 | 39.36 | 15.14 | 8.67 | 7.66 | 6.80 | 3.81 | 1.78 | 1.42 |
| 29 | 98.86 | 95.60 | 85.25 | 78.55 | 70.46 | 67.40 | 63.04 | 57.32 | 49.32 | 41.59 | 36.14 | 34.56 | 14.31 | 2.47 | 1.92 |
| 30 | — | — | 99.88 | 99.69 | 97.67 | 91.20 | 69.65 | 40.82 | 19.54 | 10.01 | 5.79 | 5.40 | 2.80 | 1.44 | 0.90 |
| 31 | — | — | 99.34 | 98.65 | 96.65 | 92.27 | 86.49 | 79.69 | 74.17 | 69.65 | 65.49 | 64.39 | 28.39 | 9.94 | 2.76 |
| 32 | 91.84 | 88.68 | 78.82 | 69.94 | 56.44 | 47.84 | 40.32 | 32.12 | 24.36 | 19.42 | 17.10 | 16.56 | 3.32 | 2.95 | 2.58 |
| 33 | — | 96.32 | 85.58 | 79.08 | 61.74 | 44.64 | 34.32 | 28.56 | 25.72 | 23.78 | 22.62 | 22.42 | 9.98 | 4.47 | 2.51 |
| 34 | — | — | 90.72 | 89.29 | 82.88 | 74.24 | 60.77 | 33.89 | 9.84 | 4.50 | 3.78 | 3.74 | 2.19 | 1.68 | 1.22 |
| 35 | — | — | 99.76 | 99.42 | 97.78 | 94.35 | 88.80 | 74.00 | 45.38 | 28.92 | 24.06 | 23.64 | 12.93 | 8.50 | 5.00 |
| 36 | — | — | — | 98.86 | 92.94 | 82.14 | 65.42 | 42.14 | 28.28 | 23.80 | 22.04 | 21.70 | 21.00 | 12.86 | 3.67 |
| 37 | — | — | 96.42 | 93.40 | 80.77 | 66.88 | 54.84 | 41.85 | 29.92 | 15.93 | 7.15 | 6.17 | 3.61 | 3.35 | 3.09 |
| 38 | — | — | 83.31 | 78.31 | 73.13 | 69.06 | 62.10 | 52.45 | 42.28 | 35.24 | 31.26 | 30.64 | 9.12 | 4.18 | 4.06 |

| | | | | | | | | | | | | | | | |
|---|---|---|---|---|---|---|---|---|---|---|---|---|---|---|---|
| 39 | — | 99.35 | 93.83 | 80.58 | 50.68 | 37.68 | 29.05 | 21.01 | 16.44 | 11.60 | 7.61 | 6.98 | 6.70 | 6.27 | 2.88 |
| 40 | — | — | 99.45 | 99.22 | 95.40 | 86.02 | 68.40 | 54.12 | 40.04 | 26.34 | 16.45 | 14.99 | 3.82 | 1.53 | 0.51 |
| 41 | 96.60 | 90.40 | 73.84 | 63.77 | 48.17 | 37.77 | 30.37 | 23.81 | 18.97 | 18.77 | 13.27 | 12.73 | 4.35 | 2.00 | 1.50 |
| 42 | — | 92.84 | 67.84 | 53.48 | 38.08 | 29.48 | 23.28 | 18.40 | 15.32 | 13.22 | 11.62 | 11.22 | 9.74 | 1.19 | 0.54 |
| 43 | — | 97.93 | 91.17 | 83.63 | 61.42 | 40.21 | 22.71 | 9.86 | 5.90 | 3.43 | 2.38 | 2.24 | 1.46 | 0.36 | 0.18 |
| 44 | — | 87.04 | 56.20 | 42.40 | 30.36 | 23.72 | 18.96 | 14.88 | 11.64 | 9.56 | 8.06 | 7.82 | 1.70 | 0.27 | 0.09 |
| 45 | — | — | 96.20 | 90.64 | 72.04 | 54.16 | 40.94 | 31.12 | 23.18 | 17.34 | 12.02 | 11.56 | 3.23 | 2.21 | 1.53 |
| 46 | — | — | — | 99.93 | 98.76 | 96.25 | 85.96 | 66.93 | 43.28 | 22.26 | 15.40 | 14.88 | 8.42 | 3.53 | 3.08 |
| 47 | — | 96.32 | 87.38 | 81.40 | 74.13 | 68.98 | 62.14 | 49.72 | 35.34 | 26.16 | 20.74 | 19.72 | 3.62 | 2.07 | 1.38 |
| 48 | — | — | 94.52 | 84.63 | 75.15 | 70.07 | 60.45 | 45.83 | 20.82 | 10.84 | 7.87 | 7.46 | 3.06 | 2.50 | 2.33 |
| 49 | — | 94.96 | 87.69 | 81.81 | 71.27 | 64.47 | 57.79 | 47.63 | 38.49 | 33.37 | 30.09 | 29.59 | 13.61 | 1.73 | 1.47 |
| 50 | — | — | 97.40 | 93.98 | 83.58 | 74.18 | 65.08 | 53.24 | 41.10 | 32.33 | 26.87 | 25.42 | 11.58 | 9.09 | 6.75 |
| 51 | — | 99.13 | 86.08 | 67.68 | 51.37 | 44.73 | 38.53 | 30.33 | 22.46 | 16.77 | 12.28 | 11.72 | 2.16 | 1.62 | 1.08 |
| 52 | — | — | — | 99.88 | 98.00 | 92.00 | 83.32 | 69.34 | 54.14 | 42.98 | 34.70 | 33.38 | 10.38 | 6.92 | 3.46 |
| 53 | — | 95.64 | 82.59 | 74.66 | 62.09 | 52.60 | 45.24 | 37.15 | 30.36 | 24.40 | 19.98 | 18.98 | 4.66 | 1.54 | 1.47 |
| 54 | — | 90.26 | 66.36 | 55.94 | 42.82 | 34.57 | 25.76 | 18.77 | 14.60 | 11.37 | 11.04 | 7.16 | 6.20 | 3.10 | 1.03 |
| 55 | — | 99.03 | 92.62 | 86.55 | 70.95 | 56.37 | 39.45 | 27.11 | 19.52 | 15.02 | 12.45 | 11.72 | 10.81 | 1.52 | 1.02 |
| 56 | — | 95.59 | 84.37 | 76.88 | 63.15 | 52.05 | 42.40 | 30.49 | 21.01 | 12.57 | 5.03 | 3.53 | 3.08 | 2.58 | 1.92 |
| 57 | — | — | 99.24 | 97.92 | 94.19 | 91.22 | 86.29 | 76.34 | 57.69 | 36.32 | 25.49 | 24.48 | 10.60 | 7.99 | 5.00 |
| 58 | — | — | 91.71 | 88.75 | 84.66 | 81.60 | 78.99 | 75.38 | 71.62 | 68.42 | 66.23 | 65.89 | 39.94 | 3.40 | 2.55 |
| 59 | — | 90.38 | 74.54 | 68.55 | 61.96 | 56.16 | 49.29 | 39.31 | 30.79 | 23.06 | 19.59 | 18.89 | 16.73 | 8.29 | 2.34 |
| 60 | 95.79 | 89.43 | 81.59 | 66.84 | 44.97 | 34.94 | 29.62 | 24.38 | 20.61 | 17.09 | 15.05 | 14.65 | 9.43 | 4.53 | 3.68 |
| 61 | 98.24 | 92.37 | 77.08 | 72.24 | 67.24 | 63.96 | 59.43 | 54.48 | 44.63 | 29.83 | 22.05 | 21.01 | 12.09 | 6.95 | 5.00 |
| 62 | — | — | — | 92.94 | 71.16 | 65.71 | 64.52 | 60.30 | 27.94 | 9.16 | 5.87 | 5.62 | 3.35 | 2.78 | 2.32 |
| 63 | — | 97.34 | 92.05 | 87.79 | 81.28 | 77.41 | 70.84 | 59.37 | 43.11 | 35.65 | 33.77 | 33.53 | 15.16 | 10.04 | 2.61 |
| 64 | — | — | 75.14 | 92.43 | 78.38 | 63.61 | 51.26 | 40.09 | 32.63 | 23.08 | 16.39 | 15.26 | 7.08 | 4.15 | 0.51 |
| 65 | — | — | 99.88 | 99.70 | 98.98 | 96.40 | 84.58 | 67.91 | 48.35 | 32.37 | 15.01 | 12.93 | 9.75 | 2.05 | 0.77 |

*Mean* This represents the average of a series of readings and several formulae have been suggested for the calculation of the mean. Inman (1952) suggested the formula $M\phi = \frac{1}{2}(\phi16 + \phi84)$. Folk and Ward (1957) indicated that Inman's formula provided a good result for fairly normally distributed curves, but if the curves were asymmetrical, or bimodal in character then the results were not so satisfactory. They have suggested the following formula: $M_z = \phi16 + \phi50 + \phi84/3$. They indicated that the $\phi16$ represents the average of the coarsest third of the sample, and $\phi84$ the average size of the finest third, while the $\phi50$ gives the average value of the middle third which will provide a more complete view of the distribution.

In 1962 McCammon provided other formulae which included more percentiles; the efficiency of the commonly used formulae and his formulae have been discussed and compared (McCammon, 1962).

|  | Efficiency (percentage) |
|---|---|
| Inman (1952) | |
| $M\phi = \frac{1}{2}(\phi16 + \phi84)$ | 74 |
| Folk and Ward (1957) | |
| $M_z = \dfrac{(\phi16 + \phi50 + \phi84)}{3}$ | 88 |
| McCammon (1962) | |
| $M\phi = (\phi20 + \phi50 + \phi80)/3$ | 88 |
| $(\phi10 + \phi30 + \phi50 + \phi70 + \phi90)/5$ | 93 |
| $(\phi5 + \phi15 + \phi25 + \phi35 + \phi45 + \phi55 + \phi65 + \phi75 + \phi85 + \phi95)/10$ | 97 |

*Standard Deviation (sorting)* The degree of sorting in a sample is essentially a measure of dispersion. The best method is that which makes use of points representing most of the cumulative curves, as the more of a curve that enters a sorting measure, the more accurate the measure will be. Trask (1930) used the upper and lower quartiles on the cumulative frequency curve, that is the 75th and 25th on the millimetre scale; $S_o = (Q_1/Q_3)$.

Krumbein (1936) proposed a $Q$ analogue to Trask's, so the quartile deviation $QD\phi = (\phi75 - \phi25)/2$. It is clear that this formula takes less note of the tail of the distribution and thus fails to give a good indication of the sorting.

Inman (1952) following Otto (1939) in suggesting a parameter called the phi diameter measure: $\sigma\phi = \frac{1}{2}(\phi84 - \phi16)$. Inman's formula gives good results for a normal distribution but is not adequate to describe all sediments, as it is also based on the central part of the cumulative curve only and ignores at least a third of the sample at either end of the range of sizes.

To overcome this difficulty, more of the distribution curves should be included in the sorting measure. Folk and Ward (1957) suggested a sorting measure which they call the Inclusive Graphic Standard Deviation:

$$\sigma 1 = \frac{\phi 84 - \phi 16}{4} + \frac{\phi 95 - \phi 5}{6.6}$$

They suggested a verbal scale which can be used to describe sorting:

| | |
|---|---|
| $\sigma$ 1 under 0.35 | very well sorted |
| 0.35–0.5 | well sorted |
| 0.5–1.0 | moderately sorted |
| 1.0–2.0 | poorly sorted |
| 2.0–4.0 | very poorly sorted |
| over 4.0 | extremely poorly sorted |

McCammon (op. cit.) proposed a new measure and compared the statistical efficiencies of various measures:

Efficiency (percentage)

Inman (1952)

$(\phi 84 - \phi 16)/2$     54

Folk and Ward (1957)

$(\phi 84 - \phi 16)/4 + (\phi 95 - \phi 5)/6.6$     79

McCammon (1962)

$(\phi 85 + \phi 95 - \phi 5 - \phi 15)/5.4$     79

$(\phi 70 + \phi 80 + \phi 90 + \phi 97 - \phi 3 - \phi 10 - \phi 20 - \phi 30)/9.1$     87

The above formulae show that the efficiency improves as more of the tail of the sample is included in the account.

*Skewness* The deviation of the frequency curve from the symmetry of a normal distribution is expressed as skewness. In a symmetrical distribution the mean and the median coincide and there is no skewness. Trask (1932) suggested the following formula to measure the skewness.

$$Sk = Q_1 \times Q_3 / Md^2$$

where $Q_1$ and $Q_3$ represent the diameter in millimetres corresponding to the 25th and 75th percentiles respectively and $Md$ is the median diameter in millimetres, but since this formula does not cover the entire curve, Inman (1952) suggested two measures of skewness

$$a\phi = \frac{M\phi - Md\phi}{\sigma\phi}$$

one for the central part of the distribution and the other to determine the asymmetry of the extremes and called it the second phi skewness, based on the 5th and 95th percentile diameters

$$a2\ \phi = \frac{\frac{1}{2}(\phi 5 + \phi 95) - Md\phi}{\sigma\phi}.$$

Folk and Ward (1957) developed a modification to the two skewness formulae of Inman and combined them in one formula which they called the Inclusive Graphic Skewness:

$$Sk_1 = \frac{\phi16 + \phi84 - 2\phi50}{2(\phi84 - \phi16)} + \frac{\phi5 + \phi95 - 2\phi50}{2(\phi95 - \phi5)}.$$

Symmetrical curves have $Sk_1 = 0.00$, the mathematical limits are $-1.00$ to $+1.00$ and a few curves have skewness beyond $-0.80$ or $+0.80$.

Folk and Ward (1957) have suggested the following verbal limits:

| | |
|---|---|
| $Sk_1$ from $-1.00$ to $0.3$ | very negative skewed |
| $-0.3$ to $-0.1$ | negative skewed |
| $-0.1$ to $+0.1$ | nearly symmetrical |
| $+0.1$ to $+0.3$ | positively skewed |
| $+0.3$ to $+1$ | very positive skewed |

Negative values indicate that the sample has a 'tail' of coarser grain, whereas positive value indicates a 'tail' of finer material.

*Kurtosis* This is a measure of peakness and measures the ratio of the sorting in the extremes of the distribution compared with the sorting in the central part; as such it is a sensitive and valuable test of the normality of a distribution. Inman (1952) defines the phi kurtosis measure as

$$\beta\phi = \frac{\frac{1}{2}(\phi16 - \phi5) + \frac{1}{2}(\phi95 - \phi84)}{\sigma\phi}.$$

For a normal distribution $\beta\phi$ has a value of 0.65, but if the curve is less peaked, the value will be greater than 0.65 and for a more peaked curve, than the normal curve the value will be less than 0.65.

Folk and Ward (1957) developed a measure of graphic kurtosis:

$$K_G = \frac{\phi95 - \phi5}{2.44(\phi75 - \phi25)}$$

where normal curves have $K_G = 1.00$, the mathematical minimum is 0.41. They suggested that for plotting graphs and for statistical analyses, it is better to use the normalized function

$$K'_G = \frac{K_G}{K_G + 1}.$$

The following verbal limits have been suggested:

| | |
|---|---|
| $K_G$ under $0.67 = K'_G$ under $0.4$ | very platykurtic (tails are better sorted than the central portion of the curve) |
| $0.67–0.9 = 0.4–0.47$ | platykurtic |
| $0.9–1.11 = 0.47–0.52$ | mesokurtic (the sorting of the central portion of the |

|  | curve is equal to that of the tails) |
|---|---|
| 1.11–1.5 = 0.52–0.60 | leptokurtic (better sorted in the central area than in the tails) |
| 1.5–3 = 0.60–0.75 | very leptokurtic |
| $K_G$ over 3.0 = $K'_G$ over 0.75 | extremely leptokurtic |

For the present work statistical parameters used in describing the grain size properties of the sediments are those proposed by Folk and Ward (1957).

*Parameter variations* Sixty-five samples were statistically analysed by the method outlined before. From the cumulative curves (Figure 5.17) different weight percentiles were obtained to calculate the different size parameters. These percentiles are: 5, 16, 25, 50, 75, 84 and 95, and are given in Table 5.5. The results of the statistical analyses are shown in Table 5.6. There is no significant relationship between the parameter value of individual sampling point and their distance from the sea. Higher or lower values are obtained in various areas. The mean size ($M_z$) value of the samples shows an absolute

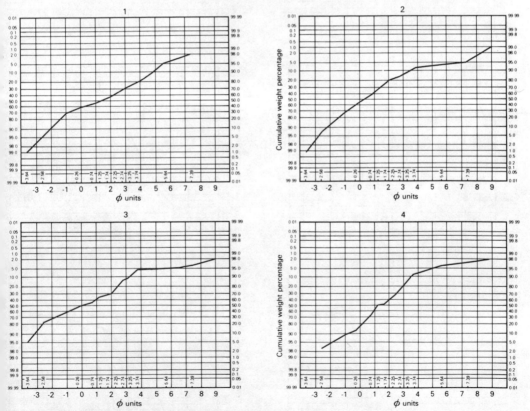

**Figure 5.17** *Cumulative curves of the samples*

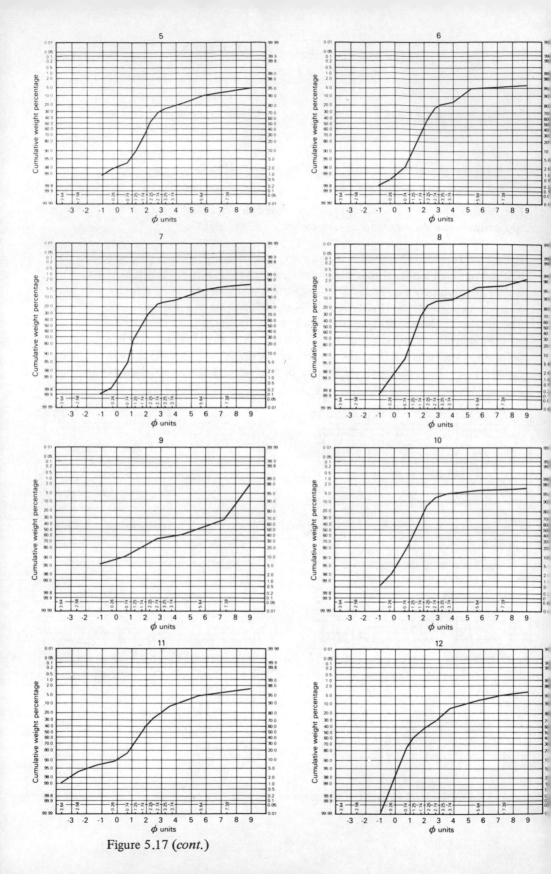

Figure 5.17 (*cont.*)

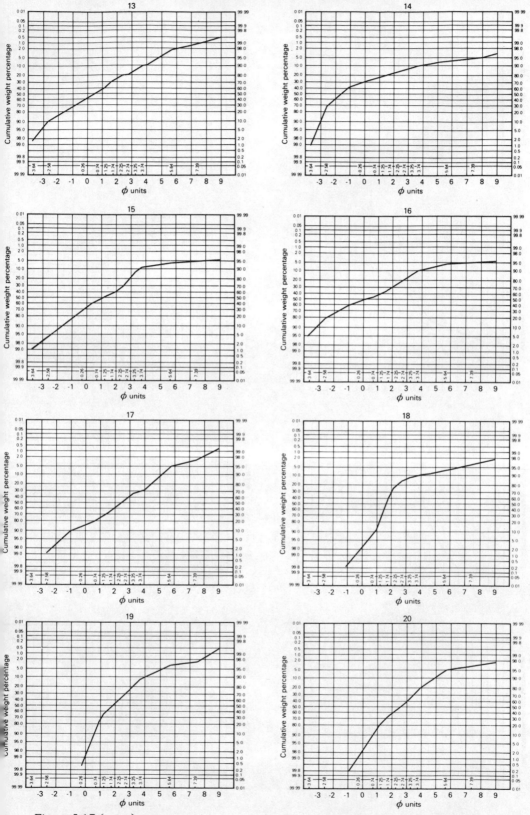

Figure 5.17 (*cont.*)

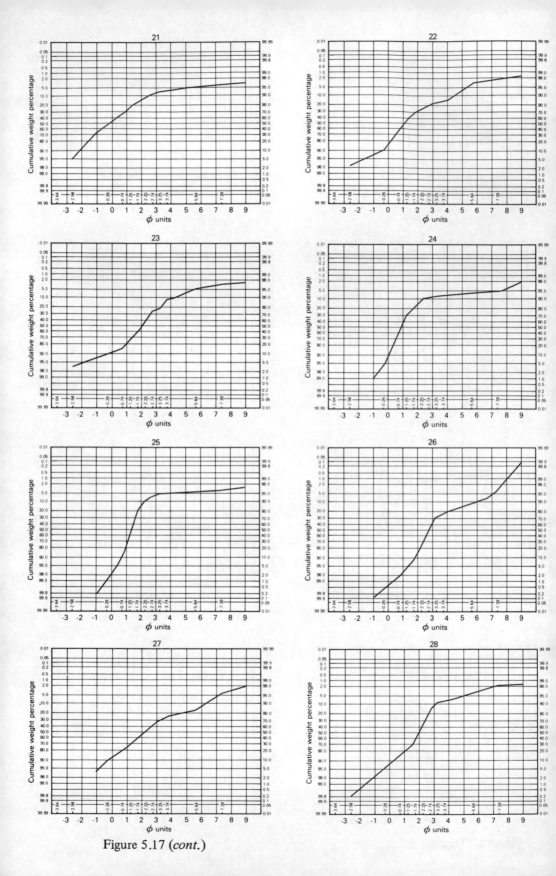

Figure 5.17 (*cont.*)

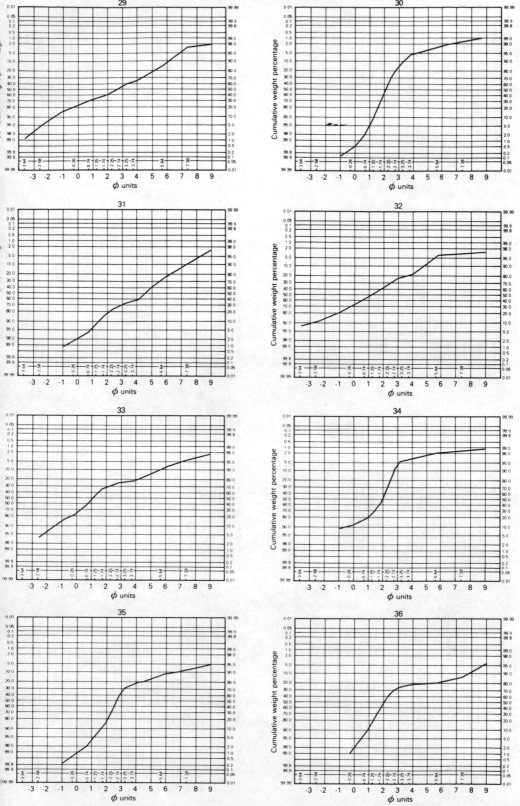

Figure 5.17 (*cont.*)

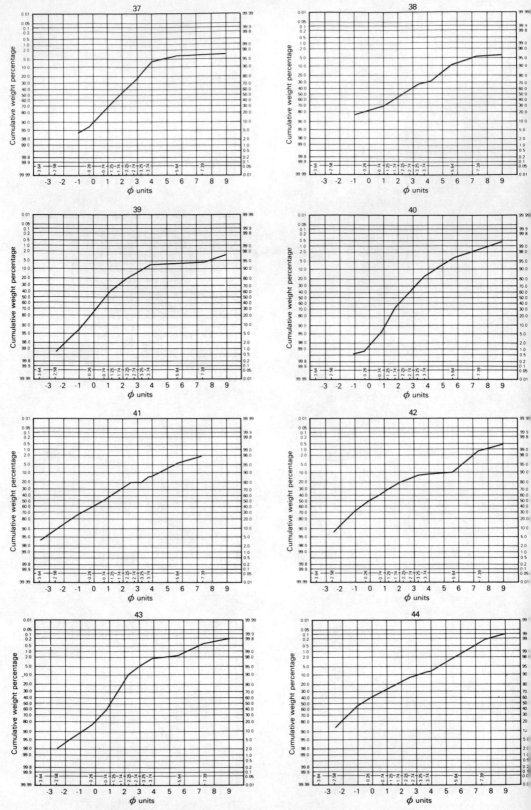

Figure 5.17 (*cont.*)

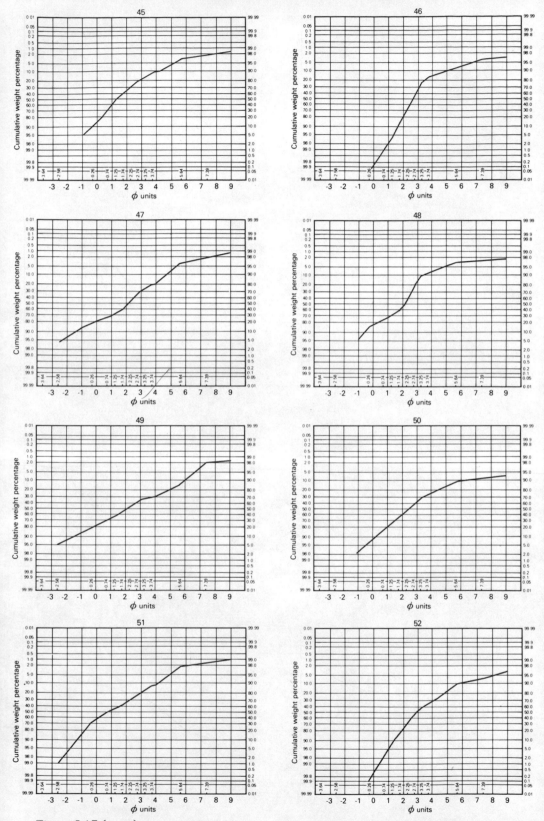

Figure 5.17 (*cont.*)

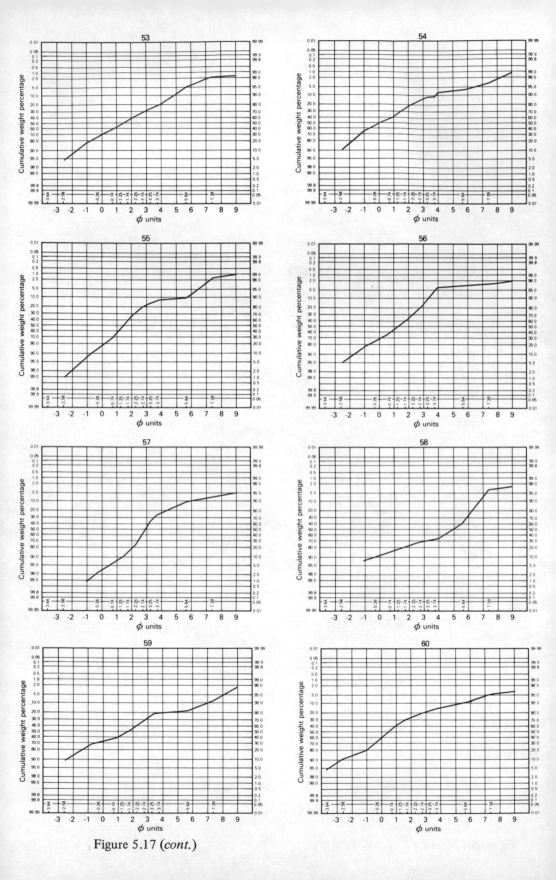

Figure 5.17 (*cont.*)

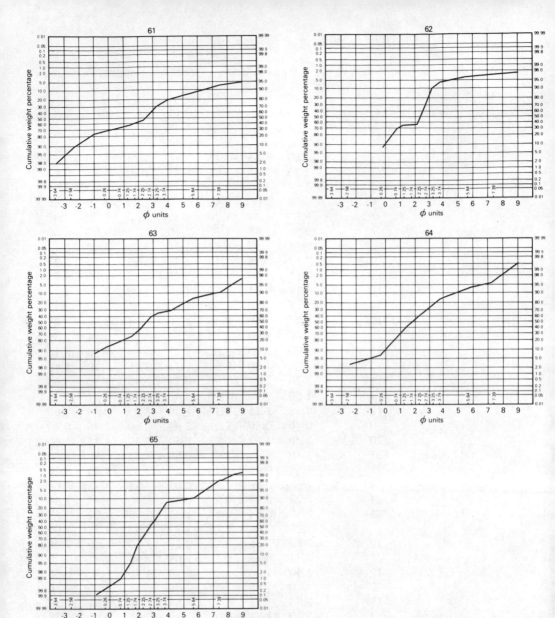

variation from $-0.61$ $\phi$ (1.53 millimetres) to $4.87$ $\phi$ (0.034 millimetres) which reflects the wide range of grain size present in the area. The standard deviation ($\sigma_I$) values range from $0.82$ $\phi$ moderately sorted to $3.54$ $\phi$ very poorly sorted. Values of skewness ($Sk_I$) range from very negative skewness $-0.43$ $\phi$ to very positive skewness $0.63$ $\phi$. The transformed values of $K'_G$ have been applied and the result shows an absolute variation from a minimum value of $0.43$ $\phi$ to a maximum of $K'_G = 0.77$ $\phi$ which reflects the environments prevailing in the area. However, an apparent variation appears when comparing all the samples from a particular terrace with the beach samples. The mean size value was obtained by averaging the results of the

**Table 5.5** *Percentiles used for the calculation of the mean, standard deviation, skewness and kurtosis*

| Location | Sample no. | 5 | 16 | 25 | 50 | 75 | 84 | 95 |
|---|---|---|---|---|---|---|---|---|
| | 1 | −2.60 | −1.65 | −1.15 | 1.40 | 3.25 | 4.20 | 5.55 |
| | 2 | −2.75 | −1.65 | −1.06 | 0.45 | 1.70 | 2.68 | 7.43 |
| Kathma I | 3 | −3.64 | −2.84 | −2.30 | 0.15 | 2.25 | 2.63 | 5.90 |
| | 4 | −1.84 | −0.05 | −0.40 | 1.20 | 2.80 | 3.10 | 5.00 |
| | 5 | 0.95 | 1.55 | 1.80 | 2.22 | 3.30 | 4.70 | 9.00 |
| | 6 | 0.98 | 1.45 | 1.65 | 2.10 | 2.70 | 4.00 | 6.00 |
| | 7 | 0.76 | 1.05 | 1.17 | 1.72 | 3.05 | 3.00 | 6.32 |
| | 8 | 0.52 | 0.98 | 1.10 | 1.48 | 1.95 | 2.30 | 5.25 |
| | 9 | −1.12 | 1.30 | 2.05 | 5.45 | 7.55 | 7.85 | 8.55 |
| | 10 | 0.14 | 0.73 | 0.95 | 1.40 | 1.90 | 2.14 | 3.90 |
| | 11 | −1.68 | 0.70 | 1.02 | 1.68 | 2.65 | 3.30 | 5.52 |
| | 12 | 0.25 | 0.65 | 0.86 | 1.70 | 3.05 | 3.60 | 7.20 |
| Kathma II | 13 | −3.00 | −1.90 | −1.15 | 0.64 | 2.05 | 3.14 | 4.85 |
| | 14 | −3.20 | −2.80 | −2.62 | −1.53 | 0.80 | 2.50 | 8.18 |
| | 15 | −2.25 | −1.00 | −0.40 | 1.20 | 2.76 | 3.10 | 8.40 |
| | 16 | −3.70 | −2.67 | −1.95 | 0.44 | 2.40 | 3.10 | 8.60 |
| | 17 | −1.50 | 0.20 | 1.10 | 2.48 | 4.17 | 4.67 | 5.90 |
| | 18 | 0.52 | 1.15 | 1.35 | 1.70 | 2.22 | 2.80 | 7.00 |
| | 19 | 0.40 | 0.80 | 1.05 | 1.95 | 3.00 | 3.45 | 5.30 |
| | 20 | 0.36 | 1.02 | 1.38 | 2.60 | 3.52 | 4.25 | 5.60 |
| Ghidhai | 21 | −2.50 | −1.65 | −1.25 | 0.00 | 1.15 | 1.90 | 5.50 |
| | 22 | −1.60 | 0.05 | 0.40 | 1.10 | 2.25 | 3.20 | 8.10 |
| | 23 | −1.60 | 0.80 | 1.25 | 2.05 | 2.95 | 3.53 | 5.64 |
| | 24 | −0.22 | 0.24 | 0.44 | 0.88 | 1.40 | 1.95 | 7.45 |
| | 25 | 0.33 | 0.84 | 0.96 | 1.32 | 1.73 | 1.97 | 3.85 |
| | 26 | 1.35 | 2.04 | 2.26 | 2.73 | 3.45 | 4.75 | 7.05 |
| | 27 | −0.80 | 0.35 | 0.10 | 2.20 | 3.70 | 5.40 | 7.00 |
| | 28 | −0.37 | 0.85 | 1.35 | 2.04 | 2.50 | 2.72 | 4.90 |
| | 29 | −2.40 | −1.00 | 0.20 | 2.70 | 4.70 | 5.50 | 6.80 |
| | 30 | 1.00 | 1.45 | 1.63 | 2.08 | 2.56 | 2.90 | 4.10 |
| | 31 | 0.96 | 1.95 | 2.70 | 4.64 | 5.90 | 6.65 | 8.30 |
| Mudairah | 32 | −3.70 | −1.74 | −0.70 | 1.10 | 2.72 | 4.02 | 5.30 |
| | 33 | −2.30 | −0.85 | 0.00 | 1.10 | 2.80 | 4.65 | 7.18 |
| | 34 | −1.25 | 0.55 | 1.20 | 1.95 | 2.36 | 2.55 | 3.15 |
| | 35 | 1.16 | 1.92 | 2.20 | 2.65 | 3.65 | 5.00 | 9.00 |
| | 36 | 0.52 | 1.18 | 1.45 | 2.05 | 3.10 | 6.35 | 8.70 |
| | 37 | −0.63 | 0.52 | 0.95 | 1.90 | 2.87 | 3.22 | 4.20 |
| | 38 | −1.40 | −1.05 | 0.40 | 2.35 | 4.25 | 4.90 | 7.00 |
| | 39 | −1.22 | −0.40 | −0.04 | 0.80 | 1.97 | 2.74 | 7.90 |
| | 40 | 0.78 | 1.30 | 1.55 | 2.40 | 3.30 | 3.80 | 5.35 |
| Al-Bahra I | 41 | −3.25 | −1.85 | −1.15 | 0.65 | 2.15 | 3.46 | 5.45 |
| | 42 | −2.65 | −1.85 | −1.38 | −0.05 | 1.60 | 2.65 | 5.10 |
| | 43 | −1.65 | −0.30 | 0.20 | 1.05 | 1.65 | 1.95 | 2.90 |

| Location | Sample no. | 5 | 16 | 25 | 50 | 75 | 84 | 95 |
|---|---|---|---|---|---|---|---|---|
| | 44 | −2.80 | −2.35 | −1.85 | −0.70 | 1.10 | 2.08 | 4.50 |
| | 45 | −0.80 | 0.20 | 0.65 | 1.40 | 2.65 | 3.40 | 5.20 |
| | 46 | 1.33 | 1.80 | 2.05 | 2.60 | 3.15 | 3.70 | 6.75 |
| | 47 | −2.22 | −0.55 | 0.65 | 2.20 | 3.35 | 4.24 | 5.40 |
| | 48 | −1.10 | −0.20 | 0.75 | 2.10 | 2.64 | 2.95 | 4.75 |
| | 49 | −2.58 | −0.50 | 0.40 | 2.10 | 4.40 | 5.35 | 6.60 |
| | 50 | −0.45 | 0.72 | 1.20 | 2.40 | 3.95 | 5.00 | 9.00 |
| | 51 | −1.70 | −0.94 | −0.55 | 0.85 | 2.60 | 3.40 | 4.90 |
| | 52 | 1.06 | 1.70 | 2.05 | 2.95 | 4.45 | 5.10 | 8.10 |
| Al-Bahra II | 53 | −2.44 | −1.14 | −0.30 | 1.45 | 3.16 | 4.20 | 5.55 |
| | 54 | −2.73 | −2.00 | −1.48 | 0.20 | 1.80 | 2.55 | 6.30 |
| | 55 | −1.37 | −0.06 | 0.50 | 1.42 | 2.38 | 3.10 | 6.40 |
| | 56 | −2.45 | −1.00 | −0.12 | 1.35 | 2.54 | 3.00 | 3.75 |
| | 57 | 0.60 | 1.90 | 2.30 | 2.94 | 3.80 | 4.90 | 9.00 |
| | 58 | −1.20 | 0.85 | 2.20 | 4.90 | 6.05 | 6.45 | 7.20 |
| | 59 | −2.72 | −1.80 | 0.25 | 1.70 | 3.10 | 5.80 | 8.10 |
| Al-Bahra III | 60 | −3.44 | −1.45 | −0.65 | 0.52 | 2.18 | 3.50 | 7.15 |
| | 61 | −2.90 | −1.60 | −0.70 | 2.50 | 3.55 | 4.80 | 9.00 |
| | 62 | −0.34 | 0.25 | 0.60 | 2.40 | 3.80 | 3.02 | 4.20 |
| | 63 | −1.20 | 0.35 | 1.40 | 2.52 | 4.65 | 5.58 | 8.30 |
| | 64 | −0.95 | 0.38 | 0.78 | 1.80 | 3.10 | 3.80 | 6.85 |
| | 65 | 1.34 | 1.76 | 2.03 | 2.70 | 3.44 | 3.74 | 6.45 |

**Table 5.6** *Results of statistical analysis of particle size curves*

| Location | Sample no. | $M_z\phi$ | $\sigma_I$ | $Sk_I$ | $K_G$ | $K_G{}'$ |
|---|---|---|---|---|---|---|
| Kathma I | 1 | 1.32 | 2.7 | −0.01 | 0.76 | 0.43 |
| | 2 | 0.49 | 2.62 | 0.20 | 1.51 | 0.60 |
| | 3 | −0.02 | 2.81 | 0.06 | 0.86 | 0.46 |
| | 4 | 1.42 | 2.13 | 0.16 | 1.17 | 0.54 |
| | 5 | 2.82 | 2.01 | 0.63 | 2.20 | 0.69 |
| | 6 | 2.52 | 1.40 | 0.52 | 1.96 | 0.66 |
| | 7 | 1.92 | 1.33 | 0.48 | 1.21 | 0.55 |
| | 8 | 1.59 | 1.05 | 0.42 | 2.28 | 0.70 |
| | 9 | 4.87 | 3.10 | −0.27 | 0.72 | 0.42 |
| | 10 | 1.42 | 0.92 | 0.19 | 1.62 | 0.62 |
| | 11 | 1.89 | 1.74 | 0.16 | 1.81 | 0.64 |
| | 12 | 1.98 | 1.79 | 0.44 | 1.30 | 0.57 |
| Kathma II | 13 | 0.63 | 2.45 | 0.03 | 1.01 | 0.50 |
| | 14 | −0.61 | 3.05 | 0.61 | 1.36 | 0.58 |

Table 5.6 (*cont.*)

| Location | Sample no. | $M_z\phi$ | $\sigma_I$ | $Sk_I$ | $K_G$ | $K_G{}'$ |
|---|---|---|---|---|---|---|
| | 15 | 1.10 | 2.64 | 0.14 | 1.38 | 0.58 |
| | 16 | 2.90 | 3.31 | 0.13 | 1.16 | 0.54 |
| | 17 | 2.45 | 2.24 | −0.05 | 0.99 | 0.50 |
| | 18 | 1.88 | 1.39 | 0.48 | 3.06 | 0.75 |
| | 19 | 2.07 | 1.40 | 0.25 | 1.03 | 0.51 |
| | 20 | 2.62 | 1.60 | 0.08 | 1.00 | 0.50 |
| Ghidhai | 21 | 0.08 | 2.10 | 0.22 | 1.37 | 0.58 |
| | 22 | 1.45 | 2.26 | 0.39 | 2.15 | 0.68 |
| | 23 | 2.13 | 1.78 | 0.04 | 1.75 | 0.64 |
| | 24 | 1.02 | 1.59 | 0.50 | 3.28 | 0.77 |
| | 25 | 1.38 | 0.82 | 0.29 | 1.87 | 0.65 |
| | 26 | 3.17 | 1.54 | 0.50 | 1.96 | 0.66 |
| | 27 | 2.65 | 2.44 | 0.25 | 0.89 | 0.47 |
| | 28 | 1.87 | 1.27 | −0.09 | 1.88 | 0.65 |
| | 29 | 2.37 | 3.04 | −0.13 | 0.84 | 0.46 |
| | 30 | 2.14 | 0.83 | 0.22 | 1.37 | 0.58 |
| | 31 | 4.41 | 2.29 | −0.07 | 0.97 | 0.48 |
| Mudairah | 32 | 1.13 | 2.8 | −0.03 | 1.08 | 0.52 |
| | 33 | 1.63 | 2.81 | 0.29 | 1.39 | 0.58 |
| | 34 | 1.68 | 1.17 | −0.43 | 1.55 | 0.61 |
| | 35 | 3.19 | 2.65 | 0.57 | 2.21 | 0.69 |
| | 36 | 3.19 | 2.53 | 0.64 | 2.03 | 0.67 |
| | 37 | 1.88 | 1.41 | −0.03 | 1.03 | 0.51 |
| | 38 | 2.07 | 2.76 | −0.02 | 0.89 | 0.47 |
| | 39 | 1.05 | 2.17 | 0.40 | 1.86 | 0.65 |
| | 40 | 2.50 | 1.32 | 0.21 | 1.07 | 0.52 |
| Al-Bahra I | 41 | 0.75 | 2.65 | 0.08 | 1.08 | 0.52 |
| | 42 | 0.25 | 2.30 | 0.26 | 1.07 | 0.52 |
| | 43 | 0.90 | 1.25 | −0.19 | 1.29 | 0.56 |
| | 44 | −0.32 | 2.21 | 0.55 | 1.01 | 0.50 |
| | 45 | 1.67 | 1.71 | 0.26 | 1.23 | 0.55 |
| | 46 | 2.70 | 1.30 | 0.34 | 2.02 | 0.67 |
| | 47 | 1.96 | 2.35 | −0.15 | 1.16 | 0.54 |
| | 48 | 1.62 | 1.67 | −0.28 | 1.26 | 0.58 |
| | 49 | 2.32 | 2.85 | 0.05 | 0.94 | 0.48 |
| | 50 | 2.71 | 2.50 | 0.31 | 1.41 | 0.59 |
| | 51 | 1.10 | 2.09 | 0.20 | 0.86 | 0.46 |
| | 52 | 3.25 | 1.92 | 0.36 | 1.20 | 0.55 |
| Al-Bahra II | 53 | 1.50 | 2.55 | 0.04 | 0.95 | 0.49 |
| | 54 | 0.25 | 2.51 | 0.20 | 1.13 | 0.53 |
| | 55 | 1.49 | 1.97 | 0.17 | 1.69 | 0.63 |
| | 56 | 1.12 | 1.94 | −0.20 | 0.96 | 0.49 |
| | 57 | 3.25 | 2.02 | 0.53 | 2.30 | 0.70 |
| | 58 | 4.07 | 2.67 | −0.40 | 0.89 | 0.47 |
| | 59 | 1.90 | 3.54 | 0.13 | 1.57 | 0.61 |

| Location | Sample no. | $M_z\phi$ | $\sigma_I$ | $Sk_I$ | $K_G$ | $K_G{}'$ |
|----------|-----------|-----------|------------|--------|-------|----------|
| Al-Bahra III | 60 | 0.86 | 2.84 | 0.23 | 1.53 | 0.60 |
| | 61 | 1.90 | 3.40 | −0.09 | 1.15 | 0.53 |
| | 62 | 1.89 | 1.39 | −0.38 | 0.85 | 0.46 |
| | 63 | 2.82 | 2.75 | 0.19 | 1.20 | 0.55 |
| | 64 | 1.99 | 2.04 | 0.23 | 1.38 | 0.58 |
| | 65 | 2.73 | 1.27 | 0.34 | 1.49 | 0.60 |

four parameters from each of the six terraces in the areas as well as those from the top of the escarpment and the beach samples (Figure 5.18, Table 5.7). The results show that:

*Mean size ($M_z$)* The mean size fluctuates from $M_z = 0.90 \phi$ on the top of the escarpment to a value of $0.78 \phi$ on the First terrace. These high values reflect the dominant mode of grains on them as a result of the presence of gravel of medium and small size. A gradual decrease in the size appears towards the lower terraces as the sediment becomes more sandy until it reaches its finest size on the Fifth and Sixth terraces ($M_z = 2.53 \phi$ and $2.52 \phi$). The mean size increases again towards the beach samples $M_z = 2.3\phi$ indicating an increase of the particle size possibly resulting from the loss of the fine grains which is expected for the beach sands in general.

*Standard deviation ($\sigma_I$)* The solid line indicates the area of very poorly sorted sand with standard deviation of $2.58 \phi$ on the top of the escarpment and on the First terrace. Similar poor sorting is attained on the Fifth and Sixth terraces with values of $\sigma_I = 2.54 \phi$ and $2.68 \phi$. The second area is concerned with the Second and Third terraces which, although characterized by being very poorly sorted (over $2 \phi$), is better sorted than the first area mentioned. The Second terrace has a mean of standard deviation of $2.16 \phi$ and $2.04 \phi$ for the Third terrace. From there the line declines to the third better-sorted area on the Fourth terrace, $\phi_I = 1.73 \phi$ where identified marine sediment has been recognized in the field. The second area of similar better sorting is on the present beach with a standard deviation of $1.83 \phi$.

*Skewness ($Sk_I$)* On the top of the escarpment, the sediment is nearly symmetrical (symmetrical limit $−0.1$ to $+ 0.1 \phi$). This is because a pure modal fraction of gravel size is predominant, $Sk_I = 0.08 \phi$. Similar to this area is the First terrace which appears to have sediment of two modes that are nearly equal (gravel and sand), but, as the two modes are mixed, with the majority being of the coarse fraction mode, the mean of the skewness in the First terrace attains a positive skewness. This can be noticed as the line joining the mean of the skewness of the top of the escarpment rises to the value of $Sk_I = 0.21 \phi$. Addition of small quantities of silt to the dominant sand mode produced

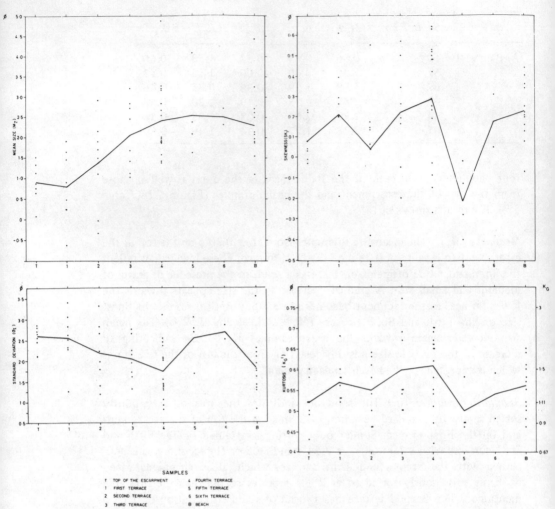

SAMPLES

| | | | |
|---|---|---|---|
| T | TOP OF THE ESCARPMENT | 4 | FOURTH TERRACE |
| 1 | FIRST TERRACE | 5 | FIFTH TERRACE |
| 2 | SECOND TERRACE | 6 | SIXTH TERRACE |
| 3 | THIRD TERRACE | B | BEACH |

The dots represent the value of each analysed sample at each locality. The solid line represents the mean value by averaging the results from each of the eight locations.

**Figure 5.18** *Parameters' variation across the research area*

positive skewness, which seems to justify the positive skewness on the Third and Fourth terrace. The line declines again to negative skewness of $Sk_I = -0.21\ \phi$ which reflects the characteristic of the sediment. It rises again to positive skewness as the sediments on the Sixth terrace contain a higher proportion of finer material ($0.18\ \phi$) than the beach samples ($Sk_I = 0.23\ \phi$). In these cases this may have been caused by the addition of more silt and clay from the Tigris and Euphrates river system as opposed to aeolian material on the Sixth terrace.

**Table 5.7** *The mean size values of the four parameters (mean, standard deviation, skewness and kurtosis) for the samples from the top of the escarpment, the six terraces and the beach*

| Location | Sample no. | $M_z\phi$ | $\sigma_I$ | $Sk_I$ | $K_G$ | $K_G$ |
|---|---|---|---|---|---|---|
| | 1 | 1.32 | 2.70 | −0.01 | 0.76 | 0.43 |
| Top of | 13 | 0.63 | 2.45 | 0.03 | 1.01 | 0.50 |
| the | 21 | 0.08 | 2.10 | 0.22 | 1.37 | 0.58 |
| escarpment | 32 | 1.13 | 2.80 | −0.03 | 1.08 | 0.52 |
| | 41 | 0.75 | 2.65 | 0.08 | 1.08 | 0.52 |
| | 53 | 1.50 | 2.55 | 0.04 | 0.95 | 0.49 |
| | 60 | 0.86 | 2.84 | 0.23 | 1.53 | 0.60 |
| | Average | 0.90 | 2.58 | 0.08 | 1.11 | 0.52 |
| | 2 | 0.49 | 2.62 | 0.20 | 1.51 | 0.60 |
| First | 14 | −0.61 | 3.05 | 0.61 | 1.36 | 0.58 |
| terrace | 22 | 1.45 | 2.26 | 0.39 | 2.15 | 0.68 |
| | 33 | 1.63 | 2.81 | 0.29 | 1.39 | 0.58 |
| | 42 | 0.25 | 2.30 | 0.26 | 1.07 | 0.52 |
| | 43 | 0.90 | 1.25 | −0.19 | 1.29 | 0.56 |
| | 54 | 0.25 | 2.51 | 0.20 | 1.13 | 0.53 |
| | 61 | 1.90 | 3.40 | −0.09 | 1.15 | 0.53 |
| | Average | 0.78 | 2.53 | 0.21 | 1.38 | 0.57 |
| | 3 | −0.02 | 2.81 | 0.06 | 0.86 | 0.46 |
| | 15 | 1.10 | 2.64 | 0.14 | 1.38 | 0.58 |
| Second | 16 | 2.90 | 3.31 | 0.13 | 1.16 | 0.54 |
| terrace | 23 | 2.13 | 1.78 | 0.04 | 1.75 | 0.64 |
| | 34 | 1.68 | 1.17 | −0.43 | 1.55 | 0.61 |
| | 44 | −0.32 | 2.21 | 0.55 | 1.01 | 0.50 |
| | 55 | 1.49 | 1.97 | 0.17 | 1.69 | 0.63 |
| | 62 | 1.89 | 1.39 | −0.38 | 0.85 | 0.46 |
| | Average | 1.36 | 2.16 | 0.04 | 1.28 | 0.55 |
| | 4 | 1.42 | 2.13 | 0.16 | 1.17 | 0.54 |
| | 17 | 2.45 | 2.24 | −0.05 | 0.99 | 0.50 |
| | 24 | 1.02 | 1.59 | 0.50 | 3.28 | 0.77 |
| Third | 35 | 3.19 | 2.65 | 0.57 | 2.21 | 0.69 |
| terrace | 45 | 1.67 | 1.71 | 0.26 | 1.23 | 0.55 |
| | 46 | 2.70 | 1.30 | 0.34 | 2.02 | 0.67 |

Table 5.7 (*cont.*)

| Location | Sample no. | $M_z\phi$ | $\sigma_I$ | $Sk_I$ | $K_G$ | $K_G'$ |
|----------|------------|-----------|------------|--------|-------|--------|
| | 56 | 1.12 | 1.94 | −0.2 | 0.96 | 0.49 |
| | 63 | 2.82 | 2.75 | 0.19 | 1.20 | 0.55 |
| | Average | 2.05 | 2.04 | 0.22 | 1.63 | 0.60 |
| | 5 | 2.82 | 2.01 | 0.63 | 2.20 | 0.69 |
| | 6 | 2.52 | 1.40 | 0.52 | 1.96 | 0.66 |
| | 7 | 1.92 | 1.33 | 0.48 | 1.21 | 0.55 |
| | 8 | 1.59 | 1.05 | 0.42 | 2.28 | 0.70 |
| Fourth | 9 | 4.87 | 3.10 | −0.27 | 0.72 | 0.42 |
| terrace | 10 | 1.42 | 0.92 | 0.19 | 1.62 | 0.62 |
| | 18 | 1.88 | 1.39 | 0.48 | 3.06 | 0.75 |
| | 25 | 1.38 | 0.82 | 0.29 | 1.87 | 0.65 |
| | 26 | 3.17 | 1.54 | 0.50 | 1.96 | 0.66 |
| | 27 | 2.65 | 2.44 | 0.25 | 0.89 | 0.47 |
| | 28 | 1.87 | 1.27 | −0.09 | 1.88 | 0.65 |
| | 36 | 3.19 | 2.53 | 0.64 | 2.03 | 0.67 |
| | 37 | 1.88 | 1.41 | −0.03 | 1.03 | 0.51 |
| | 47 | 1.96 | 2.35 | −0.15 | 1.16 | 0.54 |
| | 57 | 3.25 | 2.02 | 0.53 | 2.30 | 0.70 |
| | 64 | 1.99 | 2.04 | 0.23 | 1.38 | 0.58 |
| | Average | 2.40 | 1.73 | 0.29 | 1.72 | 0.61 |
| | 29 | 2.37 | 3.04 | −0.13 | 0.84 | 0.46 |
| Fifth | 38 | 2.07 | 2.76 | −0.02 | 0.89 | 0.47 |
| terrace | 48 | 1.62 | 1.67 | −0.28 | 1.26 | 0.58 |
| | 58 | 4.07 | 2.67 | −0.40 | 0.89 | 0.47 |
| | Average | 2.53 | 2.54 | −0.21 | 0.97 | 0.50 |
| Sixth | 49 | 2.32 | 2.85 | 0.05 | 0.94 | 0.48 |
| terrace | 50 | 2.71 | 2.50 | 0.31 | 1.41 | 0.59 |
| | Average | 2.52 | 2.68 | 0.18 | 1.18 | 0.54 |
| Beach | 11 | 1.89 | 1.74 | 0.16 | 1.81 | 0.64 |
| samples | 12 | 1.98 | 1.79 | 0.44 | 1.30 | 0.57 |
| | 19 | 2.07 | 1.40 | 0.25 | 1.03 | 0.51 |
| | 20 | 2.62 | 1.60 | 0.08 | 1.00 | 0.50 |

| Location | Sample no. | $M_z\phi$ | $\sigma_I$ | $Sk_I$ | $K_G$ | $K_G{'}$ |
|----------|-----------|-----------|-----------|--------|--------|---------|
| | 30 | 2.14 | 0.83 | 0.22 | 1.37 | 0.58 |
| | 31 | 4.41 | 2.29 | −0.07 | 0.94 | 0.48 |
| | 39 | 1.05 | 2.17 | 0.40 | 1.86 | 0.65 |
| | 40 | 2.50 | 1.32 | 0.21 | 1.07 | 0.52 |
| | 51 | 1.10 | 2.09 | 0.20 | 0.86 | 0.46 |
| | 52 | 3.25 | 1.92 | 0.36 | 1.20 | 0.55 |
| | 59 | 1.90 | 3.54 | 0.13 | 1.57 | 0.61 |
| | 65 | 2.73 | 1.27 | 0.34 | 1.49 | 0.60 |
| | Average | 2.30 | 1.83 | 0.23 | 1.29 | 0.56 |

*Kurtosis* $(K_G)$ The mean of the kurtosis values rises from the top of the escarpment where it attains a value of $K_G{'} = 0.5$ (Normal curve) indicating a predominance of gravel mode. It rises to the First and Second terraces of values 0.57 $\phi$ and 0.55 $\phi$ (leptokurtic) with one mode dominant. The same characteristic can be noticed in the values of the Sixth terrace $K'_G = 0.54 \phi$ and those of the beach samples $K'_G = 0.56 \phi$ indicating better sorting in the central part of the curves than of their tails. More progress in the sorting of the centre of the curves is noted in the Third and Fourth terrace values $K'_G = 0.6 \phi$ and 0.61 $\phi$ respectively.

### 5.3.1a *Student's* t *test*

This was applied to determine the significance of the differences between the four parameters of the top of the escarpment, the six terraces and the beach samples. The differences will reveal whether there is a close relationship between their parameters and whether a correlation can be drawn between them. In the present work the probability (*p*) has been adopted as less than 0.5 in order for differences to be significant. As has been mentioned before, there is evidence of mixed sedimentary environments in the area. The only samples of definite known environment which were collected are those of the beach area. Accordingly, it was decided that the four parameters (mean, standard deviation, skewness and kurtosis) of these samples were to be used for comparisons with other parameters of the samples of the seven mentioned areas (taking into consideration the original field notes of the samples).

It can be noticed (Tables 5.8 and 5.9) that for the mean size parameter, Student's *t* test shows that there are significant differences between the mean of the beach samples' environment and those of the top of the escarpment as well as the First and Second terrace. The probability of these differences being due to chance was $p = 3.947$ for the samples from the top of the escarpment versus those from the beach, $p = 3.951$ for the First terrace versus

**Table 5.8** *The results of Student's t test of the mean, standard deviation, skewness and kurtosis*

| Location | Parameter | Degree of freedom | Probability of the t test | Probability of the 5% level of significance | Remarks |
|---|---|---|---|---|---|
| Top of the escarpment | mean | 17 | 3.947 | 2.110 | Significant $> 5\%$ |
| First terrace | mean | 18 | 3.950 | 2.101 | Significant $> 5\%$ |
| Second terrace | mean | 18 | 2.300 | 2.101 | Significant $> 5\%$ |
| Third terrace | mean | 18 | 0.890 | 2.101 | Not significant $< 5\%$ |
| Fourth terrace | mean | 26 | 0.120 | 2.056 | Not significant $< 5\%$ |
| Fifth terrace | mean | 14 | 0.234 | 2.145 | Not significant $< 5\%$ |
| Sixth terrace | mean | 12 | 0.176 | 2.179 | Not significant $< 5\%$ |
| Top of the escarpment | Standard deviation | 17 | 3.904 | 2.110 | Significant $> 5\%$ |
| First terrace | Standard deviation | 18 | 3.01 | 2.101 | Significant $> 5\%$ |
| Second terrace | Standard deviation | 18 | 1.465 | 2.101 | Not significant $< 5\%$ |
| Third terrace | Standard deviation | 18 | 1.217 | 2.101 | Not significant $< 5\%$ |
| Fourth terrace | Standard deviation | 26 | 0.133 | 2.056 | Not significant $< 5\%$ |
| Fifth terrace | Standard deviation | 14 | 2.574 | 2.145 | Significant· $> 5\%$ |
| Sixth terrace | Standard deviation | 12 | 2.479 | 2.179 | Significant $> 5\%$ |
| Top of the escarpment | Skewness | 17 | 3.454 | 2.110 | Significant $> 5\%$ |
| First terrace | Skewness | 18 | 0.625 | 2.101 | Not significant $< 5\%$ |
| Second terrace | Skewness | 18 | 2.11 | 2.101 | Significant $> 5\%$ |
| Third terrace | Skewness | 18 | 0.50 | 2.101 | Not significant $< 5\%$ |
| Fourth terrace | Skewness | 26 | 0.211 | 2.056 | Not significant $< 5\%$ |
| Fifth terrace | Skewness | 14 | 4.710 | 2.145 | Significant $> 5\%$ |
| Sixth terrace | Skewness | 12 | 0.656 | 2.179 | Not significant $< 5\%$ |

| Location | Parameter | Degree of freedom | Probability of the t test | Probability of the 5% level of significance | Remarks |
|---|---|---|---|---|---|
| Top of the escarpment | Kurtosis | 17 | 1.418 | 2.110 | Not significant < 5% |
| First terrace | Kurtosis | 18 | 0.172 | 2.101 | Not significant < 5% |
| Second terrace | Kurtosis | 18 | 0.329 | 2.101 | Not significant < 5% |
| Third terrace | Kurtosis | 18 | 1.111 | 2.101 | Not significant < 5% |
| Fourth terrace | Kurtosis | 26 | 1.563 | 2.056 | Not significant < 5% |
| Fifth terrace | Kurtosis | 14 | 1.652 | 2.145 | Not significant < 5% |
| Sixth terrace | Kurtosis | 12 | 0.826 | 2.179 | Not significant < 5% |

**Table 5.9** *The relationship between the parameters of the beach samples and those of the other areas*

| mean | + | + | + | − | − | − | − |
|---|---|---|---|---|---|---|---|
| standard deviation | + | + | − | − | − | + | + |
| skewness | + | − | + | − | − | + | − |
| kurtosis | − | − | − | − | − | − | − |
| location | T | 1 | 2 | 3 | 4 | 5 | 6 |

The numbers indicate their location, e.g. T, Top of the escarpment, 1, First terrace etc., (+) indicates significant differences in the parameter compared with that of the beach, (−) indicates that there is no significant difference.

the beach samples and $p = 2.30$ for the Second terrace versus the beach samples, while the Third, Fourth, Fifth and Sixth terraces failed to reveal any significant differences in mean grain size between their environments. Student's $t$ test results are as follows from Third to Sixth terraces: $p = 0.89$, 0.12, 0.234 and 0.176.

By applying Student's $t$ test to the standard deviation it was found that the differences are significant between the sorting of the beach samples and other areas (terraces) and not significant in others. The probability of differences being due to chance between the beach, the top of the escarpment and the six terraces descending from the highest to the lowest one being as follows: $p = 3.904$ (significant), $p = 3.01$ (significant), $p = 1.465$ (not significant), $p = 1.217$ (not significant), Fourth terrace $p = 0.133$ (not significant),

Fifth terrace $p = 2.574$ (significant), and the Sixth terrace probability values $p = 2.479$ (significant) respectively.

The result of Student's $t$ test for the skewness indicates that the significant differences between the beach samples and the other areas are as follows: $p = 3.454$ for the top of the escarpment samples; $p = 2.11$ for the Second terrace and $p = 4.71$ for the Fifth terrace. The test also shows that there is no significant difference between the samples of the beach and the First terrace ($p = 0.625$), Third terrace ($p = 0.50$), Fourth terrace ($p = 0.211$) and the Sixth terrace ($p = 0.656$).

Finally, application of Student's $t$ test for kurtosis values failed to point out any significant differences between the beach samples and those of the terraces and the top of the escarpment.

Consequently, this technique has in general succeeded in revealing the significant differences between not only the beach samples and those of the top of the escarpment as well as the six terraces, but also shows differences in the parameters of the terraces themselves and the top of the escarpment with the beach. Table 5.9 summarizes the results of Student's $t$ test (all the results whether significant or not are related to the beach samples).

This shows that, for instance, the probability of differences is significant between the mean, standard deviation and skewness for the top of the escarpment and those of the beach, but failed to do so with kurtosis.

Student's $t$ test of the mean, standard deviation, skewness and kurtosis of the First terrace and the beach indicates that there is a significant difference between their mean and standard deviation, but no significant difference in skewness and kurtosis. The results from the Second terrace show that the probability of its mean and skewness being different from those of the beach is significant but not significant in the case of the standard deviation (the measure of sorting) and kurtosis. A close relationship exists between the four parameters of the beach samples and those of the Third and Fourth terraces. Similarity between the deposits of both have been recognized for some of the terraces in the field but were not thought to give such similarity when the test was applied.

For the Fifth and Sixth terrace, Table 5.9 shows that they both agree with their means and the beach, which indicates a similarity between their grain size as well as with the Fourth and Third terraces, but differs from the upper three areas (top of the escarpment, First and Second terraces). Also the standard deviations of the Fifth and Sixth terraces show significant differences between theirs and the beach. For the skewness parameter, the Fifth terrace characteristic differs from the beach and the Sixth terrace, the latter having a positive relationship with three of the beach samples. Kurtosis results for the Fifth and Sixth terraces proved not to be significant. However, kurtosis so far has failed to show any significant difference between the environments existing in the area.

## 5.3.1b *Interpretation of the four size parameters*

Six basic scatter plot diagrams have been drawn for the four size parameters (Figures 5.19 to 5.24) against each other in order to find out the relationship between them and whether they add more criteria for identifying the environments of their samples. Each two size parameters of the eight areas between the top of the escarpment and the beach were plotted against each other to show their relationship.

Figure 5.19 is of the scatter plot diagram of the mean size versus standard deviation; it shows that the best sorting values are attained by medium-to-fine sands at mean size of 1.38 $\phi$ (0.38 millimetres) and 2.13 $\phi$ (0.22 millimetres), but sorting becomes worse as the samples get either finer or coarser, which agrees with the conclusion arrived at by Inman and Chamberlain (1955) and Folk and Ward (1957). Some of the samples from the top of the escarpment as well as the First and Second terraces which were found in the field to contain higher percentages of medium-to-fine gravels, have in the diagram high sorting values (very poorly sorted). Most of Fifth terrace samples and the two samples from the Sixth terrace are very poorly sorted, with a mean size between fine sand to silt. Several samples of the Second, Third and Fourth terraces fall in the field of the majority of the beach samples. They correspond to the area represented by medium-to-fine sand mean size and they are not too badly sorted with an inverted peak of moderately sorted. The result of plotting these two parameters gave results similar to those obtained by Student's *t* test. Moreover, three characteristic environments seem to exist.

1 The better sorted areas which include most of the beach samples as well as others from other terraces and those of the Fourth terrace with sorting less than 2 $\phi$.
2 Area of coarse grains, corresponding to the top of the escarpment, the First terrace as well as the Second terrace samples and some of the Fifth, with standard deviation value over 2.5 $\phi$.
3 Area of mixing between all the environments described above and attained on the Second and Third terraces.

In the scatter plot diagram of mean size versus skewness (Figure 5.20) it can be noticed that there is a good relationship between the mean size and the skewness. A region of symmetry occurs in the pure sand mode from some samples of the terraces as well as from the top of the escarpment where the sands and gravels are equal. The samples attain very positive skewness of $Sk_I = 0.61$ $\phi$ at $M_z = -0.61$ $\phi$ (1.53 millimetres) as the amount of gravels exceeds that of the sand in the samples. As the mean size of the sediment decreases, due to the addition of more silt and clay, a positive skewness will result.

The mixing of the two modes with abundant sands produces negative to very negative skewness. Folk and Ward (1957) concluded that the pure mode fractions are in themselves nearly symmetrical, but when the two modes are

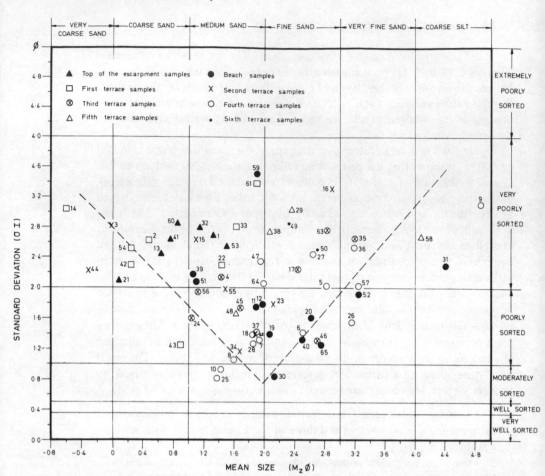

**Figure 5.19** *Scatter plot diagram of mean size versus standard deviation*

mixed negative skewness will result if the fine mode is more abundant, and positive skewness if the coarse mode is abundant. It can be noticed that most of the beach samples and those suspected of being of marine origin have positive skewness. This is believed to be due to the location of the research area close to the north of the Gulf where there is a continuous discharge of fine particles. Khalaf (1969) came to the same conclusion that the beach sediment here is usually of a clay texture in composition, i.e. they have pronounced positive skewness for samples of this area as compared with negative skewness for those of the southern coast of Kuwait.

Figure 5.21 is a scatter plot diagram of mean size versus kurtosis. There is a general tendency for the kurtosis to change from platykurtic to very meso-kurtic which coincides with decreasing the mean from left to right. As the kurtosis measures the sorting in the 'tails' of the distribution, it can be seen

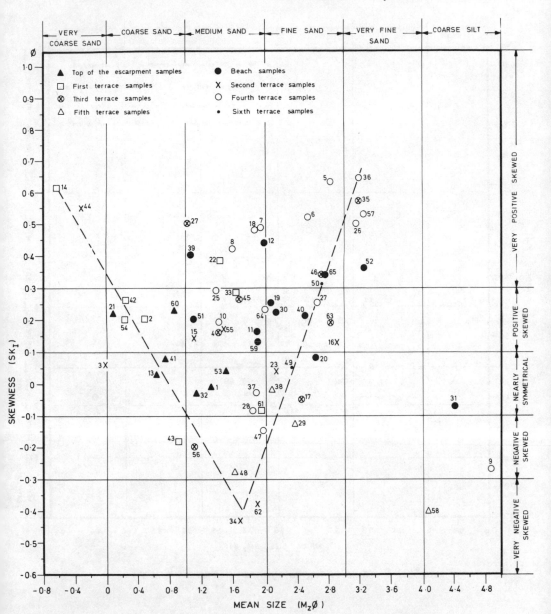

**Figure 5.20** *Scatter plot diagram of mean size versus skewness*

that the pure gravel or sand gives a normal curve $K_G = 1.00$ ($K'_G = 0.5$). The addition of small percentages of about 10 per cent with a maximum of 20 per cent from another mode result in good sorting in the middle part of the curves but worsened in the tails (leptokurtic) which characterize most of the samples except those from the top of the escarpment and some of the other terraces and

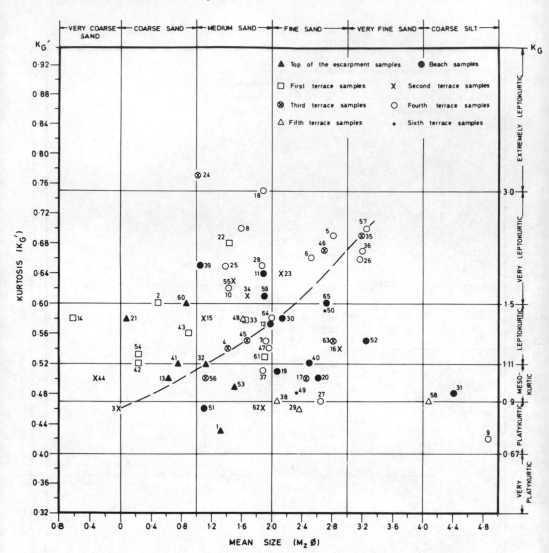

**Figure 5.21** *Scatter plot diagram of mean size versus kurtosis*

beach samples. Further addition of another mode brings bimodal sediment and platykurtic characteristics (better sorting in the tails than the central curves).

After examining the mean size of all the samples versus their sorting, skewness and kurtosis, additional information has been added to the information already known from the field notes as well as those from Student's *t* test. It can be said at this stage that there are three main mode characteristics in the sediments indicating their depositional environments. These are (1) the gravelly sand mode given the symbol of GS, and (2) the sandy mode of

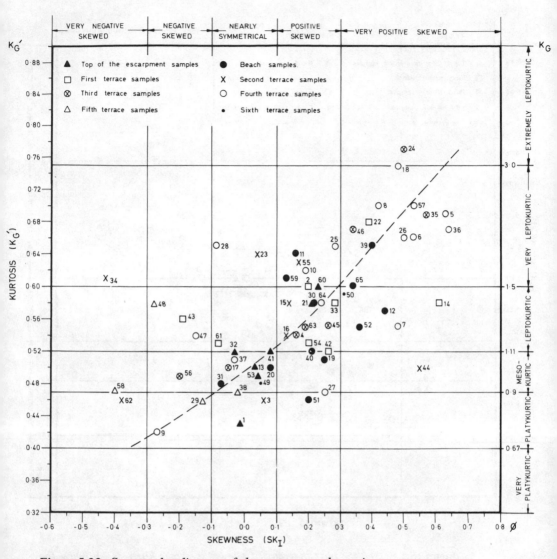

**Figure 5.22a** *Scatter plot diagram of skewness versus kurtosis*

beach samples and samples from other terraces given the symbol B. The third mode of aeolian environment, is characterized by a high percentage of fine sands ranging to silt, clay fractions and given the symbol A.

Figures 5.22a and b are scatter plot diagrams of skewness against kurtosis. Mason and Folk (op. cit.) mentioned that plotting these parameters against each other was the best way to differentiate between the beach, dune and aeolian flats. Figure 5.22a shows that the changes of the skewness from very negative to very positive skewness is associated with changes of the kurtosis from platykurtic to extremely leptokurtic. Figure 5.22b is a scatter plot

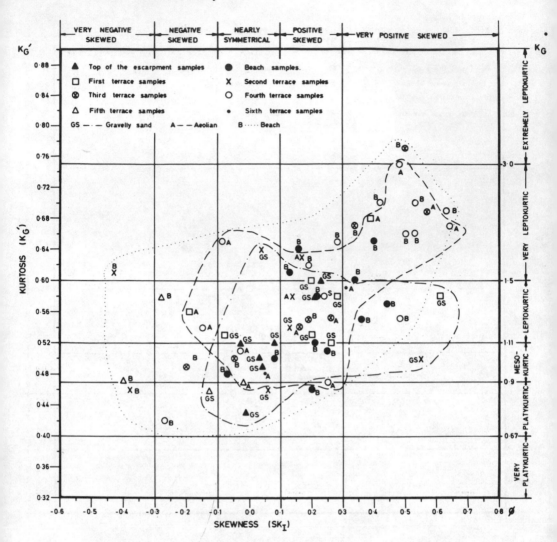

**Figure 5.22b** *Scatter plot diagram of skewness versus kurtosis, showing the depositional environments of the samples*

diagram of skewness against kurtosis of the same samples but with their depositional environments. The result shows also that most of the samples of the mode gravel exhibit mesokurtic to leptokurtic traits. Those of the sandy mode samples have negative to positive skewness and range from platy-kurtic to leptokurtic. The third mode samples have mesokurtic to very lepto-kurtic. However, this diagram does not show a clear separation of the three fields and a mixing between them occurs.

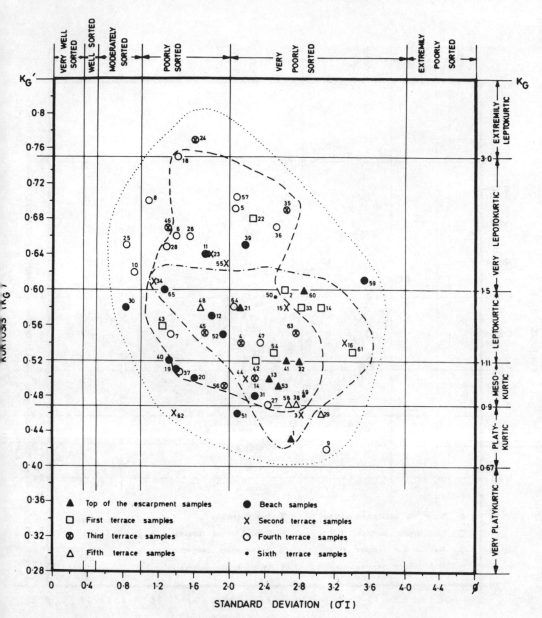

**Figure 5.23a** *Scatter plot diagram of standard deviation versus kurtosis*

Figures 5.23a and b are scatter plot diagrams of standard deviation against kurtosis. Figure 5.23a shows that the sorting decreases from moderately to very poorly sorted which is accompanied by decrease of the kurtosis values. It can be noticed that the three modes of environment are overlapping in

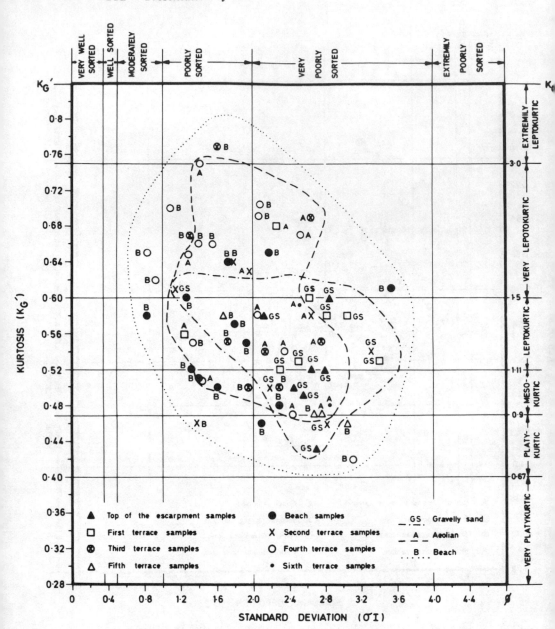

**Figure 5.23b** *Scatter plot diagram of standard deviation versus kurtosis, showing the depositional environments of the samples*

some respects. Several other characteristics, however, also appear from this diagram. Figure 5.23b, which shows the depositional environments of the samples of Figure 5.23a, indicates that the samples from the top of the escarpment as well as from other terraces which are characterized by gravelly sand environments concentrate in the area between platykurtic and leptokurtic, as well as being very poorly sorted. Samples of the aeolian environments which come from some of the terraces are characterized by being mesokurtic and very leptokurtic. The sorting of some of these samples and most of the first environment – gravelly sand – is very poor, but some are slightly better by being poorly sorted. The previous characteristic indicates that the samples from these groups are in general better sorted in the centre of the curves than in their tails. The samples of the third environment of the beach and those of similar characteristics have the best sorting compared with the last two, and they are moderately to poorly sorted with few very poorly sorted. Their kurtosis ranges from platykurtic to extremely leptokurtic, indicating that the beach samples are unimodal and bimodal mode depending on the sedimentary supplies (silt and clay coarse sands).

Figures 5.24a and b show the results of plotting the two parameters of standard deviation versus skewness. Figure 5.24a indicates that sorting for all the samples ranges between moderately sorted to very poorly sorted and from very negative skewed to very positive skewed. It can be seen also that the plotting of the assumed environment of each sample against each other (Figure 5.24b), although it shows no clear separation between the fields, is very successful in showing that the result in general agrees with those of Student's *t* test for the same parameters. It shows that most of the beach samples and those similar are moderate to poorly sorted (some samples of the Second, Third and Fourth terraces), while those from the top of the escarpment and the First and Fifth terraces (except for a few of each of them) with the Sixth terrace are characterized by also having their special characteristics: (1) the gravelly sand samples mainly from the top of the escarpment as well as the First terrace and Second terrace are in the field of very poorly sorted and range from symmetrical to very positive skewness; (2) those of the assumed aeolian environment range between symmetrical (except two samples) to very positive skewness, but they differ from the gravelly sand by being better sorted (compared to the gravelly sands only); (3) those of the beach samples have in general the best sorting of all the samples in the area. They range from moderately sorted to very poorly sorted. The skewness of these samples ranges from very negative skewness to very positive skewness, the positive skewness apparently being inherited from the adjacent areas to the north.

*5.3.1c Correlation and comparison between the size distribution curves*

Each size distribution curve of the analysed samples has been first studied by itself to find out the characteristic of its distributions. Using arithmetic probability papers for plotting the curves has proved to be helpful in identifying the processes involved in transporting and depositing the sediments, as samples which have a more or less symmetrical size distribution will appear as a straight line when plotted on this kind of paper and any deviation from

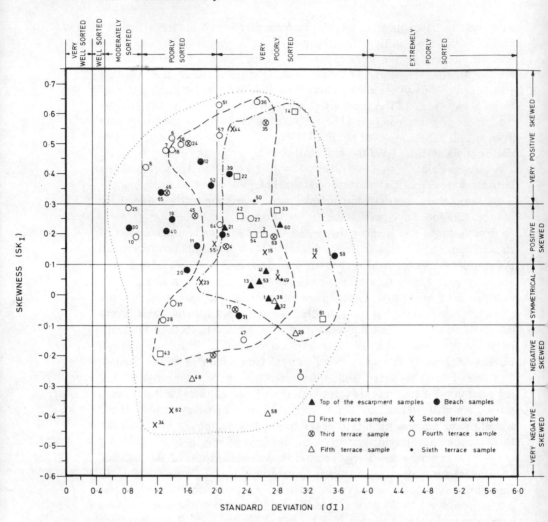

**Figure 5.24a** *Scatter plot diagram of standard deviation versus skewness*

the symmetical distribution will clearly appear. The result shows the existence of the following three populations, indicating the processes involved in deposition:

1 *Suspension population*
This includes grains smaller in size than 4.0 $\phi$ (0.062 mm) and not exceeding a maximum size of 3.32 $\phi$ (0.1 mm), but mixed with another population they may exhibit sizes larger than 0.1 mm; in some cases they were found to have a size of 0.21 mm (2.25 $\phi$).

2 *Saltation population*
The sizes of its grains range between a minimum of 3.74 $\phi$ (0.075 mm) and

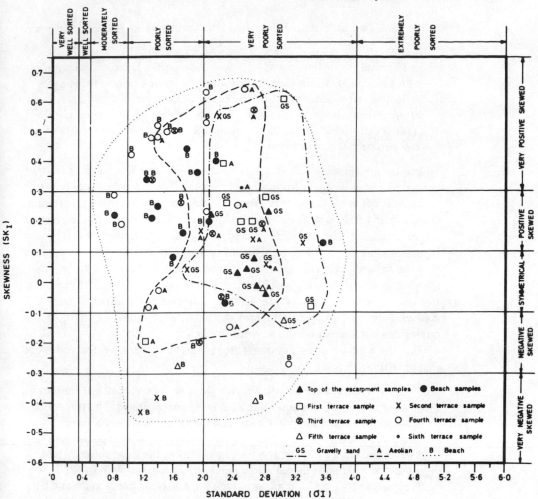

**Figure 5.24b** *Scatter plot diagram of standard deviation versus skewness, showing the depositional environments of the samples*

a maximum of about 1.74 $\phi$ (0.3 mm) to 0.74 $\phi$ (0.6 mm) with unstable percentages.

3 *Rolling or creep population*

It has a grain size diameter from about 0.74 $\phi$ (0.6 mm) to > 0.6 mm (0.74 $\phi$) coarse to fine and medium gravels. The percentage of this population varies in different curves.

The grain size distribution curves of all the samples from the eight areas, viz. the top of the escarpment, the six terraces and those of the beach, include samples extending laterally from Kathma I in the west to Al-Bahra III in the east. The purpose of this plotting is tentatively to find out two main points:

1   To reveal the differences as well as the similarities between the samples collected from different transects of the eight groups mentioned above.
2   To find out whether plotting the curves of each group together, reflects different depositional environments, or whether they have the same characteristics which mean that they are all the result of one process of transportation and deposition.

The results (Figures 5.25 to 5.32) show that there are areas of distinct characteristics as well as of mixed environment. For example, there is a clear difference between the curves from the top of the escarpment samples, (Figure 5.25) and those from the beach (Figure 5.32). Some of the terraces exhibit characteristics of either one of the previous environments and some have a mixture of two. More important, a third kind of environment appears to exist between the two. The three environments are thought to be sandy gravel, aeolian and beach environments. The result shows also that in general there is a similarity between the samples collected from different areas but belonging to one group. There are also some exceptions which show the mixing of several environments on one terrace.

The three environments thought to be in the area have the following characteristics:

1   Gravelly sand environment: this has three well-developed populations of suspension, saltation and rolling (or creep) populations. The truncation between the suspension population and the saltation occurs between 2.74 $\phi$ (0.15mm) and 4.0 $\phi$ (0.062 mm). The suspension population is very distinct and consists of about 6 to 22 per cent of the distribution. The truncation points for the saltation population occur between 0.74 $\phi$ (0.6 mm) and $-1$ $\phi$ (2.0 mm), the population varying between 25 and 51 per cent of the distribution. The rolling population is very well developed in this environment and with percentages between 38 and 60 is larger than those in the other environments.
2   Aeolian environment; this has been found in some of the samples collected from the terraces between the beach and the top of the escarpment. The curves are characterized by a high percentage of suspension population, a high percentage of saltation population, but a smaller percentage of the rolling population than those of the gravelly sand environment. The truncation of the suspension population occurs between 3.25 $\phi$ (0.110 mm) and 3.74 $\phi$ (0.075 mm). The percentage is between 8 and 33 of the distribution. The distribution of the saltation population is the best, with a truncation point between 0.74 $\phi$ (0.6 mm) and 1.25 $\phi$ (0.42 mm), its population being between 35 and 79 percent of the distribution. The curves 'tail off' to the right near the suspension population because of the additions of fine particles. The rolling popula-

tion ranges between 2 and 36 per cent with the majority at about 10 per cent of the distribution.

3 Marine environment; the curves are distinctly different from those of the top of the escarpment and the aeolian curves. Generally, it is the nearest to a normal curve with a small percentage of fine and coarse ends. The majority of the suspension population ranges between 6 and 20 per cent, but reaches about 40 per cent. The truncation points between the suspension and saltation populations are between 2.25 $\phi$ (0.21 mm) and 3.74 $\phi$ (0.75 mm). The second population (saltation) ranges in size between −0.26 $\phi$ (1.19 mm) and 1.25 $\phi$ (0.42 mm), making up between 51 and 92 per cent of the distribution. The rolling (or creep) population in the beach samples is the smallest, and is absent in some samples. In the majority it is between 1 and 10 per cent of the distribution, with a few exceptions.

## *Distinguishing the depositional environment of the curves*

The results of plotting together the curves of the samples for the top of the escarpment (Figure 5.25) from Kathma I to Al-Bahra III were found to be very significant. The curves tend to be horizontal, indicating the similarity between the percentages of the three populations. Although the samples came from different locations, this indicates that they are of the same origin. These

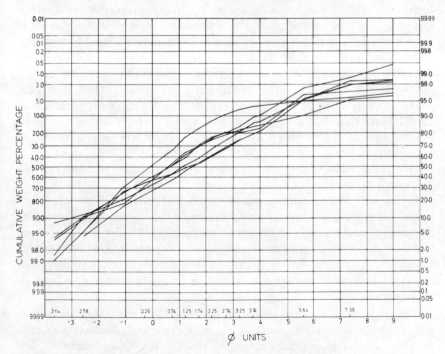

**Figure 5.25** *Grain size distributions: top of the escarpment*

curves have the characteristics of the gravelly sand environment. In Figure 5.26 for the samples of the First terrace, the curves are in general similar to those of the top of the escarpment. There are exceptions where some of the curves seem to have a smaller percentage of the gravelly material and more of the sandy textures. Figure 5.27 represents the size distribution curves of the Second terrace. They seem to be a mixture of those of the gravelly sand samples and those of the aeolian samples. However, there is an improvement in the shape of the curves as a result of curves with a higher percentage of silt and clay like some of the samples identified as being of marine origin.

Descending to a lower terrace (No. 3), the curves show that they are better sorted than those of the upper terrace (Figure 5.28). There is a tendency towards curves of aeolian material with very small amounts of gravel, as well as curves with beach characteristics.

Terrace No. 4 exhibits samples identified as being of marine origin and was traced along the escarpment. The replotting of these samples, as well as others collected from this terrace, illustrates that they are in general similar to the aeolian curves, all having a sharp bend to the right with a horizontal extension (Figure 5.29). The high percentage of the suspension population is due to the addition of fine particles brought by the dust storms which prevail during the summer and especially from May to July. There is a larger saltation population and the percentage of the rolling population is small or negligible. As far as the samples of marine origin are concerned, while they can be distinguished from the aeolian samples, their graphical identity is not as clear. Figure 5.30 represents the grain size distribution of the Fifth terrace. It is an area of mixed environments and all the curves have different shapes. The middle two curves represent sandy-to-gravelly sand deposits, and the upper and lower ones are believed to be of marine origin. All the curves except the upper one have a high percentage of suspension population. Figure 5.31 is the grain size distribution of two samples which came from the Sixth terrace of the Al-Bahra area. It has been mentioned before that deposits of terrestrial and marine origin were found scattered in the area. The lower curve represents the sample which is mixed with marine deposits, and the upper one is the terrestrial sample. Both have a suspension population of more than 30 per cent of the distribution.

Figure 5.32 illustrates the curves of the samples collected from the present beach. They are characterized by having small tails at the coarse end. The deposits are sandy or silty with varying content of silt, the suspension population varying from about 6 to 30 per cent but reaching to about 42 per cent in one of the samples. This is due to the large supply of fine particles from the Tigris–Euphrates river system as well as to the dust storms brought by the north wind.

The identification of the origin of the samples by comparing their grain size distribution curves, although with clear limitations, is reasonably successful. The occurrence of the three populations – suspension, saltation and rolling – with different sizes and percentages led to the identification of three

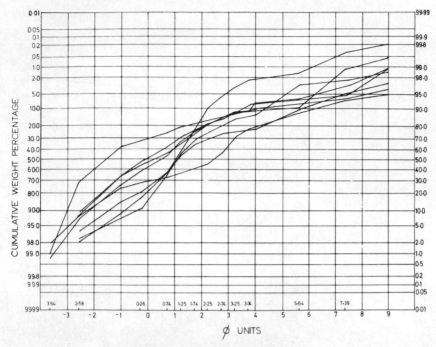

**Figure 5.26** *Grain size distributions: First terrace*

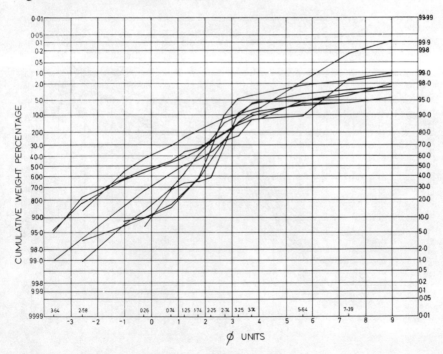

**Figure 5.27** *Grain size distributions: Second terrace*

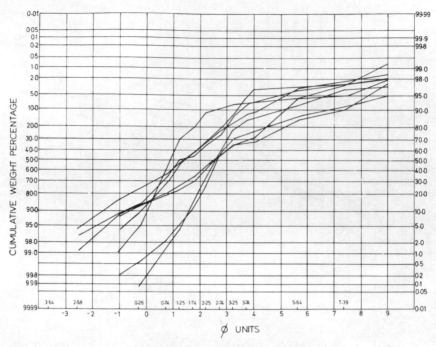

**Figure 5.28** *Grain size distributions: Third terrace*

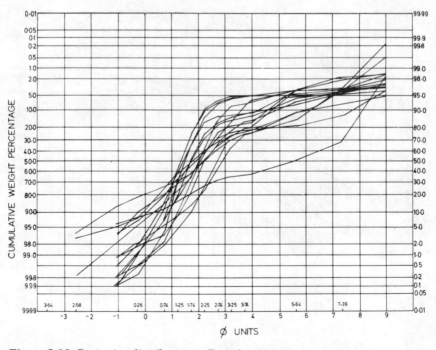

**Figure 5.29** *Grain size distributions: Fourth terrace*

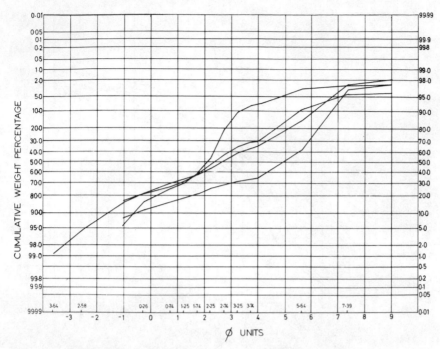

**Figure 5.30** *Grain size distributions: Fifth terrace*

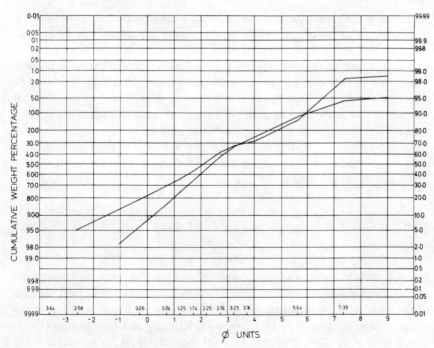

**Figure 5.31** *Grain size distributions: Sixth terrace*

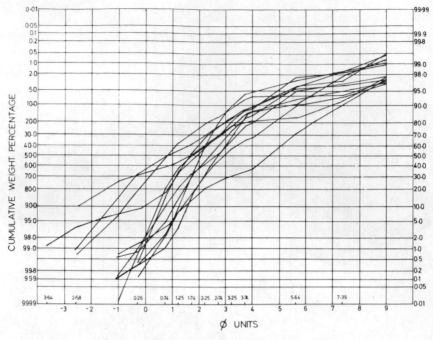

Ø UNITS

**Figure 5.32** *Grain size distributions: the beach*

main sedimentary environments and a fourth zone representing the mixing of two or more environments. These environments are believed to be gravelly sand, aeolian and marine. Identification of the origin of the six terraces as well as the top of the escarpment and the beach samples has been possible and in some cases samples belonging to one terrace but coming from different areas showed similarity between their curves. Also, it has been shown that the area under research is an active environment, with sediments of different origin often being mixed with one another, mainly by the north wind but also the south-east wind. Finally, the location near the head of the Gulf causes the continuous mixing of the coastal grains with those of the fine detritus of the Tigris and Euphrates river systems.

### 5.3.2 *Interpretation of surface textures by SEM*

The results of applying scanning electron microscope (SEM) analysis show that the surface textures of the grains are associated either with subaqueous or aeolian environments or carry the characteristics of superimposed textures of the two environments. Krinsley and Funnel (1965), Krinsley and Donahue (1968), Krinsley and Margolis (1969) and Krinsley and Doornkamp (1973) have provided detailed information about the characteristics of each environment and this has been followed in interpreting the samples. The main characteristic textures for subaqueous and aeolian environments can be summarized as follows:

*Subaqueous environments* Surfaces are characterized by V-shaped patterns which may have resulted from the collisions between grain and grain: straight or slightly curved grooves caused by the drawing of a sharp edge of a sand grain across another. V-shaped patterns may be found oriented along the axis of the grooves. Blocky conchoidal breakage patterns differ from those in aeolian environments in having regular rather than curved sides.

*Aeolian environments* The surface textures of the quartz grain of the aeolian environments are characterized by having upturned plates, but through abrasive action, the corners are removed and the grain tends to be rounded. According to Krinsley and Doornkamp (1973), rolling topography is produced because of the solution and precipitation which tends to modify the plates; grains from hot deserts are largely affected by this last action.

Meandering ridges are formed as a result of the impact of grains against one another during transportation which causes the wearing of the breakage blocks. The breakage patterns differ from those of the subaqueous environment in having curved rather than regular sides.

Graded arcs occur in series and form fan-shaped patterns which may represent percussion fractures. A pitted surface is also one of the aeolian environment characteristics.

The following are the results of examining the surface textures of the sample quartz sand grains in terms of these characteristics. The locations of the samples are illustrated in Figures 5.4, 5.6, 5.8, 5.10, 5.12, 5.15 and 5.16.

*Samples associated with subaqueous environment* Plate 19A is for sample No. 5. This is from the fossiliferous bed on the Fourth terrace west of profile Kathma I. The characteristic features of beach origin are very clearly shown on this grain. It is densely covered by V-shaped patterns of different sizes. The grain in general has rounded protruding edges, straight and slightly curved grooves with some V-shaped patterns developed along the axis of the grooves.

Plate 19B is for sample No. 6. This sample was collected from the deposits which are immediately below the fossiliferous bed (sample No. 5). It has a smooth surface as well as V-shaped patterns having a limited degree of orientation. Some grooves are partly associated with V-shaped and irregular breakage patterns.

Plate 19C is for sample No. 8. This represents a smooth surface of a portion of a quartz grain with some V-shaped depressions and irregular breakage patterns. Silica precipitation adheres to the surface. Curved depressions exist which may have resulted from aeolian environment.

Plate 19D is the surface texture of sample No. 17 from the Third terrace in Kathma II; it shows V-shaped patterns with high relief, typical of beach texture. Blocky breakage patterns are also present.

Plate 19E is a portion of one of the quartz grains; the surface texture appears to be generally smooth although this sample (No. 25) is from the fossiliferous bed in terrace Four found at Ghidhai. Faint V-shapes can be seen on the surface.

The beach sample (No. 31) from Ghidhai (Plate 19F) exhibits V-shaped patterns and grooves. The surface has silica precipitation covering large parts of the grain.

The surface textures of high relief seen in sample No. 34 which come from Mudairah reflect a beach environment. The sample is from the main fossiliferous bed on the Second terrace. Plate 20A shows several blocky conchoidal breakage patterns and V-shaped patterns. Irregular curved grooves can be seen at the left of the plate. These are V-shaped patterns oriented along the axis of the grooves. A little silica precipitation is also present on the surface.

Plate 20B is for sample No. 40 which was originally collected from the present beach. It shows a clear curved groove to the left associated with V-shaped depressions and upturned plates.

A typical surface texture of beach origin (Plate 20C) is observed in sample No. 46 collected from the Third terrace at Al-Bahra I. The surface of the grain is almost covered by mechanically formed V-shaped depressions and irregular breakage patterns. Straight and slightly curved grooves are scattered on the surface with some of the V-shaped patterns oriented along the axis of the grooves.

The second sample (No. 48) of marine origin is shown in Plate 20D on the Fifth terrace of Al-Bahra I; it also comes from a fossiliferous bed. Although the surface texture of portions of the quartz sand shows a smooth surface, it also has several clear V-shaped patterns of different sizes scattered on the surface. Silica precipitations adhering to the surface and covering large parts of the grain indicate the hot desert environment of the area.

The last sample shown by SEM to be of beach origin comes from the Fourth terrace in Al-Bahra II, sample No. 57. Plate 20E shows V-shaped patterns of various sizes and a generally smooth surface. Blocky conchoidal breakage patterns are present and what seem to be 'chatter marks', originating from the skipping of a portion of one grain across another.

*Samples associated with aeolian environment* Plate 21A illustrates the surface texture of a sand grain from sample No. 18 in Kathma (profile II). It shows the dish-shaped concavities with a deep one in the middle, and a certain amount of solution and precipitation occurring on the surface. According to Kirnsley and Doornkamp (1973) the dish-shaped forms probably resulted mechanically during periods of violent abrasion related to strong wind storms.

Plates 21B, C and D are typical examples of quartz sand grains of aeolian environments. Plate 21B represents a group of aeolian quartz grains. Although not all of them are smooth, round grains, most of them are fairly rounded or in the process of rounding and many show the upturned plates. Plate 21C is of the middle grain in the upper part of the plate. The grain is very smooth with rounded edges which shows that this grain may have undergone mechanical abrasion for a considerable time. There is silica precipitation adhering to the surface, with a larger part on the upper surface of the grain. Plate 21D is a close-up of the large grain on the right of the plate. The upturned plates have been subjected to solution precipitation which leads to smoothing of the surface; rolling topography is predominant in this portion of the grain. It is possible that the second rough part of the grain, which can be seen also in the lower right corner of Plate 21B, may achieve the rolling characteristic after a longer period of time. This sample, No. 37, comes from the Mudairah area, on the Fourth terrace.

*Samples associated with superimposed environments* Plates 22A and 22B are from sample No. 11. Although this sample was collected from the present beach, it shows characteristics of aeolian as well as littoral environments, i.e. Plate 22A shows a well-rounded grain with several dish-shaped depressions of aeolian character. Plate 22B is a detailed surface of another grain from the same sample with faint V-shaped indentation and upturned plates. There is silica precipitation adhering to the surface which may further smooth the surface. This mixing of the characteristics of the grain may be explained by the fact that these grains are originally of aeolian environments but have been carried to the beach by the wind storms which usually blow actively in Kuwait during the summer.

Plates 22C and D are of quartz sand grains from sample No. 42. Plate 22C is a single grain showing the rolling and smooth topography of the grain. Several irregular depressions are developed on the right side of the grain.

There are also upturned plates with smooth surfaces. Plate 22D is a close-up of the upper left portion of the grain. The characteristics indicating aeolian environment are the dish-shaped features and the smooth surface, but a close examination shows also characteristics of subaqueous environment, such as V-shaped patterns and straight or slightly curved grooves which in some cases are associated with V-shapes. It appears that this grain has superimposed subaqueous and aeolian environments with the first being the original then giving way to the aeolian.

Plates 23A and B are for a quartz sand grain from the top of the escarpment, sample No. 13; here is another example of superimposed environments. Plate 23A is a single grain which carries the characteristics of the aeolian environment, e.g. smooth surface and round edges, irregular depressions which may have resulted from mechanical chipping and solution precipitation, and silica precipitation in the depressions and adhering to the surface (especially top left) which will help in smoothing and rounding the surface. Plate 23B is a close-up of the southern portion which in fact indicates subaqueous environments with V-shaped depressions and grooves with V-shaped developments along the axis. A crack has developed in the lower right of the plate, a result of weathering with silica precipitation helping in the weathering.

Plate 23C is a portion of sand grain from sample No. 32 from the top of the escarpment in Mudairah. It indicates subaqueous environment with V-shaped patterns and deep grooves. However, it seems that these features have been subjected to solution precipitation which after some time may change the characteristic of the grain.

Plate 23D is a portion of a sand grain from sample No. 60 collected from the top of the escarpment in Al-Bahra III. By very careful examination of this plate, very faint V-shapes can be recognized; the original surface of the grain is almost hidden by particles adhering to the surface which changes the character of the original grain. It is thought that the previous example (Plate 23C) is an earlier stage of the present example. Both samples originated from subaqueous environments and were then subjected to aeolian environments.

The conclusions which one may draw from using the scanning electron microscope in this research are that the technique has revealed two environments of deposition: (1) subaqueous, which according to Krinsley and Doornkamp (op. cit)., includes all environments in which sand grains are transported, abraded and deposited by water, including marine and non-marine and (2) aeolian. Some grains carry the characteristics of the two environments with one being predominant. The results show that eleven samples are of beach origin, these include samples Nos. 5, 6, 8, 17, 25, 31, 34, 40, 46, 48 and 57, and two of aeolian environments, samples No. 18 and 37. Five samples carry superimposed environments, Nos. 11, 13, 32, 42 and 60 of which four (Nos. 13, 32, 42 and 60) are believed to be of subaqueous origin while the last one (No. 11) is originally of aeolian environment but carried to the beach environment.

For further application of these results we have to consider them in the context of other data (see Chapter 6).

# Chapter 6

# Evidence for changing sea-level along the north coast of Kuwait Bay

## 6.1 Introduction

This chapter is concerned with the interpretation of the results of the methods which have been applied in investigating the changes in sea-level along the north coast of Kuwait Bay. The changes of sea-level may result from several causes but it has been generally agreed that they have occurred as a result of the following processes acting alone or together, and affected by the isostatic processes later described.

1  Tectono-eustasy, which involves variation in the capacity of the ocean basin, while the volume of oceanic water remains constant.
2  Sedimento-eustasy, a result of outpouring of volcanic lava and the deposition of land-derived sediments in the ocean basins which reduce the capacity of the ocean basin and raise the level of the sea.
3  Glacio-eustasy, which results from climatic changes and is caused by changes in the volume of ice sheets.

All the above-mentioned processes have a relative influence on changes of sea-level as a world-wide phenomenon, while the changing volume of ice sheets has been the most important influence in the Quaternary Period. Emerged and submerged features all over the world have been recorded as evidence or changes in sea-level. Accordingly, glacio-eustasy will be discussed in further detail as it is believed that it affected the present area of research.

During the Quaternary Period, world-wide climatic changes produced glacial and interglacial phases. At the time of glaciation, a considerable volume of water was locked up as ice sheets on the land and as sea ice, causing the sea-level to fall; during interglacial and interstadial periods water returned to the sea and the sea-level rose. The concept of glacio-eustasy was first introduced by MacLaren (1842) and developed in the first half of this century by De Lamothe (1911, 1918), Chaput (1917), Depéret (1918–22), Daly (1934) and others who accepted the theory as an explanation of the former strandlines and sea-level fluctuations during the Quaternary. The amplitude of sea-level fluctuation resulting from the melting and accumulation of ice has been estimated by several authors, e.g. Antevs (1928) who estimated a range of 93 metres vertical fall in sea-level for the last glaciation. Daly (1934) suggested that sea-level was about 75 metres below the present for the last glaciation, while Fairbridge (1961) put it at 100 metres below the present. The highest sea-water level (Sicilian) at the beginning of the Pleistocene Period was estimated by Depéret (1918–22) to be at 90–100 metres above the present.

The Mediterranean has been the classic area for the study of Pleistocene high stages of sea-level. The work was initiated by De Lamothe (1911) and followed by that of Depéret (1918–22) who presented the Mediterranean sequence of high shorelines named as: Sicilian (90–100 m), Milazzian (55–60 m), Tyrrhenian (28–30 m), and Monastirian which is subdivided into main Monastirian (18–20 m) and late Monastirian (6–8 m).

However, the uniformity of the Mediterranean shorelines described by De Lamothe and Depéret has been questioned by other workers, including Baulig (1935), Johnson (1931) and Castany and Ottmann (1957).

The beginning of the postglacial rise in sea-level (Flandrian Transgression) began after the melting of Würm ice sheets with a rapid rise of sea-level between 17,000 and 6,000 years ago with many minor fluctuations to reach the present level. There is less agreement about the time the sea-level reached its present level as well as its fluctuation above and below its present level as will appear in later discussion. A detailed account of the Quaternary changes of sea-level is given by Zeuner (1959) as well as by Fairbridge (op. cit.).

Although the accurate study of the movements of shorelines as a result of eustatic changes should be carried out in an area which has not been exposed to upward and downward tectonic movements, it is very difficult in many cases to find an absolutely stable region. Isostatic/tectonic movements have a principal role in determining strandline levels, many of which have been found at heights of more than 200 metres above present sea-level. These resulted not only from the eustatic changes of sea-level, but because parts of the earth's crust responded isostatically to ice formation and ice melt, or were tilted or deformed by local crustal movements.

The weight of large ice caps causes localized depression of the earth's crust during glaciation, but this slowly recovers when the ice melts; the amount of the depression will depend on the thickness of the ice. The recovery and balance of a land mass from the depression caused by the weight of ice is usually a slow process, although it is believed that recovery is faster in the marginal regions where the depression is less than near the centre which suffers from greater depression and where the ice stays longer. Evidently, in areas such as Scandinavia, the pattern of terraces and beaches is extremely complicated as it is the result of interaction of both a rising sea-level and the recovery of a land mass from its depression by an ice cap.

One element in the interpretation of ancient shorelines is connected with certain geodetic possibilities that involve changes in the Earth's motion and shape as a whole. Fairbridge (1961) stated that these may be related to change in the rotational rate of the Earth, and change in the gravitational forces both internal and extra-telluric. Both are intricately related. A redistribution of mass will change the moment of inertia, and hence the rotational rate, but it will also affect gravity. Also involved will be the Polar wobble, the angular velocity and its direction. Under centrifugal force, the Earth's geoid swells at the equator and shrinks at the poles. A change in the angular velocity would result in the hydrosphere reacting differently from the lithosphere. Acceleration would cause a rise of sea-level in the equatorial belt and a lowering at the poles. Deceleration would have the opposite effect. According to several authors, these changes have affected the level of the sea. As the geoid corresponds with the level of the sea at any given time, accordingly the geoid itself may change with the cycles of world climate. The sea-level, and hence the geoid, oscillates between three modes as illustrated by Fairbridge (1961). A minimum dimension is assumed during the Glacial Period, when much of the Earth was covered by ice sheets, and this limit is referred to as a glacial geoid. In the interglacial stages, similar to that of today, although most of the ice caps have melted, there is still water glacially tied up, as in the Antarctica and Greenland ice sheets. A curve corresponding to the interglacial geoid may be shown through the positive peaks of Fairbridge's sea-level curve (ibid., Figure 10, page 133), data relating to these peaks being well established mainly in North Atlantic regions. A complete melting of the ice caps did not occur during each interglacial but would reach its maximum dimension in a period when the Earth was free of ice. As a result, the interglacial curve may not represent an accurate picture of the deglacial geoid and hence the latter curve deviates from the interglacial geoid which, according to Fairbridge, would reach a point 50 metres above present sea-level today (allowing for isostatic adjustment).

As most of the Pleistocene sea-level curves come from continental coastlines, and hence at the edge of the surface loading, it is therefore expected that they undergo complicated movement patterns. Areas of glacio-isostatic rebound (as in the case of North America and Europe) are experiencing larger movements than those areas which are only affected by the water-level changes. Since, as with any real body, the Earth is exposed to deformation and has a finite rigidity, any load on the surface level would cause stress and surface displacements. The eustatic changes of sea-level which result from the shifting of loads from the ice-covered areas to the oceans will produce a redistribution of loads over the Earth's surface and will cause deformation of the solid Earth; this crustal sensitivity to water is called hydro-isostasy. The crustal sensitivity to ice (glacio-isostasy) as well as to water (hydro-isostasy) form the eustatic curves of sea-level recorded from different parts of the world.

There are strong arguments for a hydro-isostatic deformation of the ocean floor; Daly (1934) speculated about the effect of the changing of the Pleistocene sea-level on the isostatic adjustment of the floors of the ocean, while Jensen (1972) discussed the reasons for the differences in eustatic sea-level curves and the effect of deglaciation in changing the shape of the geoid. The glacio-isostasy, which occurs as a result of the withdrawal of ice masses, is in itself a non-global effect; meanwhile, the rising of water all over the globe will create an elastic deformation of the solid Earth, and also an isostatic adjustment (hydro-isostasy), both on a global base. Jensen (ibid.) indicated that the effect of the hydro-isostatic change is smaller than that of the glacio-isostatic, since the equivalent water is much smaller than the ice thickness. Bloom (1967) studied the effect of the hydro-isostatic changes on continental coast and oceanic islands, and indicated that the oceanic islands record different shoreline levels from those of the continental coasts and are the best place to study glacially controlled sea-level changes. Mörner (1970, 1972) mentioned that consideration should be given to the hydro-isostatic effect when discussing supposed eustatic curves and maintained that the decrease in ocean volume associated with the building-up of glaciers had little effect on the ocean floor. On the other hand, the transformation of water from the melted ice to the oceans would hydro-isostatically deform the ocean floor by about $\frac{1}{3}$ of the thickness of the added water body.

Walcott (1974) used several rheological models of the Earth as the elastic theory and elastic parameters for the Earth, which can be used to find out the quantitative relationship between surface loads and the displacement of the surface. He indicated (1972) that during and following the melting of the Pleistocene ice caps, several deformational effects should occur and stated that 'The actual movements at any particular point over a specific time-interval will be the sum of all three movements (elastic, hydro-isostatic and postglacial rebound)'. As mentioned in Chapter 2 the Gulf during the Pleistocene Period was occupied to a varying extent by oceanic water. Crustal deformation below and above present sea-level may have resulted from associated geoidal hydro-isostatic changes if not from glacio-eustasy. So far, however, no quantitative measurement of the effect of these processes on the general physiography of the Gulf has been possible.

We now turn to the correlation of the levelled terraces and discuss them in relation to the world-wide changes of sea-level; an attempt will also be made to elucidate whether these terraces have been formed as a result of eustatic changes of sea-level or whether other factors have also played a part in their formation. The interpretation is based on the assumption that in the absence of crustal movements, ancient shorelines will be horizontal identifiable physiographic features. Hence, if the terraces exposed on land in the present research area are the result of a fall in sea-level alone, the terraces of the Al-Bahra area in the east would be of the same or similar height to the terraces elsewhere, i.e. at Mudairah, Ghidhai and Kathma in the west. The problem of interpretation becomes complicated when both localized and regional crustal as well as eustatic changes of sea-level are involved in the area. In this case, terraces of the same age may not be found at the same height in different areas, while on the other hand the fact that the terraces are found at the same or similar height does not necessarily mean that they are of the same age.

## 6.2 Basic assumptions and sources of error

First, some of the basic assumptions concerning the techniques described in the previous chapter must be examined, with particular reference to any source of error in the data obtained.

*Basic assumptions*

*1 Tide range constant* It has been assumed that fluctuations of the tidal range in Kuwait Bay were no greater in Pleistocene times than they are today. The tidal levels now observed in the Bay are as follows:

| | |
|---|---|
| Mean Higher High Water Springs | + 3.58 metres |
| Mean Lower Low Water Springs | −0.72 metres |

Levels refer to Kuwait Land Chart Datum, which is 0.47 metres above Admiralty Chart Datum (Shwaikh Port Authority). However, it is possible that during the Quaternary this range varied, as the morphometry of the Gulf changed with fluctuating sea levels.

2 Sample taken from transect lines are representative of terrace sedimentary environments. The number of the analysed samples has been decided according to two factors: (i) the condition of the samples when they arrived in the laboratory; some samples were abandoned due to breakage of their containers; (ii) that at least a representative sample from each terrace is included. However, although the results obtained from analysis of the samples and the shape of their diagrams (Figures 5.19 to 5.32) show general similarities, it is worth while mentioning here that the samples and their results are mainly representative of their particular locations along the levelled transects (as indicated in Figures 5.4, 5.6, 5.8, 5.10, 5.12, 5.14 and 5.16), and hence reflect the sedimentary environments along the transects. Nevertheless, it is believed that as the transects themselves are dispersed in different locations in the research area, and the results still show similarities, it can be held that the transects are significantly representative of the type of depositional environments which exist not only along the transect lines, but also in the intervening areas.

*Sources of error*

It is believed that all three methods are exposed to some degree of error which could affect the results obtained. The degree of error varies from one method to another, and it is believed that the radiocarbon dating results may be most liable to error. Accordingly, the results presented here for the three methods are preliminary, and further research must be considered. However, it is also believed that correlation of the results of all three methods has reduced the degree to which errors become significant, and are below the level which would be obtained if only one method was adopted.

*1 Levelling* The error in levelling will mainly occur due to the difficulty of closing the levelled transects. The unavoidable reason, previously referred to, was the lack of trigonometrical stations or bench-marks near the closing point. However, the preliminary levelling (carried out before the levelling began) indicates that the possible closing error of each transect is of the order of ± 1 metre, and this value is not significant in comparison with the range of terrace heights obtained in the area (see Table 5.1).

Another possible error arises from unequal forward- and back-reading of distances between levelling stations. The distances were largely determined by the topography of the area, with narrow widths in the upper terraces, and increasing widths in the case of the lower terraces. As a result, the inequality of the distances between the levelling points introduced some error in the levelling results. However, this question has been referred to specialists in this field, who have indicated that although the procedure adopted would introduce a geodetic error, it is not significant in relation to the research in hand, with an error value of about 10 centimetres over a distance of about 5 kilometres.

*2 Radiocarbon dating* Sources of error in the carbon dating procedure may have arisen for several reasons. One of these is statistical – a result of submitting the shells to several laboratories; although the existence of this source of error was recognized, it was not possible to determine its precise value. Accordingly, for this and other reasons which will be discussed further, only the inner fraction of the dated samples was counted in calculation, and the outer fraction, which is more exposed to contamination, was ignored. There is also a possibility that contamination of the fossil shells may have occurred in the field before collection as a result of the handling of some of the species by human agencies, as well as by intermingling of geologically older and younger species. Mollusca add a certain proportion of radioactively 'dead' carbon derived from old rocks to their tissue, with the result that the radioactivity will be too low, and subsequently the indicated age will be too great.

*3 Mixture of samples on the terraces* When we come to analyse the characteristics of the material of which the terraces – identified by levelling – are
composed, and which cover the surface of the terraces, we meet one major
problem of special importance to an interpretation of fossil materials.

During the levelling along the named transects, the nature of superficial
deposits was observed along the line and also in a wider zone on each side of
the transect line. During this process, the presence, sometimes over extensive
areas, of richly fossiliferous beds was noted at various altitudes.

As will be seen later in this chapter, the identification of fossil material is
of considerable importance, but in the case of the fossiliferous beds the
question which has to be asked, and which cannot always be satisfactorily
answered, is whether these beds represent discontinuous exposures of lithological material in the parent bedrock, or whether they represent later deposition on the bedrock.

The fossiliferous beds have been correlated and examined with the aid of
the cross-sections which were constructed through the Jal-Az-Zor escarpment
by Fuchs *et al.* (1968). These cross-sections show the occurrence of a fossiliferous formation of Tertiary age (exposed Neogene). The composition of the
collected fossiliferous samples and their locations resemble those illustrated
by Fuchs *et al.* and accordingly some of the collected samples are thought to
be of the same formation. These samples came from the First terrace in
Ghidhai and from the Second and Third terraces in Mudairah as well as from
some parts of the research area. As for the fossiliferous bed west of Kathma I,
and that traced on the Fourth terrace on Ghidhai, it is probably a mixture
between the old and more recent formation.

The fossiliferous marine deposits which were found to overlie the Lower
Fars fossiliferous bed exposed in some parts of Kathma (II) are sufficiently
physically distinctive to be considered as of more recent deposition (Figure 5.6
and Plate 4). The same applies to the fossiliferous rocks found on the lowest
terraces in the Al-Bahra area on the three transects AI, AII and AIII (Figures
5.12, 5.14 and 5.16).

In addition, over thirty fossiliferous rock samples have been further
examined by the geologists Dr G.A.L. Johnson of the Geology Department
of the University of Durham, Dr J. D. Taylor and Mr C.P. Nuttal of the
British Museum (Natural History), and Mr C.C.S. Davies of British Petroleum
(formerly Kuwait Oil Company). Dr Johnson examined some of the samples
collected from the Kathma area and indicated that no precise age can be given
to them, but they are probably Tertiary to Recent. Dr Taylor and Mr Nuttal
examined a large number of samples and concluded that the material is very
poorly preserved, but that the age probably ranges from Pliocene to Recent.
As for the samples examined by Mr Davies, no definite conclusion could be
drawn to their state of preservation. Purely from lithological and palaeonto-
logical examination of the fossiliferous samples collected from selected sites,
we can go no further than the conclusion reached in Chapter 5.

## 6.3 The terraces as physiographic features

In Chapter 3, it was noticed that the area north of Kuwait Bay is structurally unstable, but study of the area has not been sufficiently detailed for the intensity of this instability to be precisely determined.

The detailed levelling of the various transects not only helped in the identification of the terraces but also gave indications of the degree to which crustal changes have affected the areas.

The number of the levelled terraces between Kathma and Al-Bahra district varies between six in Al-Bahra (profile AI) to four terraces east of Al-Bahra (AIII) as well as in Kathma. Figure 6.1, which has been drawn from the combined results of the field survey and from information constructed by the help of aerial photographs and topographic maps, shows that throughout the area, there is clear evidence of several breaks of slope representing remnants of terraces; the bedrocks of these terraces are mainly of Miocene and Pliocene age. They are found either exposed on the surface or overlain by Pleistocene and Holocene marine and terrestrial deposits.

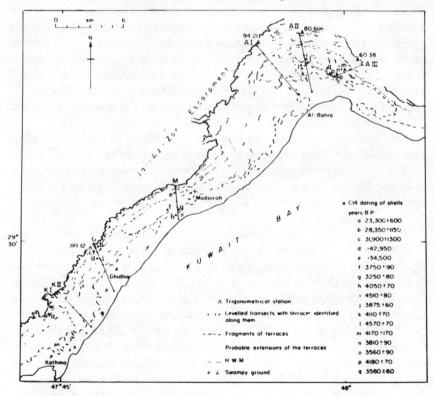

**Figure 6.1** *Tentative genetic correlation of terraces north of Kuwait Bay (from Kuwait Oil Company maps, 1961; aerial photograph, 1962, field investigations (T.A.A))*

The mean heights of the levelled terraces range between a maximum of 92.62 metres for the highest terrace found in Ghidhai and a minimum of 5.99 metres above Kuwait Land Chart Datum (KD) for the lowest height of terrace in Al-Bahra III. Table 5.1 gives the mean height of the surveyed terraces; it clearly indicates that from Kathma in the west to Al-Bahra in the east, the mean heights of the terraces above KD, not only decrease, but also there are local decreases and increases in height. This can be noted from the heights of the First terrace where, as in Kathma, it has a mean height of 90.60 m above KD in KI and a mean height of 81.53 m above KD in KII, while in Ghidhai area, the First terrace exhibits higher elevation than that in KII and KI. East of Ghidhai and at the border of Mudairah, the mean height decreases to a level of 71.12 metres above KD. In Al-Bahra district, the First terrace in AI rises to 79.85 m above KD, and then gradually decreases to 63.72 m above KD in Al-Bahra AII until it reaches a mean height of 33.11 m above KD in Al-Bahra AIII. Similar characteristics are found for the other terraces in that from Ghidhai the height of the terraces gradually decreases until they reach the lowest level in Al-Bahra III. The height of the Fifth terrace which has been levelled in Ghidhai, Mudairah and Al-Bahra (profile I and II) has its highest mean elevation in Ghidhai at 33.60 m above KD, then it decreases to a mean height of 11.61 metres in Mudairah. In Al-Bahra I, it rises to a mean height of 22.32 metres above KD and has an elevation of 14.43 m in the middle of Al-Bahra (AII).

The levelling results indicate that:

1 There are six terraces observable between Kathma and Al-Bahra.

2 These terraces do not have a constant height, but generally decrease in height from west to east.

3 Beside the general eastward decrease of their elevation, there are indications supported by the differences in heights that the area in the middle between Ghidhai and Al-Bahra has suffered from some local structural warping.

Therefore, it seems that although the levelling has thrown some light on the existence of the terraces and their distribution in the area, it has meant also that it is impossible to correlate them solely according to their height and the results of the other methods applied in this research are necessary to a better understanding of the relations between the terraces.

*C14 dating correlation*

During field investigation, several fossil shell species were found either scattered or cemented onto the surface of the terraces in different areas and at different heights (Figures 5.4, 5.8, 5.10, 5.14 and 5.16).

The shells have been identified and some of them submitted for radiocarbon dating. They were identified for two reasons:

1   To investigate whether they are of marine or freshwater origin for the reasons explained already on page 75.

2   To find out whether they correspond to those species described by Cox and Rhoades (1935) and Fuchs *et al*. (op. cit.) as being of the fossiliferous Lower Fars Formation which is exposed in some places between Kathma and Al-Bahra, or whether they correspond to more recent deposition. The species which belong to the Recent period have also been described by Cox and Rhoades, Perry and Al-Refai 1958 and Steininger (1968). Although, it is known that complete separation between old and new species during geological time is not possible for some species, as they may have existed long before the Pleistocene and may be still flourishing in present seas, it is possible to locate some of the species which lived for a limited period of time. An attempt has been carried out to compare the shells which were collected and partly submitted for C14 dating with those referred to by the previous authors as belonging to the fossiliferous Lower Fars Formation of Miocene age.

The results indicate that the shell samples include both old and more recent species. The older group, including *Ostrea sp., Spondylus sp.* and *Turbo sp.*, has been found at different heights. *Ostrea sp.* have never been found on the lowest terraces (i.e. terrace No. 6) but have been found in Kathma west of the levelled line of KI on the Third terrace and the upper part of the Fourth terrace. They have also been found in Ghidhai on the Third, Fourth and Fifth terraces. In Mudairah, they are scattered on the Second, Third and Fourth terraces and at some places on the higher terraces in Al-Bahra.

*Turbo sp.*, have been found in Ghidhai on the Third terrace and on the First terrace east of Al-Bahra (AIII), but have not been found near the present coastline. *Spondylus sp.*, which have not been found on the higher terraces as the previous two species, are represented only in Mudairah below the Fifth terrace (Figure 5.10). However, the last two species *Turbo* and *Spondylus*, although thought to be only of Miocene age of the Lower Fars Formation, have been reported on the southern coastal area of Kuwait and on some of the adjacent islands by Steininger (1968). Therefore, one is left with only the *Ostrea sp.* which has not been reported as Recent in the available literature. The rest of the species must probably be thought of as Recent as well as of earlier provenance and similar to some of the other Recent species described by Steininger (ibid.) and to those which have been found by the author on the coastal area of Al-Dhba'iyyah (Table 5.2). Those which are reported by Steininger include *Barbatia sp., Cerithium sp., Dosina sp., Glycymeris sp., Plicatula sp.* and *Spondylus sp.* Of the supposedly Recent shell species, a few of them are located on the higher terraces such as *Cerithium sp., Dosina sp.* and *Pitar hagenowi sp.*

The question is whether these old and Recent species are helpful in indicating the age of the terraces on which they were found, or are they spread throughout the area without any regularity in age, and is the C14 dating able to indicate whether they belong to old or more recent deposition? Also, the dating of the shells will be helpful in correlating those terraces already identified by levelling but which cannot be correlated solely according to height. For example, can a terrace fragment in the Al-Bahra area be correlated with other fragments, sometimes at different heights, in Mudairah, Ghidhai and Kathma?

Two samples of *Ostrea sp.* which at the moment are thought only to belong to the Miocene formation were submitted for dating. The first, from the Fifth terrace in Ghidhai at a height of 46.51 metres above KD (Figure 5.8), gave a C14 dating of > 42,950 BP. The other sample, from the Fourth terrace in Mudairah at a height of about 40–42 metres above KD, gave an age of > 34,500 BP. C14 dating of *Cerithium sp.* from a higher level (63.30 metres) above KD on the Third terrace in Ghidhai gave an age of 28,300 ± 1150 BP.

At similar heights, two further shell samples have been identified; they are composed of broken indeterminate shells of mixed species and were collected from the top of a clear Fourth terrace covered by a fossiliferous bed. This terrace and the fossiliferous bed has been described in Chapter 5 and both field investigation and aerial photographs confirmed its location at the foot of the Jal-Az-Zor escarpment. These two samples were collected from two different areas, the first from Kathma west of the levelled line KI, and the second from the Fourth terrace in Ghidhai (Figures 5.4 and 5.8). The results were 23,300 ± 600 BP for the sample in Kathma at elevation of about 48 metres above KD and 31,900 ± 300 BP for the sample in Ghidhai at a height of about 52 metres above KD.

The other samples all came from the lower terraces and gave a maximum age of 4,570 ± 70 BP and will be discussed later.

The result from the higher terraces indicates several points. First, that although the *Ostrea sp.* samples do not come from the highest altitudes, they gave the greatest age (> 42,950 BP and > 34,500 BP) for heights of 46.51 metres and 40–42 metres above KD. By contrast, some younger samples were taken from higher altitudes, e.g. sample (SUA.86) 28,350 ± 1150 BP, height 63.30 metres above KD, and sample (I.7610) 31,900 ± 1300 BP, height about 52 metres above KD and sample (I.7609) 23,300 ± 600 BP, at elevation of about 48 metres above KD.

Second, the dated *Cerithium sp.*, which have also been found in the southern coast of Kuwait and are still living at present, have an age of 28,350 ± 1150 BP which is younger than that of the *Ostrea sp.* samples although the former come from a much higher elevation.

Third, the two samples (I.7610 and I.7609) taken from the Fourth terrace have given disappointingly different results, 31,900 ± 1300 BP for that from Ghidhai and 23,300 ± 600 BP for the Kathma sample. They also gave different ages from those of the *Ostrea sp.* and *Cerithium sp.*

Fourth, although the *Ostrea sp.* samples were found at lower altitudes, they seem to belong to the exposed fossiliferous Lower Fars Formation of the oldest age.

Fifth, the fossil shell bed found on the Fourth terrace and from which samples I.7610 and I.7609 were collected – although from a terrace clearly identifiable physiographically in the field – gave a different age. These differences may have resulted from the mixing of old and recent species to various degrees. Hence, the fossiliferous bed (Lower Fars Formation) has been washed down by water and different kinds of erosion, and may have been mixed with products of deposition associated with later marine transgression depositing more recent sediment and reworking the two at the same time. Last, the C14 dating indicates that the age of the higher terraces is possibly Pleistocene or older, two of the samples being earlier than 34,500 and 42,950 BP.

In the case of the lower terraces which are close to the present coastline, all the species are found on sediments more recent than the Lower Fars Formation. The samples dated came from Mudairah and Al-Bahra, and C14 dating results give similar ages and are generally close to each other. The ages range between a maximum of 4,570 ± 70 BP (T.1056) from a sample in Al-Bahra AII (Table 5.3 and Figure 6.1) and a minimum of 3,250 ± 80 BP (T.1062) in Mudairah which would indicate a Holocene age. Twelve samples have been dated, three from Mudairah (T.1062 to T.1064), four samples from the middle of Al-Bahra (AII) (T.1054, HV.4770, T.1055 and T.1056) and five samples from east of Al-Bahra (AIII) (T.1057, T.1058, T.1059, T.1060 and T.1061).

Most of these dated shell samples are thought to be *in situ* due to their occurrence in dense masses and in some cases they are cemented on to the terraces. Exceptionally, those collected from the Third terrace in AIII were found scattered sporadically in the area. As pointed out earlier in this study, the terrace sequence One to Six refers to physiographically identifiable terraces in each transect and there may not necessarily be a firm correlation between individual terraces in different transects. In the case of the Third terrace however, levelling, other field survey and an analysis of aerial photographs, do not suggest a continuity between transect AIII, AII and AI. In Kathma, Ghidhai and Mudairah C14 dates for the Third and Fourth terraces are all older than 23,300 ± 600 BP. C14 dating results for Al-Bahra transects show that sample (T.1057) which was found on the Third terrace along transect AIII to have an age similar to samples from the Fourth and Fifth terraces. The C14 dating for this sample is 4,170 ± 170 BP and is totally different from the Third terrace sample dates from Kathma and Mudairah equivalents. It is suggested, therefore, that the apparent age of this sample is too young for this terrace and that the C14 content may have been distorted by human activity. Figure 6.1 shows the distribution of C14 dating for the lower terraces; it indicates that the ages of the samples for the middle of Al-Bahra are generally close to those in AIII, ranging between a maximum of 4,570 ± 70 BP (T.1056) and a minimum of 3,560 ± 60 BP (T.1059). Similar dates have been obtained for the samples in Mudairah, where the C14 results range from 4,050 ± 70 BP (T.1064) to 3,250 ± 80 BP (T.1062). The above samples of Al-Bahra and Mudairah include four samples which were collected below the lowest terrace in the two areas. Two of the samples, HV.4770, age 3875 ± 60 BP and T.1055 dated 4,110 ± 70 BP, come from the lowland embayment within the Fifth terrace in AII, while the other two T.1062 of 3,250 ± 80 BP and T.1064 of 4,050 ± 70 BP have been collected from below the Fifth terrace in Mudairah. Although these last four samples came from lower altitudes than those on the adjacent terraces, they do not have different ages. They probably belong to the terraces lying at a slightly greater height but have been carried down either by human or physical agencies, or both.

The shell samples located on the lowest terraces in Mudairah and Al-Bahra are at the following heights: about 11 metres in Mudairah, 15.18 metres and 9.77 metres above KD in AII (middle of Al-Bahra), at 8.87 metres, 8.27 metres, 7.44 metres and 4.60 metres above KD to the east of Al-Bahra (AIII). This difference in heights agrees with the general results of the levelling which proved that there is no regular change in the heights of the sets of terraces between one area and another but there is a general decrease in height from west to east. Figure 6.1 shows that there is a continuation of part of the levelled terraces from Al-Bahra AIII to AII, AI and another continuation in Mudairah as well as west of Mudairah. The dotted line represents a probable extension of the fragment of the terraces in the area.

As the dating results, with one or two obvious anomalies, gave similar sequences in all the terraces and since gradation in heights is expected, it is possible to hypothesize that the fragments of terraces observable between the transects are remnants of one continuous terrace which extended from Al-Bahra in the east at least as far as Mudairah; it may also extend further west to Ghidhai (evidence of aerial photographs) and even to Kathma, but this latter extension cannot be identified from available aerial photographs and has not been identified by C14 sampling.

The result of fossil identification and correlation with the old and more recent marine shell species as well as the C14 dating of the shell samples implies:

(1) that there is a noticeable mixing between shell species of the Lower Fars Formation exposed in the area and those presumably of younger age, this applying particularly to the upper four terraces;

(2) that the age given for the higher dated terraces (above 40 m) suggests Pleistocene age at least, and

(3) the other result determined by C14 dating suggests that the lower terraces in each of Mudairah and Al-Bahra are remnants of one terrace dated between 4,570 ± 70 BP and 3,560 ± 60 BP. The mean heights of this terrace in each of the previous areas are 11.61 metres in Mudairah, 14.43 m in the middle of Al-Bahra (AII) and 5.99 m above KD east of Al-Bahra (AIII).

It is probable that the sample of shells which came from Al-Dhbai'yyah area (SUA.85) and gave a date of 940 ± 80 BP was introduced by human agencies. Fossil shells have been noticed covering vast parts of the coastal area of Al-Dhbai'yyah at different levels. Recently, this area has been covered by an almost continuous belt of seaside cottages and buildings. Hence, the age obtained by C14 dating for the sample which comes from an elevation of about 5 m above KD has given a younger age compared with other samples collected from the research area at a similar height. However, a definite explanation can not be given until further dating and investigations have been carried out in this area.

### Interpretation of sediment investigation

Until now, it has been possible to identify the number of the terraces in the research area as well as their heights which, together with some radio-carbon evidence, positively proved that the area is not stable. Marine shell dating has suggested possible ages for the higher and the lower levelled terraces.

### Origin of the terraces

The origin of these terraces is not definitely known and we now turn to studying the deposits covering the terraces to see whether this will indicate their origin, although there is a possibility that they, or some of them, may have been cut by different agents than might be indicated by the superficial deposits. In this section therefore some sediment analysis results are discussed in the context of other research results already noted and of other geological studies.

The result of the application of sediment research by particle-size analysis and to a limited degree by scanning electron microscope seems, in general, to provide a good indication of the origin of the deposits covering the terraces and the adjacent areas at the top of the escarpment and on the present beach. Student's *t* test (Table 5.9) has shown that there is no relationship between the samples from the top of the escarpment and the beach samples, with regard to sediment mean size, standard deviation and skewness. The results of the plotting of the parameters against each other have shown that samples from the top of the escarpment fall in the gravelly sand category. Also, the composition of the particle size curves (Figures 5.25 to 5.32) shows that the curves of sediments from the top of the escarpment (Figure 5.25) are different from those of the six terraces and from those of the beach. The results of three samples from the top of the escarpment which have been examined by scanning electron microscope (samples 13, 32 and 60) from Kathma, Mudairah and Al-Bahra, indicate the occurrence of subaqueous environment as well as aeolian with the former being the dominant agent of deposition. Krinsley and Doornkamp (1973) indicated that the subaqueous environments include both marine and non-marine water. The literature relevant to the whole region refers to freshwater deposits of gravels covering the north and west of Kuwait (Moody, 1947; Higginbottom, 1954; and Fuchs *et al.*, 1968), these deposits being laid down by active rivers which originated in the interior of Arabia during the Pleistocene. The evidence thus given concerning the origin of sediments on top of the escarpment fits with the results of this investigation which indicate that the deposits covering the bedrocks of the top of the escarpment are mainly of fluviatile origin.

As far as the First and Second terraces are concerned, the results seem to show that their deposits are similar to each other but that the First terrace is closer in character to the top of the escarpment than to the Second terrace. The mean sizes of the sediments on the First and the Second terraces are different from that of the beach sediments indicated by Student's *t* test which agree with the result of the field investigation. The sorting of the sediments of the First terrace seems to be worse than that of the Second terrace and of the beach and is similar to that of the top of the escarpment. As for skewness, the situation is reversed; this can be understood when one remembers that some of the beach samples have positive skewness. The difference in skewness results may have been obtained because some parts of the Second terrace carry marine deposits. The result of plotting the parameters of the First and Second terrace samples (Figure 5.24b) shows that all the First terrace samples, except one, fall in the gravelly sand category with the top of the escarpment samples. The same applies, except for three samples, to those of the Second terrace. The combined curves of the First and Second terraces (Figures 5.26 and 5.27) illustrate that the curves of the First terrace, although generally similar to those of the top of the escarpment, in some cases have higher percentages of the suspension population which distort the shape of the graphs. The graphs of the Second terrace are more uniform as they include samples of marine origin. Sample 42 from Al-Bahra (Figure 5.12) indicates a superimposed environment when examined by scanning electron microscope. The sample (Plate 22C and D) was first deposited by water and later exposed to aeolian action; sample 34 (Plate 20A) which comes from the Second terrace in Mudairah is of beach origin. It can therefore be stated that the First terrace exhibits deposits similar to those of the top of the escarpment, with indications of both fluviatile and aeolian origin. As for the Second terrace, traces of marine deposits have been found in the area (Figures 5.8, 5.10, 5.12 and 5.16) and hence one would expect to find more evidence of marine origin than would be found in the First terrace; it also carries sediments of fluviatile and aeolian origin.

The Third and Fourth terraces have been observed to contain fossiliferous beds of possibly old and more recent deposits, and extend from Kathma to Al-Bahra. Student's *t* test (Table 5.9) shows that there is a complete agreement between the four parameters of the samples of these two terraces and those of the present beach. These parameters, when plotted against each other, show that some of the Third terrace samples fall into the gravelly sand field as well as the aeolian and beach environments, a result which does not completely agree with Student's *t* test (Figure 5.24b). The samples of the

Fourth terrace have all fallen in the beach field and in the aeolian field except one sample in the gravelly field. Investigation of the origin of the samples according to their shape characteristics and the three populations (rolling, saltation and suspension) indicates that the Third terrace (Figure 5.28) shows characteristics of aeolian curves. As for those of the Fourth terrace, they have special characteristics with a higher percentage of suspension population indicating mixed environments. The results of scanning electron microscopy on two samples, one from Kathma (No. 17) and from Al-Bahra (No. 46) agree with the result of the particle size analysis and show that they are of marine origin. Samples Nos 5, 6, 8, 18, 25, 37 and 57, collected from the Fourth terrace between Kathma and Al-Bahra, possess features on the grains that indicate marine origin. In conclusion, one can say that the Third and Fourth terraces show that there is a mixing of the three environments, although there are only very limited samples of gravelly sand deposits of fluvial origin.

Only four samples have been analysed for the Fifth terrace and two from the Sixth terrace. Student's *t* test shows a close relationship with the parameters of these samples and those of the beach, especially of the Sixth terrace, but the mean size and skewness correlation is negative. The result of plotting the parameters for the Fifth and Sixth terraces shows that two of the samples of the Fifth fall in the beach field and one in the aeolian field, while the fourth has gravelly sand. Those of the Sixth terrace sample all fall in the aeolian field.

Thus, the distribution of the sediments covering the bedrock of the terraces and the study area can be summarized as follows:

1   The gravelly sand deposits are concentrated on the top of the escarpment, the First, Second and parts of the Third terraces; they are also found sporadically on some of the lower terraces.

2   The sediments of the aeolian environment are in some cases very difficult to separate from the other two environments because they were deposited during all periods and hence are widespread in the whole area. However, the aeolian material is most noticeable in the middle zone between the higher terraces and high-water mark, i.e. on the Third, Fourth and on a fragment of the Sixth terrace.

3   The third and last environment of deposition is that of the beach and this, as well as being found on the present coastline where samples exhibit characteristics of the adjacent area's sediments to the north of the Gulf, has been also identified on the Third, Fourth and Fifth terraces, as well as having a very limited distribution on the Second terrace, especially in Al-Bahra area.

4   The fossiliferous beds found on some of the terraces, e.g. below the First terrace in Ghidhai, are of Miocene age (Lower Fars Formation); the same applies also to those in the Mudairah area on the Second and Third terraces, and to some of the exposed fossiliferous beds in between

the previous areas and Al-Bahra. The problems arising from the presence of this non-Recent material were considered earlier in this chapter.

It is now proposed to give a first tentative statement on the possible origin of these terraces in relation to sea-level changes. The small amount of relevant literature, together with information provided by geologists in Kuwait – partly in the form of personal communication – has indicated: first that this area of research is tectonically unstable and that this instability has affected the general topography of the area. Second, the Bahra anticline has been associated with the Kuwait arch which extends to the south of Kuwait and is possibly still active. Third, a general dip towards the north-east has been noticed, which may accord with a general subsidence of the northern part of the Gulf. Fourth, a probable northward block tilting as suggested by C. C. S. Davies (personal communication). Fifth, there are indications of marine fossils of recent species on higher levels than would be expected either in the absence of positive vertical movement of land or of a general falling of sea-level. The existence of several levels of terraces at the foot of the escarpment reflecting sea-level changes during the Pleistocene has already been postulated (Fuchs *et al.*, 1968 and personal communication).

In addition to these basic observations one may cite the widespread occurrence of fluviatile materials on the northern and western land surface of Kuwait, which have been interpreted as being deposited by rivers during the Pleistocene and possibly late Pliocene (see pp. 22, 23). The fossil remnant of one of these rivers is the Wadi Al-Batin in the west of the country and possibly the Al-Musannat in the south-west. The sedimentological results embodied in the present research support the view that fluviatile materials are present in this area, e.g. the gravels at the top of the escarpment and on the upper terraces. The sediment evidence for marine action becomes stronger as one proceeds down the terrace sequences from the escarpment.

On the basis of these points a tentative correlation of the origin of the terraces in terms of present knowledge may be attempted. The terraces in the area seem to be attributed to two main agents of erosion and deposition, these agents being marine and freshwater action. The latter is more evident on the higher two, and possibly three terraces, while marine action has been responsible for the cutting and deposition – of the lower terraces (which include the Fourth and other lower terraces). This correlation is based on the types of deposition found on the terraces even though there is a general mixing of the kinds of deposits. Terraces Nos 1, 2 and 3, together with the top of the escarpment, carry sediment deposits of gravelly sand and are dissected by several dry drainage systems. The fossiliferous beds found on some of the First terrace in Ghidhai and on the First and Second in Mudairah, are partly of Miocene age, while those of the lower altitudes carry marine deposits of more recent age which rest upon the Miocene fossiliferous formation, which in turn represents the bedrock of these terraces.

The probability that the upper terraces have been partly formed by rivers is strengthened when one considers the evidence for past widespread fluvial action in the area. Whether this fluvial system was a previous align-ment of the Wadi Al-Batin or a quite separate system which deposited the gravels in the north and west of the country is not known.

The alluvial agents of freshwater deposition no longer exist under present conditions, as annual rainfall does not exceed 195.8 millimetres. Accordingly, it is probable that the sediments covering those terraces with incised wadis originated during past periods of heavier rainfall, coinciding with global climatic changes (during the Pleistocene) and fluctuations of sea-level along with regional and local tectonic movements.


## Ancient climate

At this stage, a brief consideration of ancient climates and their development in the surrounding areas is worth while. The present climate does not justify the existence of several morphological features, as for example, the dendritic wadis in Arabia, the higher advance of sea-level to more than 150 metres above present sea-level at the early stages of the Pleistocene Period as indi-cated by the height of old deltas of Wadi Al-Batin and Wadi Sahbah (Holm, 1960), as well as the existence of sabkhahs and east-facing cliffs, at about 150 metres height in eastern Saudi Arabia. The raised beaches of 373 metres in Oman (Lees, 1928) which carry marine fauna in a state of preservation similar to that of sub-Recent raised beaches, may have been formed during the high stages of sea-level during Early Pleistocene. Other indications have been discussed by Lees (ibid.) and others (see Chapter 2).

The effect of climatological variations and their associated features has made it possible to clarify the factors involved in the development of the present topography of the research area. Butzer and Hanson (1968) indicated that during the Late Tertiary the climate of Egypt was semi-arid, accom-panied by concentrated run-off. Chapman (1971) referred to the climatic history of the Eastern Province of Saudi Arabia during the Pliocene as having a temperature approximately the same as at the present time, being consider-ably moister in mid-Pliocene and semi-arid in Late Pliocene. As for the Pleistocene, the main relevant feature was the great development of glaciers, when millions of cubic kilometres of ocean water were locked in the Conti-nental ice masses, with a resultant lowering of the sea-level. During the warmer interglacial periods, when water was released, the sea-level rose. Schwarzbach (1963) reported that in the period of glaciation, particularly in the Northern Hemisphere, the west wind belt was forced equator-ward; consequently, at least the poleward limits of the deserts received a more abundant rainfall, and a glacial phase in a polar region corresponds to a 'pluvial' with reduced temperatures near the equator. During the interglacial stages, Schwarzbach believes that the climate was drier, and either as warm or slightly warmer than at present, while the higher latitudes were subjected to glaciation and deglaciation and the arid lands were exposed to moister (pluvial) and drier (interpluvial) periods. The pluvial periods were characterized by cooler temperatures and considerable rainfall, and by the formation of terraces and wadi cutting.

The interpluvial, on the other hand, were warm and semi-arid with short periods of appreciable rainfall alternating with longer periods of drought. The pluvial period was defined by Butzer (1961) 'as a phase of widespread, long-term rainfall increase, of sufficient duration and intensity to be of geological significance'. Penck (1913), Büdel (1939) and Fairbridge (1961) have discussed this phenomenon, and put forward two hypotheses to explain it. The first is the uniform migration of climatic belts, equator-wards, in glacial periods and towards the pole in the interglacials. The equatorial belt was narrowed down during the cold periods and expanded during the warm periods. The second hypothesis is the pluvial–arid alternation, during which the glacial phases were characterized by almost complete suppression of arid zones and extensive increase in precipitation, while wide desert belts were developed during the interglacial phases.

Schwarzbach (1963) indicated that every present-day desert area has been influenced by pluvials. In North America, during the glacial period, the Great Basin area was flooded by extensive lakes such as Lake Bonneville; the former high feature level is indicated by the old lake terraces. In Asia, the Caspian, Aral and Black Seas were connected, while in the Dead Sea the water level was 400 metres higher than it is today, with fifteen raised beaches. In Arabia, several examples have been presented regarding the climatic changes which occurred, one of which is the occurrence of several wadi drainages in areas which are now desert and relics of wetter climates such as the wadi channels and fluvial gravels which occur on the southern edge of the Rub al-Khali of Saudi Arabia, an area which at present lacks a permanent flow of water. According to Glennie (1970) these features originated at periods of increased wadi flow, e.g. during the Pleistocene pluvial periods.

Correlation between pluvial and glacial periods has been broadly suggested on the basis of sea-level correlations, although exceptions do occur, as in the Mediterranean area, where it has been found that only the early parts of low sea-level periods were moister, while later parts were much drier. Also, while some periods were generally dry, other periods were warm and moist (Butzer, 1963). The glacial periods were associated with marine regression and river degradation, while the interglacials were accompanied by marine transgression and river aggradation.

For the Holocene or Recent Period, Butzer (1961) indicated that the Sahara experienced a full aridity about 8,000 BC, and between about 5,500 BC and 2,350 BC, the climate was more moist than today, this being indicated by faunal, botanical and geological evidences. The period between 2,350 and 800 BC was intensely dry with evidence of sand-dunes invading parts of the Nile Valley, and the decline of the Nile floods associated with famines. In south-west Asia, there was a similar climate to that of the Sahara, with fluctuations of markedly greater humidity and aridity (Butzer, 1961). The evidence of climatic changes of postglacial periods in the Gulf are recorded in the submarine terraces at different levels (Houbolt, 1957; Kassler, 1973). Godwin *et al*. (1958), Evans *et al.* (1969) and Taylor and Illing (1969) also refer to marine transgressions of that period.

## Further possibilities of the origin of Terraces

After considering the climatic change in the macro-region of which Kuwait is part, it may now be possible to consider further possibilities as to the origin of the terraces besides those already obtained from the applied methods of investigation by returning to the question of land surface alluvial deposition.

When one examines the topography of Kuwait (see Figure 3.5), one notes the existence of channels of gravels aligned south-west to north-east in the area between the Jal-Az-Zor escarpment and Wadi Al-Batin in the west. This phenomenon is not observable between the escarpment and the coastline; instead marine deposits cover some of the terraces at different altitudes.

The north and west of Kuwait is dissected by several drainage systems and as the present climate does not permit the existence of such drainage, it is obvious that they originated during some of the pluvial periods of the Pleistocene or possibly earlier. The edge of the escarpment is dissected by wadis which are most prominent in the west. Their channels cut through the terraces and represent periods of rejuvenation of erosion and deposition influenced by repeated regional tectonic movements and sea-level changes. The present staircase topography which is most prominent between Kathma and Mudairah and the deposits covering them and the dissection, show that the terraces may have been formed as a result of land and sea movements since at least the beginning of the Pleistocene. It is possible therefore that the terraces were first cut by marine action during high stages of sea-level. As the sea-level dropped to a lower level, stream erosion would have been increased and streams would be deeply incised, with the heavier rains washing down the fluvial deposits from the top of the escarpment on to the lower altitudes. If the sea-level rose again, stream erosion would decrease and streams would tend to aggradate their loads. These changes occurred either because of an eustatic drop of sea-level or a local and/or regional tectonic movement, or both.

From Kathma to Mudairah, the upper two or three terraces have narrow widths compared to those of the Al-Bahra area. Usually, if the sea maintained its level for a long period, the original cliff would retreat inland and the wave-cut terrace would be broad, But, if the sea-level was not maintained for a long time, or if a sudden change of coastal movement occurred, the width of the wave cut terrace would be small. Hence it is possible that the upper two, and possibly the third, terraces between Kathma and Mudairah, had a different tectonic history from those in Al-Bahra; they may have been exposed to local positive movement during which the sea-level dropped to a lower stage, while the area of Al-Bahra had a generally quiet tectonic history or had been rising very slowly in accordance with the movement of the Bahra anticline. The indication that the area between Kathma and Mudairah up to the border of Al-Bahra was exposed to a different tectonic history is first given by the results of topographic levelling and by the clear phenomenon of wadis which are cut straight into the terraces. The other possibility is that an increase in stream erosion and the even better preservation of the higher terraces from Kathma to Mudairah (which are also higher than those of Al-Bahra) may relate to the general subsidence of the north of the Gulf, and as Al-Bahra is closer to that area, it is possible that Al-Bahra, especially the eastern part, was affected by that movement. Lees and Falcon (1952) have suggested that the northern part of Bubiyan Island which is close to the Al-Bahra area is undergoing subsidence because of the general movement at the north of the Gulf. More recently, Kassler (1973), quoting an unpublished oil company report written by V. S. Colter, indicated that the latter estimated the subsidence of the Kuwait part of the delta to be as much as 37 metres below sea-level in the last 5,000 years (see p. 9).

It seems that the Fourth terrace, which clearly extends along the foot of the escarpment from Kathma to Mudairah and appears discontinuously in the Al-Bahra area, was probably cut by marine action only. It carries fossiliferous beds of old and younger ages. It may have originated during the last stages of the Pleistocene when the world climate became warmer and the sea-level consequently rose, a change in accordance with which the climate of Arabia including Kuwait tended to become less moist. As a result there would have been a decrease of the amount of rainfall and possibly the ending of the alluvial action which originated from the highlands of Arabia, leaving the area affected by marine transgression only. Another reason for the end of the freshwater deposition in this area and particularly on the Fourth terrace, may be the block tilting towards the north, as C. C. S. Davies suggested. That tilting was accompanied by stream migration from an original Musannat–Kuwait Bay to the more recently developed channel of Wadi Al-Batin. However, the C14 dating of fossil shell samples from the higher terraces, which are believed to be younger than the shells of the Lower Fars Formation, have age ranges between a maximum of $> 42,950$ BP for sample No. C5/I from Ghidhai (at a height of 46.51 metres above KD) and a minimum of $23,300 \pm 600$ BP for sample I.7609 from Kathma (at an elevation of about 48 metres above KD), while the sample which was collected from Mudairah at a height of 40–42 metres above KD (Birm. 285) gave an age of $> 34,500$ years BP. The fourth sample (SUA.86) at a height of 63.30 metres above KD gave an age of $28,350 \pm 1150$ BP from the Third terrace in Ghidhai

*Eustatic changes of sea-level*

At present, little is known about the eustatic changes of sea-level during the period between 80,000 and 20,000 years BP. Fisk (1959) reported an age of 23,400 BP for the shells 50 feet (15.24m) below sea-level on Padre island, off the coast of southern Texas. Frye and Willman (1961) mentioned that there was an interstadial at 25,000 BP called Farmdalian with an ice advance before and after. Fairbridge (1961) estimated the level to be about −40 metres around that date, while Curray (1961) thought it was about −15 metres as indicated from remnants of shoreline deposits, off Freeport, Texas, which gave an age of about 30,000 years. McFarlan (1961) reported that the sea-level rose to its present level about 3,000 years ago in two stages; the sea-level was about −450 feet (−137.2 m) more than 35,000 years ago, it then rose from −450 feet to −250 feet (−76.2 m) and stayed at that height until 18,500 years ago. The second stage started at that time and continued until about 3,000 years ago. In 1963 Shepard declared the existence of an inter-stadial sea-level which may belong to the Farmdalian. The evidence was obtained from terraces at levels of between 1.5 and 3.7 metres in Oahu (Hawaii) and New Caledonia. He dated shells from terraces in Oahu and the ages obtained were 24,140 and 26,640 years BP for the 1.5 metre terrace, while the shells from the 3.7 metre terrace gave ages of 31,540 and 31,840 years BP. The study of the coral reef terraces along the north-east coast of Huon Peninsula, New Guinea (Bloom *et al.*, 1974) indicated that since about 125,000 years ago, a time of higher sea-levels than at present, five stages of sea-level maxima occurred, but none of them is above the present level. The terraces record the succession of relative transgression and regression which reflect the oscillation of glaciation superimposed on a rela-tively smoothly rising land. Fairbridge revised the dates of major Late Quater-nary events as presented by vast numbers of researchers. He referred to the Gottweig interstadial which is dated about 50,000–30,000 and the Main Würm Emergence as being between 30,000 and 17,000 years BP. None of these ages corresponds with evidence from the study area.

Also the correlation between the present terraces and those of Depéret (1918–22) in the Mediterranean, is rather difficult because of the variations in terrace height found within the study area. In addition, the Pleistocene terraces are beyond the limits of the radiocarbon method dating. It has been suggested by Zeuner (1959) that the approximate age of the Pleistocene inter-glacial terraces - Sicilian, Milazzian, Tyrrhenian and Late Monastirian - are be-tween 825,000 and 125,000 years BP. The ages of the Late and Epi-Monastirian terraces (the last was named by Zeuner, 1953) which attain heights of 6–8 and 3–5 metres, have been revised by Fairbridge (1961), who indicated that ex-trapolation to Emiliani's curve (1955) suggests that the age is of 95,000 – 90,000 years BP for the late Monastirian and 80,000 years BP for the Epi-Monastirian.

From this and previous reviews, it can be said that there is a general agreement that for the time period obtained for the Kuwait higher terraces (between > 42,950 years BP and 23,000 ± 600 years BP), sea-level fluctuated without being higher than at present. Exceptions rarely occurred, and are referred to by Shepard (1963) and Shepard and Curray (1967). Consequently, it seems that the heights of the Kuwait dated terraces are very much higher than other workers have estimated for the same Periods in other parts of the world.

## 6.4 Summary

The present ages and heights of the terraces and their relationship with the general trend of sea-level changes in the Pleistocene Period can be summarized as follows:

1  Although the heights of the terraces of the study area are in the range of the Mediterranean sequence of high sea-level, none of the terraces can be definitely correlated with any particular terrace of the Mediterranean because of the considerable height variations within the study area.
2  Although a correlation between the ages of the available shells collected from different heights of the terraces, agrees in general with dates obtained by other workers for the Late Pleistocene, they are distinctly different in their heights above sea-level.
3  The samples which have ages of 23,300 ± 600 years BP and over may either confirm their association with the Lower Fars Formation or they may represent more recent Pleistocene contamination.

With regard to the lower terraces, for which young C14 ages were obtained (between 4,570 ± 70 BP and 3,560 ± 60 years BP) the dates suggest that they are Holocene and particularly related to that stage which occurred from about 6,000 to 3,000 years ago. There is less agreement between the various researchers about the trend of sea-level during the last 6,000 years. Shepard (1964) indicates that there are three schools of thought concerning the changes in sea-level during this period:
(1) sea-level fluctuated from about −1.5 to +3 metres above the present; (2) constant sea-level since the present level was reached about 3,000 to 6,000 years ago, and (3) continuing slow rise of sea-level after about 5,000 to 6,000 years ago up to the present level. Fairbridge (1958, 1961) maintained that the sea-level fluctuated with four higher-level stages. The first occurred about 5,000 BP when the sea-level rose to +3 to +5 metres, but the actual elevation may be greater in some areas than others. The second rise reached to about +3 metres in the period from 4,000 to 3,400 BP. The third was about 2,300 BP with a positive rise up to +1.5 metres while the last rise was between 1,600 to 1,000 BP during which the sea-level rose by 0.5 to 1 metre. Shepard and Suess (1956) believed that sea-level was never above the present in the postglacial period; McFarlan (1961) held the same opinion, but believed that the sea reached its present level about 3,000 years ago. A

similar result to McFarlan's has been obtained by Jelgersma and Pannekoek (1960). More recently Tooley (1974) recorded three or four stages of higher sea-level above the present during the last 4,000 years. It is therefore suggested that the lower terraces may represent one of the higher stands of sea-level during the last 6,000 years, especially since there is world-wide as well as regional evidence from the Gulf of stages of higher sea-level. The only problem is that the height of the terraces varies from a minimum mean height of 5.99 metres above KD east of Al-Bahra to a mean height of 14.43 metres above KD in the middle of Al-Bahra, and a mean height of 16.10 metres west of Al-Bahra, to a mean height of 11.61 metres above KD in Mudairah. However, the most noticeable characteristic of these terraces is that they are better preserved than the higher terraces farther inland and the marine fossiliferous deposits here lie directly on bedrock of Miocene to Pliocene age. The lowest terrace also has its highest elevation in the west and the middle of Al-Bahra, a fact which fits with the movement of the Al-Bahra anticline, which is possibly still active. Further, there is clear observable continuity of the lowest dated terrace, especially in the Al-Bahra area (see Figure 6.1). The above conclusion is supported by the sample dating of the shell material. In other words, the present height above KD does not represent the original higher stand of sea-level because the area has been disturbed by action in Al-Bahra anticline and possibly by tilting towards the north and subsiding towards the north-east.

The only dated shell sample (SUA. 85) from the southern coast of Kuwait which comes from Al-Dhba'iyyah area at a height of about 5 metres above KD (940 ± 80 years BP), proved to be too young to be correlated with the dates obtained for the lowest terrace in the research area. However, it is doubtful whether it represents the true age of the terrace from which it was collected because of its location beside an inhabited area, but the height is close to that of the uplifted cliffs further south in Al-Jlay'ah which stand at an elevation of about 6 metres above KD and were referred to by Perry and Al-Refai (1958). Khalaf (1969) referred to a marine terrace which varies in height from a few centimetres near Al-Sabbiyah to about 4 metres at Ras-Ashairij and Al-Khiran. All the last three examples referred to by the author, Perry and Al-Refai (1958) and by Khalaf (1969) contain shells such as those which are found on the beach at the present time. Further correlation will need an extension of the area of detailed investigation, and also additional detailed studies within the area.

Chapter 7

# Implications of the Kuwait Bay findings and the geomorphic evolution of the Arabian Gulf

A correlation between the results of work on the present area of research and those relating to the adjacent areas in the Gulf cannot be definitively made at the present stage, mainly because of the absence of sufficient data. Most of the research work concerned with the physical environments of the Gulf has only been carried out during the past fifteen years and has mainly been concentrated on the study of the Holocene sedimentation. Other studies of the Pleistocene and associated features, especially those related to sea-level fluctuations, are very limited. The difficulty of correlation has been particularly felt in dealing with the higher terraces of the research area, which gave ages of 23,300 ± 600 years BP and over. These terraces suggest a Pleistocene age about which information from other parts of the Gulf is sparse.

To correlate each individual terrace with similar phenomena from other areas in the Gulf is a difficult task for several reasons. First, general studies of similar features elsewhere in the Gulf area lack detailed scientific descriptions. Most studies of geomorphological features generally refer to their height and occasionally to the kind of deposition, but there is no precise dating or levelling. Second, with regard to the research area, so far the results obtained from the levelling indicate that the area under investigation has been exposed to regional and local upward and downward movements, and the possible effect of local disturbances was referred to in Chapter 3. As well as being affected by local movements, the research area is close to the Mesopotamian area and the head of the Gulf area, over which argument still continues concerning crustal movements. However, it is felt that at this stage a general correlation can be achieved in the context of understanding the tectonic framework of the Arabian Gulf as well as the palaeoclimate of the area.

The structural evolution of the Gulf and surrounding areas can be summarized by identifying the Gulf as a tectonic basin, whose general form was largely established in Late Pleistocene times. The Iranian coast is topographically controlled by Zagros orogeny. A close relationship exists between the Zagros and Oman mountains, and it is possible that the uplift of the Oman mountains continued well into the Quaternary. Recent investigation has shown that the Musandam peninsula of Oman is undergoing subsidence, and that the amount of subsidence during the last 10,000 years has exceeded 60 metres (Vita Finzi, 1973).

In Chapter 2, two other points of view were discussed with reference to the head of the Gulf; that of the archeologists, who, supported by a geologist (De Morgan, 1900), claimed that the advance of the shoreline at the Gulf towards the south, was due to the continuous silting-up caused by the accumulation of sediments brought down by the rivers Karun, Karkeh, Tigris and Euphrates. The second point of view, that of geologists who have emphasized the structural instability of the area, is mainly presented by Lees and Falcon (1952), Mitchell (1957a and 1958) and Colter (quoted by Kassler, 1973). Recently however, Larsen (1975) has argued in favour of structural stability at the head of the Gulf. Kassler (op. cit.) maintained that the effect of Quaternary tectonic movements only produced local adjustment of existing features, but that an exception exists in the Gulf of Salwa where small vertical movements considerably affected the topography.

First, a re-examination of the scattered evidence of high stands of sea-level of Pleistocene age around the Gulf will be presented. As with those of the Postglacial, an attempt will also be made to postulate their possible morphological development as a result of sea-level changes.

According to Fairbridge (1961), at the end of the Pliocene the level of the sea was about 150 metres above its present level. Holm (1960) has indicated that inland sabkhas on the coast of Saudi Arabia are found at the same height. The retreat of the sea to its present level left its mark on the coast of the Arabian Gulf in the form of marine terraces, high deltas and inland sabkhas. In the Gulf area, however, it has been found difficult to correlate the available evidence according to the height at which features are now found. For example, the marine terraces of Oman, which occur at an elevation of about 373 metres, were claimed by Lees (1928) to be sub-Recent; this is on the basis of evidence of marine shells claimed to be of this age. However, the problem of correlating these terraces with other areas in the Gulf raises two questions. First, what was the precise height of these beaches at the time of their formation, noting that the Oman mountains have been exposed to uplift movements since before the Pleistocene; the second question is how certain is the dating of the shells to the sub-Recent (apart from their similarities to present-day species). A similar question faced the author when the results of the C14 dating of shells from the research area were examined, where the sediment analysis indicated Quaternary marine deposits as well as Pleistocene fluvial deposits, the latter being laid down during the wetter periods of the Pleistocene. There is a possibility that the shells are Tertiary in age, since the species identified are not solely Recent or Quaternary in provenance, or contaminated either by mixing with other species or by handling.

Certainly the height correlation between the raised beaches found in

Kuwait, with elevation over 15 metres in Qatar (Kapel, 1967), in Saudi Arabia and Oman (Holm, 1960 and Lees, 1928) as well as those found in the Makran coast and referred to by Falcon (1947) and Butzer (1958), and others found in Das, Zirko, Ardhana and Qarnain Islands (Kassler, 1973) is not completely feasible because of the crustal movements in most of these areas. However, it is possible to indicate the weight of the evidence for high sea-levels from that presented from the present area of research, as well as from the sporadic evidence discussed at length in Chapter 2. Mitchell (1958) described recent marine fauna near Najaf in Iraq at a height of between 40 and 41 metres, pointing out possible higher sea-levels during the Pleistocene. Voute (1957) also referred to the occurrence of recent marine fauna in the Abu Dibbis depression; according to Larsen (1975) a high sea-level of about +25 metres is necessary in order to connect Abu Dibbis with the sea. These levels are similar to those found for the Fifth terrace in Kuwait (Table 8.1); and these heights also fit well with the Qatar raised beaches at +25–30 metres, which were reported by Kapel (1967) to have an age of > 39,800 years. Raised beaches at similar elevation (30 metres and higher than 80–90 metres) in the Makran coast of Iran were reported by Falcon (1947) who attributed them to uplift movements; Butzer (1958) later suggested that eustatic changes of sea-level have played a part in the formation of these beaches. Moreover, he added a 60-metre level and suggested that the whole sequence corresponded to the altimetric sequence from Sicilian to Monastirian. He also referred to the raised beach of 30 metres on Kharag Island, Qishm, as well as in Bushire.

The 60-metre raised beaches can be followed on the Makran coast as well as in Kharag Island (Butzer, 1958). Glennie's (1970) inland sabkha of Umm as-Samim in Oman suggests a relic of an arm of the sea at a height of less than 70 metres, and evidence of similar heights has been reported by Kassler (1973).

However, as noted in Chapter 6, even the features associated with Early Quaternary high sea-levels in the Gulf must also be regarded in the light of recent work on local and regional deformation of the Gulf basin by hydro-isostatic forces, as well as by the more general geoidal changes associated with varying distribution of oceanic water. As well as being affected by the world-wide eustatic changes of sea-level, the Arabian Gulf has responded to the load of water transferred to and from its basin. The Pleistocene was a period of repeated glaciation and deglaciation phases associated with periods of low and high sea-levels, from which point the volume of water in the Gulf basin alternatively fell and rose, producing hydro-isostatic changes. At the end of the Pleistocene, the sea began to rise from its minimum level of −100 metres (according to Fairbridge, 1961) or −120 metres to −130 metres (according to Guilcher, 1969) to reach its present level. It invaded the Gulf basin through the Strait of Hormuz and marked the new coastal areas with several morphological features, one of which is the formation of submarine platforms and drowned valleys.

Since then, the Gulf has experienced the pressure of the load of water on its surface and is undergoing stress and surface deformation. However, at present, there are no published detailed studies regarding such processes in the Gulf area, and one may note for consideration that any results of work on eustatic changes of sea-level in the Gulf must be concentrated on the consideration of hydro-isostasy in the area.

Apart from the evidence provided for higher sea-levels during the inter-glacial periods, represented by raised beaches or higher sabkhas, it is evident that they occur at different heights, according to the steps followed by the sea until it reached its present level.

During the Glacial Period, several wadis in the Arabian peninsula flowed into the sea. Holm (1960) referred to two main rivers, the Nisah-Sahbah, which flowed towards the south-east of Qatar, and Rimah Wadi al-Batin which extended from Najd and followed the western border of Kuwait until it reached the Tigris–Euphrates valley. These water-flows were active during the pluvial periods of the Pleistocene and carried gravels, cobbles and pebbles which were deposited as deltaic material. Chapman (1971) indicated that the wadis and gullies of the Shedgum Plateau of Saudi Arabia were cut by running water during a wetter climate. During the pluvial periods, wadi-cutting was active, even if not continuous, while during the drier intervals, wadi-cutting ceased, or at least became very intermittent. He referred to the important role of sea-level fluctuation on the development of these wadis and to the fact that the falling sea-level had resulted in the formation of fluvial terraces by increasing wadi gradients. The dry rivers and wadi channels found inland or along the coast may extend below the present sea-level. These landforms were mainly cut by rivers in a variety of climates, and their development has been influenced by both sea-level changes and repeated regional uplifts. The drowned river valleys offshore of Abu Dhabi (Kassler, 1973) and those of the Musandam peninsula (Lees, 1928 and Vita Finzi, 1973) which were of fluviatile origin, may have been drowned by the rising sea-level during the postglacial. Kassler (1973) indicated that the drowned river valleys can be mapped down to the deepest platform, indicating that the channels may have been formed during a single eustatic sea-level period. Consequently, it appears that alluvial landforms are common geomorpho-logical features, both above and below the present sea-level, noted by several researchers and related by all of them to the Pleistocene development of glacial and interglacial periods, which in general coincide with the occurrence of pluvial wet periods and interpluvial dry or semi-dry periods.

At this stage, it seems reasonable to believe that similar developments have taken place in the research area as part of the climatic succession of the area. The present area of research is characterized by the occurrence of several wadi systems (Plate 1), and although these seem to be smaller in size than those described by other authors in the surrounding area, a general similarity is implied. The west and north of Kuwait, as well as the upper part of the Jal-Az-Zor escarpment are covered by fluvial deposits laid down by running water. The remnants of these main channels, represented for example by Wadi al-Batin, were referred to by Holm (1960) as being active during the pluvial periods of the Pleistocene, and Davies (personal communication), who has also referred to similar drainage (see Chapter 3). Another wadi channel on a smaller scale is the Al-Musannat in the south-west of the country. As well as these, several wadi drainage areas in a variety of shapes cover the north and west of the country, and these river channels and wadis have responded to both climatic and sea-level changes in the area. The lowering of the sea-level during the glacial periods would have resulted in considerable active eroding, as well as lowering the base level of the wadis. During the drier periods – which may coincide with high sea-level – active wadi-cutting would decrease, tend to aggradation, and give way to further subaerial erosion.

The general correlation seems reasonable at present in the light of the available results from both the research area and from other areas around the Gulf. Any further correlation needs more detailed investigation.

During the late Würm glaciation, the sea reached its minimum level at −100 or −120 metres, and as the maximum depth of the Gulf does not exceed 100 or 110 metres near the Strait of Hormuz, the Gulf would have then remained a dry basin, except for the flow of the water of the Tigris and Euphrates rivers. Sarnthein (1972) believed that the Shatt al-Arab at that time reached the shelf margin in the Gulf of Oman, which at present stands at −110 metres. During the glacial maximum (about 70,000 to 17,000 years BP, according to Fairbridge, 1961), the Gulf experienced continental conditions and the climate of the whole area was more arid than today; Kassler (1973), quoting a personal communication with M. S. Thornton, indicated that Pleistocene limestone in cores taken from a depth of some 37 metres has undergone leaching, which probably shows sub-aerial exposure of the rocks. On the other hand, Sarnthein (1972) declared that during the post-glacial transgression, aragonitic sediments dominated the north-east area of the Gulf. At present, these carbonates can only be found along the south and south-west coast, where no rivers enter the Gulf, while those sediments in the north-east are covered by calcareous, clayey, terrigenous sediment deposited by Zagros rivers. This suggests that the climate of the Zagros mountains must have been much drier than that of today, indicated by the lower activity of Zagros rivers. The climax of development of the drowned rivers offshore of Abu Dhabi and the Musandam peninsula occurred during the maximum retreat of sea-level of the Pleistocene. Vita Finzi (1973) indicated that the drowned valleys of the Musandam peninsula are the result of subsidence of the coastal areas and the Flandrian transgression; he estimated that the vertical displacements of the north-east of this coast have exceeded 60 metres during the past 10,000 years.

The aeolianite of the Makhus Formation, which Vita Finzi (ibid.) interpreted to be of coastal dunes, was formed during that period, and accords with the last major regression. As there was no 'evidence for a subsequent transgression above present sea-level', Vita Finzi suggested that the onset of the aggradation of Makhus deposits may have occurred after approximately 35,000 years ago. The raising of the sea-level from −130 metres to −40 metres, about 11,000–9,000 years ago, eliminated most of the major sources of littoral sediments, and also indicated that the age of the upper crust of the calcareous deposits is about 10,000 years.

Coinciding with the maximum sea-level retreat of the Pleistocene glaciation, river channels and wadi degradation became active, and those facing the coastal areas of the Gulf would have experienced considerable lowering of their base level to correspond with the decrease of the water level of the Gulf. Kassler (1973) reported the occurrence of a network of channels which represent drowned river valleys, appearing most clearly in the steps between submarine terraces. According to his interpretations, these river valleys were formed when the climate was wetter than today.

The so-called 'Flandrian transgression' began about 20,000 to 17,000 years ago, and reached its present level in stages. In the following review, a correlation of the postglacial sea-level will be suggested between the available data, which include erosional and depositional features from the Arabian Gulf, and Fairbridge's (1961) eustatic curve of changing sea-level (Figure 7.1). However, it must be mentioned here that although most researchers have indicated structural stability of the Gulf during the transgression period, the possibility of small movements cannot be entirely eliminated. Examples of such movement have been presented from the north coast of the Gulf, the Iranian coast and the Musandam peninsula, as well as from the Gulf of Salwa. Along with these examples is the effect of the hydro-isostatic movement on the deformation of the Gulf floor and coasts. Nevertheless, the correlation is tentative and will show the possibility of the simultaneity of events in the Gulf with those from different parts of the world, which were presented in Fairbridge's curve.

The maximum retreat of the sea-level to a level of about −120 metres is recorded by Kassler (1973) in the form of eroded submarine platforms in the Gulf of Oman and the Strait of Hormuz, formed while the Gulf floor stayed above the level of the sea. As the sea rose eustatically to a higher level of −100 metres, or Main Würm, according to Fairbridge (1961), it formed (Kassler, op. cit.) a submarine platform at a depth of −100 metres; this platform extends along the Gulf of Oman as well as in the Arabian Gulf. A rapid rise of sea-level began about 17,000 years BP and is characterized by the formation of several wide submarine platforms, such as the −65-metres platform described by Carrigy and Fairbridge (1954) on the stable west coast of Australia. In the Gulf area, it is possible that this coincides with the formation of Kassler's −66–80 metres platform. Houbolt (1957) was one of the first to put forward evidence from the north and east of Qatar to show the postglacial rise of sea-level in the Gulf. The deepest submarine terrace to which he referred is at −55 to −73 metres (−30 to −40 fathoms). Meanwhile, Sarnthein (1972) believed that the rising sea-level transgressed the area, which at present lies at depths of between 100 and 65 metres. He presented depositional evidence to show the transgression still-stands in the Gulf at −64 to

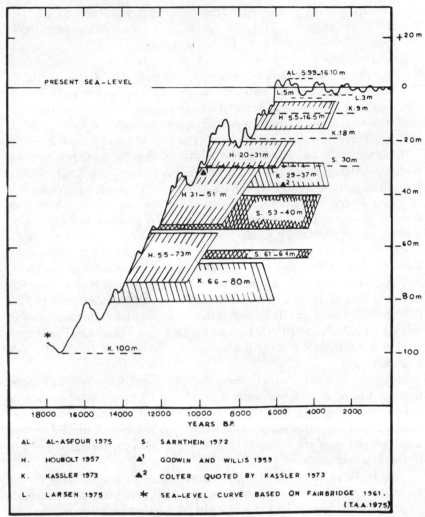

**Figure 7.1** *Tentative correlation of Late Pleistocene and Holocene sea-level changes in the Arabian Gulf*

−61 metres, and −53 to −40 metres. The transgression is indicated by the frosted quartz and ooid concentrations embedded in lithified aragonitic mud. These are interpreted by Sarnthein to be drowned sand dunes associated with a fossil ridge and trough system of dunes. He correlated his results with those of Van Andel *et al.* (1967), who described similar formations at the same depths on the Sahul Shelf of Australia. Meanwhile, Sarnthein (1972) believed that at that time the entire Arabian Gulf coastal region attained a morphological maturity, indicated by several features, among which is the break of slope along the longitudinal profile of the Gulf at a water depth of approximately 50 metres. According to Sarnthein, this feature can be followed around the entire Gulf. This does, in fact, correspond also (see Figure 7.1) to the depth of the 'Second offshore terrace' of Houbolt (1957), which occurs at −31 to −51 (−17 to −28 fathoms).

Towards the end of the last glaciation, evidence from other parts of the world recorded warm phases dated approximately 12,000 to 10,800 BP (Fairbridge, 1961). Marine platforms at −32 to −40 metres (−18 to −22 fathoms) have been recorded from all over the world. It is expected that such platforms were formed simultaneously in the Gulf at similar levels. Houbolt (1957) referred to a submarine terrace, 'The first offshore terrace' at −20 to −31 metres (−11 to −17 fathoms), which is broadly developed east and north of Qatar. Also, and from a similar depth (Figure 7.1), Kassler (1973) recognized a submarine platform at −29 to −37 metres (−16 to −20 fathoms). Moreover, Kassler indicated that a platform at that depth has been mapped from Abu Dhabi to Kuwait, and used this evidence to disagree with Colter's results (quoted by Kassler), who claimed that the Kuwait part of the Delta has subsided by approximately 37 metres over the last 5,000 years. Kassler indicated that the more or less horizontal surface which was identified by Colter at about −35 metres (−115 feet) and which carries modern deltaic sediments, is in fact within the depth range of the submarine platform (−29 to −37 metres, or −16 to −20 fathoms) which extends between Kuwait and Abu Dhabi. Kassler (1973) suggested that correlation with Fairbridge's 1961 scale indicates the age of this platform to be between 9,000 and 11,000 years BP.

Moreover, Godwin et al. (1958) and Godwin and Willis (1959) referred to the dating result of a freshwater detrital mud which represents an argamic layer at −32 metres of 9,910 ± 100 years BP. Replotted on Fairbridge's curve (Figure 7.1), this sample falls within the range −29 to −37 metres, which suggests that the sample may have come from the surface referred to by Colter as well as Kassler (1973).

About 11,000 years BP, at the commencement of the Holocene period, the sea began to rise at a rate of about 20 to 30 mm per annum to within 15 metres of its present level, the rise alternated with small pauses and reversals. Marine platforms associated with this period are universally recorded between −15 to −24 metres (−7–13 fathoms). The work of Houbolt (1957) and Kassler (1973) provides evidence of this movement within the Gulf area. The former referred to a submarine terrace ('near-shore terrace') between −5.5 and −16 to 5 metres (−3 to 9 fathoms), the latter to a submarine platform at −18 metres.

During the last 6,000 years, the sea-level has fluctuated above and below the present level, and several points of views have been presented concerning this period (Chapter 6). According to Fairbridge (1961), the highest recorded level of the sea in most places was about 3-5 metres (10-15 feet) above the present (older Peron Terrace, Australia), although he indicated that a higher figure could be obtained as a result of isostatic rebound, geodetic, tidal and other features. It is possible that the lowest terraces in the research area, which extend between Mudairah and Al-Bahra, and which have ages between 4,570 ± 70 and 3,560 ± 60 years BP corresponded to this high stage of sea-level. The difference in heights, which range from a maximum of 14.43 ± 1 metre in the middle of Al-Bahra to a minimum level of 5.99 ± 1 metre east of Al-Bahra, is presumably related to tectonic movements in and around the research area.

Sarnthein (1972), Kassler (1973) as well as Larsen (1975) have particularly emphasized that the area at the head of the Gulf has generally been structurally stable during the last 6,000 years. In the light of this evidence, it is possible that the period of deposition which occurred in the Mesopotamia area between 4,000 and 3,000 BC (about 6,000–5,000 BP) is in general accord with the world-wide sea-level fluctuation of the Holocene. Accordingly, it is possible that the positive movements of sea-level to near its present level or higher correspond to the period of river deposition during the period 4,000–3,000 BC, postulated by Woolley (1938), Lloyd (1943) and Lees and Falcon (1952). The minor erosional events and later deposition referred to by Lees and Falcon (1952) correspond to minor fluctuations of sea-level, while the main erosional event, which is probably post-Sassanian and produced the Dar-i-Khazineh evidence, has resulted from a world-wide dropping of the sea to attain its present level.

If during the Holocene general structural stability prevailed in the northern part of the Gulf in particular, and the whole Gulf in general, then the great variation in height found among the lower terraces may indicate local movements, possibly due to Bahra anticline activity, although this question requires further investigation, both in the research area and surrounding zones.

Other dated evidence from the Gulf comes from Abu Dhabi, where a detailed stratigraphic sequence indicates marine transgression from 7,000 to 4,000 BP (Evans *et al.*, 1969), while Taylor and Illing (1969) reported that the age of the strandlines in Qatar, which have heights between 1.5 and 2.5 metres, range between 3.930 ± 130 and 4,340 ± 180 years BP. However, those dated evidences, although indicating high stages of sea-level, can not be applied to any specific period of high sea-level until further research is carried out.

Evidence of undated marine transgression in the Gulf (see Chapter 2) (except for one sample from the southern coast of Kuwait) can be related to terraces in the research area or to younger stages, ranging in height from between 1.5 and 6 metres above sea-level. These fatures extend along the Arabian coast of the Gulf from Kuwait as far as Oman. Along the coast of Kuwait, Recent marine deposits containing shell fragments, similar to those found on the present beach, have been found by the author in Al-Sha'aib and Al-Dhba'iyyah areas on the southern coast. A dated sample of shells which come from Al-Dhba'iyyah at a height of about 5 metres above KD, gave an age of 940 ± 80 BP, but further investigation is necessary due to the possibility of contamination. Milton (1967) referred to these marine terrace deposits, as did Khalaf (1969) who has identified a recent marine terrace with a thickness of up to 4 metres at Ras Ashairij and at Al-Khiran. Perry and Al-Refai (1958) indicated that oolitic sandstone found at Ras Al-Jlay'ah at a height of about 6 metres above sea-level, extends into the coast of Saudi Arabia, which, they believe, suggests eustatic lowering of shorelines. Evidence of sea-level recession of 1.5 to 3 metres on the coast of Al-Hasa in Saudi Arabia was mentioned by Cornwall (1946), and included the abandonment of old settlements to more recent settlements on the Gulf coast. In 1960 Holm reported the occurrence of undisturbed shell beds at heights of 1.5 to 2 metres above sea-level, which extend from Ras al-Mish'ab to Salwah, and similar occurrences along the Trucial coast (coast of the United Arab Emirates). This level may also, as Holm (1960) suggested, correspond to the level which Cornwall (op. cit.) had in mind when he referred to the 1.5 to 2 metres recession of sea-level. Powers *et al.* (1966) referred to marine terraces of 1-3 metres in height along Saudi Arabia, but considered them to be of Pleistocene marine transgression.

Evidence of lower sea-levels in the Gulf during the last 6,000 years, which can be correlated with Fairbridge's scale of 1961, may be found in the recent data provided by Larsen (1975). According to Fairbridge (1961) the sea-level fall to −4 metres (Bahama emergence) occurred between 4,600 and 4,000 BP and is evidenced by buried peat-drowned forests and submarine platforms. Larsen (1975) referred to two submarine platforms at −5 and −3 metres, which are found in the deltaic area north of the Gulf. Both levels appear to cut into marine and perhaps estuarine clay or silt of Hammar Formation. The −3 metres submarine platform has also been observed by Larsen off Bahrain.

# Chapter 8

# Conclusion

Sea-level changes along the north coast of Kuwait Bay have been investigated by examining the coastal terraces in the areas of Kathma, Ghidhai, Mudairah and Al-Bahra. 'Staircase' topography was observed everywhere between the Jal-Az-Zor escarpment and the present coastline. In some cases, the terraces are clearly continuous for long distances, while in others they are represented by isolated terrace fragments. In general, the bedrock strata dip to the north and are frequently exposed between surfaces of more recent, unlithified sediments. A complicating factor in the reading of the superficial geology arises from the outcropping of fossiliferous beds which belong to Lower Fars Formation of Miocene age. As well as material derived from this formation, fossiliferous marine deposits, presumably younger in age, in some cases overlie the Lower Fars Formation and were also found on some of the terraces, e.g. the Fourth terrace between Kathma and Mudairah and the lowest terrace in the Al-Bahra area.

Three methods of investigation were adopted in the study of the terraces and the origin of the surface materials, viz.: (a) levelling, (b) radiocarbon dating of shells, and (c) sediment analyses, including particle size analysis and scanning electron microscopy. Each of the methods was selected in order to deal with particular problems and, consequently, each has furnished independently valuable results which can also be evaluated collectively.

## Levelling

This technique was adopted to determine the number and heights of the terraces in the area, and also provided essential data for the understanding of the structural stability or otherwise of the research area.

This part of the work consisted of surveying seven lines of levelling transverse to the alignments of the coast and the Jal-Az-Zor escarpment, two in Kathma, one each in Ghidhai and Mudairah and three lines in Al-Bahra.

Whenever possible, the lithology along the transect was recorded in detail along with the nature of the superficial deposits. Soil samples and available fossil shells were in most cases collected during the levelling procedure. The overall results of the levelling indicate that the total number of terraces or fragmentary lines of terraces do not seem to be more than six in number and these are identified as Terraces 1 to 6 in descending order.

The area as a whole has been considerably affected by tectonic movement since the terraces were formed and this has resulted in a general tilting downwards from west to east. Since the terraces are not completely continuous morphological features, their numerical classification along each levelling transect line was obtained from the sequence in which they could be topographically identified independently along each transect. Thus the sequence 1 to 4 on Kathma II transect refers solely to that transect and does not necessarily correspond to the sequence 1 to 4 in Ghidhai transect (see Table 5.1)

The use in this way of the uninterpreted levelling data exposed some clear alignment correlations as in the case of terraces 1 and 2 in all transects except the most easterly (Al-Bahra II and III), the height variations being explicable by later warping.

In the case of Terrace 3, the levelling data and/or field morphological observations showed clear correlation over the four most westerly terraces, with the exception of the Third terrace in KII which seems to correlate with the Fourth terrace elsewhere, height variation being only explicable in terms of later warping; Terrace 4 is basically of the same type but with larger height variation.

In the cases of Terraces 5 and 6 any correlation between particular sequence numbers could only be made after analytical methods were used.

The levelling data and morphological observations when displayed uncorrected, as in Table 5.1, also indicated that the Al-Bahra area as a whole could not simply be regarded as an eastward continuation of the same terrace features as were observed in the west. Within the Al-Bahra area it was also clear that the three transects could not simply be correlated on the basis of height and physical conformation.

Given the apparent anomalies in the topographic data, sediment and fossil analyses were then applied to samples from the uncorrected terrace sequences, so that any first observational bias would be avoided. The most significant facts to emerge from the first levelling and topographic observations were (a) the recognition of a set of terraces, up to six in number, and (b) evidence of structural instability during and after the period of terrace formation.

**Radiocarbon dating**

This was applied to shells, the only fossil material, in order to determine the age of the fossil material which was collected from different heights either along the transect lines or occasionally offset from the levelled lines.

The results have been treated very cautiously as the shells are subject to the seawater affect, for which empirical data are not available from the Gulf and therefore any sea correction is not possible. The shells themselves may have been exposed to contamination or may have been handled by human agencies.

A particular problem arose because of the exposure of the fossiliferous Lower Fars Formation of Miocene age from which some shell material now on the surface may have been derived. The shell species were tentatively compared with the available literature on the mollusca of Kuwait. Radiocarbon dating made it possible to make a tentative correlation for the lowest terraces only. The results show that there are two main groups of ages represented. The first includes those which range between > 42,950 years BP and 23,300 ± 600 years BP which suggests that these terraces are probably not younger than Pleistocene. There is no simple direct relationship between the height above datum and age, e.g. the highest dated sample in Ghidhai had an elevation of 63.30 metres above KD and the age obtained is 28,350 ± 1,150 years BP. The second group of dated samples has a maximum age of 4,570 ± 70 years BP and a minimal age of 3,250 ± 80 years BP suggesting their formation in the Holocene. The samples of this second group came from and below the lowest terraces in Mudairah and Al-Bahra areas.

### Sediment analyses

The third method of investigation used was the study of the origin of the deposits covering the terraces by applying two methods of sediment analysis; particle size analysis as the main technique and scanning electron microscope as a subsidiary one. The results of the mechanical analysis have been plotted as cumulative curves from which several percentages have been chosen to determine the mean, standard deviation, skewness and kurtosis. The characteristics of the four parameters of each sample as well as all the samples from a particular location, e.g. top of the escarpment, First terrace, have been studied and compared with the present beach samples.

Student's *t* test was applied in the sediment investigation to see whether there are significant differences between the parameters of the present beach samples and those of the top of the escarpment as well as with the other six terraces.

The results show that there are significant differences between the samples from each of the different levels, i.e. the top of the escarpment, the six terraces and the beach.

The sedimentation environments in which the sample materials were shaped have been identified by plotting the four stated parameters against each other. The results show that there were three kinds of sedimentary environments dominant in the historical geomorphology of the area, namely fluvial, aeolian and marine beach environments.

However, the results do not define a sharp separation between the environments as there is often material from different environments, on a single terrace. In general, the conclusion which has the highest probability is that the fluvial environment is represented mainly on the top of the escarpment, and on the First, Second and parts of the Third terrace. The aeolian environment is the most difficult one to separate from the other two and is represented everywhere, especially in the middle zone. The marine beach environment is mainly represented on the present beach as well as on the Fourth terrace, especially in Kathma, Ghidhai and Mudairah. It is represented also by material on the Sixth, Fifth and Fourth terraces in Al-Bahra.

The particle size analysis also showed that a large number of samples, especially those of the present beach, have positive skewness indicating the influence of the freshwater sedimentation of the Shattal-Arab.

Comparison between the grain size distribution curves of the samples shows that there is a clear difference between the curves obtained from material on top of the escarpment and the curves from the present beach material. The degree of similarity between each sample as well as between each group of terrace samples depends upon the origin of the samples involved. The result broadly supports the conclusions reached from the earlier-mentioned analyses.

Although the number of samples examined by the scanning electron microscope was limited, the micro-morphological features imprinted on the quartz sand grain show that the results of most of the samples correspond with those of particle size analyses.

The collective evaluation of the results of the three methods of investigtion indicates that the terraces were not only formed by sea-level changes but that the First, Second and probably the Third terraces originated because of sea-level changes, freshwater action and changes in the location which probably accompanied crustal movements. This is particularly clear in the case of the terraces between Kathma and Mudairah.

Some terraces certainly appear to have been formed by changing of sea-level accompanied by tectonic movements either during their formation or after. This is probably true of the Fourth, Fifth and Sixth terraces.

The simple correlation between each individual terrace identified in each area with others similar in numerical sequence is certainly not possible for the whole area. Problems appear especially in Al-Bahra, where the main difficulty is that heights of fragments of what is apparently the same terrace vary from one place to another. It is suggested that the reasons for altitudinal variation within the area can be attributed to one or more of the following disturbances, (a) instability associated with the Bahra anticline which is probably still going on, (b) possibly long-continued but not necessarily regular subsidence at the head of the Gulf as suggested by Lees and Falcon (1952), and (c) the possible north tilting of the area as suggested by C. C. S. Davies (recent work, in personal comminication). If all the research results are utilized, it is possible to suggest a highly tentative correlation of marine terrace alignments. Table 8.1, which is a projection from Table 5.1, indicates such a hypothetical correlation which however must remain unproven until further field investigation is possible.

The heights of the terraces fall within the range suggested for the Pleistocene high shorelines of the Mediterranean; also they are broadly similar in height to those which have been tentatively suggested for the Gulf. However, these can not with certainty be identified in detail with any particular research area because of the problem caused by variability in terrace heights.

The terraces cannot either be certainly correlated as the result of the radiocarbon dating undertaken in this study; this is particularly true for the earlier dates. A larger and longer-term investigation involving a much larger number of samples than could be taken in this research is clearly required. There would still remain the problems caused by the exposures of old fossiliferous beds of Lower Fars Formation from which fossil material has been mixed with younger shells. The resulting contamination affects C14 dating very considerably and has made it difficult at this stage to differentiate with certainty between bedrock-derived fossil shells and those of presumably younger sediments.

Accordingly, it is possible that the older dated terraces are not younger than Pleistocene. As for the more recent dates which come from Mudairah and Al-Bahra, these still create a correlation problem with terrace height variation from a mean height of 13 metres above KD in Ghidhai, 11.61 metres above KD in Mudairah to a mean height of 16.10 metres above KD west of Al-Bahra, 14.43 metres above KD in the middle and a mean height of 5.99 metres above KD east of Al-Bahra.

The other evidence of recent and continuing coastal movement may be used for providing some explanation of apparent anomalies. For example, the anomalous height in the middle of Al-Bahra probably results from Bahra anticlinal movement, the close grouping of C14 dates suggesting strongly that these samples represent a single terrace which extends between Mudairah and Al-Bahra and is of Holocene age.

However, the fossiliferous surface deposits covering the terraces need to be reconsidered in detail before firmer conclusions can be reached about the age of the terraces.

The changes of sea-level in the area have been the result of changes of water volume in the Gulf basin as a result of glaciation and deglaciation; they have also occurred because of local and regional tectonic movements in the research area and surrounding regions. The results of sediment investigation have also indicated that fluvial processes have played a significant part in the area. The levelling of the terraces indicates that as well as height variation existing from one area to another, there is a general tendency for the terrace heights to decrease from west to east. The lateral continuity of the terraces from one area to another is not always possible or easily distinguishable, and the height variations create a problem of correlation.

A tentative correlation between the results of the present research and

**Table 8.1** *Tentative genetic correlation of the terraces (all heights in metres above Kuwait Datum)**

| Terrace number | Kathma I | Kathma II | Ghidhai | Mudairah | Al-Bahra I | Al-Bahra II | Al-Bahra III |
|---|---|---|---|---|---|---|---|
| 1 | 90.60 | 81.53 | 92.62 | 71.12 | 79.85 | | |
| 2 | 77.92 | 69.65 | 79.27 | 59.57 | 56.10 | 63.72 | 33.11 |
| 3 | 67.38 | | 65 | 52.30 | 40.39 | 47.82 | 18.58 |
| 4 | 50.76 | 40.55 | 52.94 | 31.23 | 31.79? | 39.45 | 11.72 |
| 5 | | 10.70? | 33.60 | | 22.32? | 29.86 | |
| 6 | | | 13 | 11.61 | 16.10 | 14.43 | 5.99 |

* Recorded heights might be exposed to some source of errors (see text).

those from the Arabian Gulf has been presented. It indicates that, during the last 7,000 years, the sea-level has fluctuated above and below the present level. However, these fluctuations do not only represent eustatic changes of sea-level, which have been recorded from different parts of the world, but also local tectonic movements. The absolute value of the eustatic changes can not yet be decided at present. The lack of sufficient data for the interpretation has been particularly felt, especially when correlating features older than those of the Holocene. However, the evidence becomes more positive for the postglacial transgression, and hence the interpretation, although not completed, is more easily understood.

Although necessarily tentative, the conclusions put forward have been reached with some degree of confidence. There is, of course, no simple descriptive explanation which can as yet be given, which clearly differentiates between isostatic, eustatic or a simple climatic variation, but it is hoped that the complex hypothesis arrived at in this work will encourage further research and will stimulate interest in the study of Quaternary problems in this region. It is further hoped that the results of this research will draw the attention of the authorities in Kuwait to the need to slow down the demolition of the natural environment of the coastal areas of Kuwait, with all its evidence of the genetic history of the country. This destruction, through the demolition of terraces, earth and beach movement and building, has already affected much of the southern coast, and it is hoped that scientific studies can be urgently organized before it becomes too late to carry out further investigations.

It is perhaps of satisfaction, at least to the author, that the present rebuilding of the coast which is going on in the south, has not yet penetrated to the present area of research.

# Bibliography

Al-Kuwait Al-Youm (Kuwait Today), 2 March 1958, 'A Report by a Danish Expedition to the Ministry of Education', Government of Kuwait Press (*Official Gazette* in Arabic).

Anderson, E. C., Libby, W. F., Weinhouse, S., Reid, A. F., Kirshenbaum, A. D. and Grosse, A. V. (1947), 'Radiocarbon from Cosmic Radiation', *Science* N.Y., 105 (2735).

Antevs, S. (1928), 'The Last Glaciation', *Am. Geogr. Soc. Res. Ser.* N.Y., 17, pp. 292.

Apfel, E. T. (1938), 'Phase Sampling of Sediments', *Journ. Sed. Petrol.*, 8, pp. 67–8.

Arnold, J. R. and Libby, W. F. (1949), 'Age Determination by Radiocarbon Content: Checks with Samples of known Age', *Science*, N.Y., 110, pp. 678–80.

Baulig, H. (1935), 'The Changing Sea Level', *Inst. Brit. Geogr.*, London, no. 3, 46pp.

Beke, C. T. (1835), 'On the Geological Evidence of the Advance of the Land at the Head of the Persian Gulf', *Philosophical Magazine*, 7, pp. 40–6.

Biederman, M. W., Jr (1962), 'Distinction of Shoreline Environments in New Jersey', *Journ. Sed. Petrol.*, 32, pp. 181–200.

Biggs, H. E. J. (1958), 'Littoral Collecting in the Persian Gulf', *Journ. Conch.*, 24, no. 8, pp. 270–5.

Biggs, H. E. J. and Grantier, L. L. (1960), 'A Preliminary List of the Marine Mollusca of Ras Tanura, Persian Gulf', *Journ. Conch.*, no. 11, pp. 387–92.

Blanford, W. T. (1872), 'Note on Makran and Musandam on the East Coast of Arabia', *Rec. Geol. Surv. India*, 5, pp. 75–7.

Bloom, A. L. (1967), 'Pleistocene Shorelines: A New Test of Isostasy', *Bull. Geol. Soc. Am.*, 78, (2), pp. 1477–93.

Bloom, A. L., Broecker, W. S., Chappell, J. M. A., Matthews, R. K. and Mesolella, K. J. (1974), 'Quaternary Sea Level Fluctuations on a Tectonic Coast: New $^{230}$Th/$^{234}$U Dates from the Huon Peninsula, New Guinea', *Quaternary Res.*, 4, pp. 185–205.

British Standard 1377 (1967), *Methods of Testing Soils for Civil Engineering Purposes*, London, British Standards Institution.

Büdel, J. (1939), 'The Periglacial-morphologic Effects of the Pleistocene Climate over the Entire World', *Internat. Geol. Review*, 1, no. 3, pp. 1–16.

Butler, G. P. (1966), 'Early Diagenesis in the Recent Sediments of the Trucial Coast of the Persian Gulf', Univ. London, M.Sc. Dissert. (unpublished).

Butzer, K. W. (1958), 'Quaternary Stratigraphy and Climate in the Near East', *Bonner Geographische Abhandlungen.*, 24, pp. 1–57.

Butzer, K. W. (1961), 'Climatic Change in Arid Regions since the Pliocene', in *A History of Land Use in Arid Regions*, L. D. Stamp (ed.), UNESCO Arid Zone Research, 17, pp. 31–54.

Butzer, K. W. (1963), 'The Last "Pluvial" Phase of the Eurafrican Sub-tropics', in *Changes in Climate*, UNESCO Arid Zone Research, 20, pp. 211–21.

Butzer, K. W. (1964), *Environment and Archaeology: An Introduction to Pleistocene Geography*, London, Methuen.

Butzer, K. W. and Hanson, C. L. (1968), *Desert and River in Nubia*, Madison, Wisc., University Press.

Cailleux, A. (1942), 'Les Actions Eoliennes Périglaciaires en Europe', *Mém. Soc. Geol. France*, 46, pp. 1–176.

Carrigy, M. A. and Fairbridge, R. W. (1954), 'Recent Sedimentation, Physiography and Structure of the Continental Shelves of Western Australia', *Journ. Roy. Soc. West. Australia*, 38, pp. 65–95.

Castany, G. and Ottmann, F. (1957), 'Le Quaternaire Marin de la Méditerranée occidentale', *Revue Géogr. Phys. Geol. Dyn.* Ser. 2, 1, pp. 46–55.

Chapman, R. W. (1971), 'Climatic Changes and the Evolution of Landforms in the Eastern Province of Saudi Arabia', *Bull. Geol. Soc. Am.*, 82, pp. 2713–28.

Chappell, J. (1967), 'Recognizing Fossil Strand Lines from Grain-size Analysis', *Journ. Sed. Petrol.*, 37, pp. 157–65.

Chaput, E. (1917), 'Recherches sur les Terraces alluviales de la Loire et de ses Principaux Affluents', *Ann. Univ. Lyon. N. Ser.*, 1:1–303.

Cochran, W. G., Mosteller, F and Tukey, J. W. (1954), 'Principle of Sampling', in *Statistical Problems of the Kinsey Report*, pp. 309–31, Washington, D.C., Am. Stat. Assoc.

Cornelius, P. F. S., Falcon, N. L., South, D. and Vita Finzi, C. (1973), 'The Musandam Expedition 1971–72, Scientific Results: Part I', *Geogr. Journ.*, 139, pp. 400–25.

Cornwall, P. B. (1946), 'Ancient Arabia: Explorations in Hasa, 1940–41', *Geogr. Journ.*, 107, pp. 28–50.

Cox, P. T. and Rhoades, R. O. (1935), 'A Report on the Geology and Oil Prospects of Kuwait Territory', Kuwait Oil Company (Unpublished Report).

Curray, J. R. (1961), 'Late Quaternary Sea Level: a Discussion', *Bull. Geol. Soc. Am.*, 72, pp. 1707–12.

Daly, R. A. (1934), *The Changing World of the Ice Age*, New Haven, Conn., Yale University Press.

De Lamothe, L. (1911), 'Les Anciennes Lignes de Rivages du Sanel d'Alger et d'une Partie de la Côte Algérienne', *Mém. Soc. Geol. France*, Paris, 1 (6): 1–288.

De Lamothe, L. (1918), 'Les Anciennes Nappes Alluviales et Lignes de Rivage du Bassin de la Somme et leurs Rapports avec celles de la Méditerranée occidentale', *Bull. Soc. Geol. France,* 18, pp. 3, 58.

De Morgan, J. (1900), 'Délégation en Perse', *Mémoires*, tome 1, pp. 4–48.

Depéret, C. (1918–22), 'Essai de coordination chronologique des temps quaternaires', *Compt. Rend. Acad. Sci.,* Paris, 116: 480, 636, 884; 118: 868; 120: 159; 121: 212; 124: 1502, 1595.

Directorate General of Civil Aviation (1955/67), *Climatological Data for Kuwait,* Government of Kuwait, Climatological and Stations Division.

Doeglas, D. J. (1946), 'Interpretation of the Results of Mechanical Analysis', *Journ. Sed. Petrol.,* 16, pp. 19–40.

Doornkamp, J. C. and Krinsley, D. (1971), 'Electron Microscopy applied to Quartz Grains from a Tropical Environment', *Sedimentology,* 17, pp. 89–101.

Emery, K. O. (1956), 'Sediments and Water of Persian Gulf', *Bull. Am. Assoc. Petrol, Geologists,* 40, pp. 2354–83.

Emery, K. O. and Stevenson, R. E. (1950), 'Laminated Beach Sand', *Journ. Sed. Petrol,* 20, pp. 220–3.

Emiliani, C. (1955), 'Pleistocene Temperatures', *Journ. Geol.,* 63, pp. 538–78.

Evans, G. (1966), 'The Recent Sedimentary Facies of the Persian Gulf Region', *Phil. Trans. Roy. Soc. Lond.*, Ser. A. 259, pp. 291–8.

Evans, G. (1970), 'Coastal and Nearshore Sedimentation: A Comparison of Clastic and Carbonate Deposition', *Proc. Geol. Assoc.,* London, 81, pp. 493–508.

Evans, G., Kendall, C. G. St. C., Skipwith, Sir Patrick A. d'E. (1964), 'Origin of the Coastal Flats, the Sabkha of the Trucial Coast, Persian Gulf', *Nature,* 202, No. 4934, pp. 579–600.

Evans, G., Schmidt, V., Bush, P. and Nelson, H. (1969), 'Stratigraphy and Geologic History of the Sabkha, Abu Dhabi, Persian Gulf', *Sedimentology,* 12, pp. 145–59.

Fairbridge, R. W. (1958), 'Dating the Latest Movements of Quaternary Sea Level', *Trans. N.Y. Acad. Sci.*, Ser. 2, 20, pp. 471–82.

Fairbridge, R. W. (1961), 'Eustatic Changes in Sea Level', in *Physics and Chemistry of the Earth,* L. H. Ahrens *et al.* (eds.), vol. 4, pp. 99–185, Oxford, Pergamon Press.

Falcon, N. L. (1947), 'Raised Beaches and Terraces of the Iranian Makran Coast', *Geogr. Journ.*, 109, pp. 149–51.

Falcon, N. L. (1973), 'The Musandam (Northern Oman) Expedition 1971/ 1972', *Geogr. Journ.*, 139, pp. 1–19.

Falcon, N. L. (1975), 'From Musandam to the Iranian Makran', *Geogr. Journ.,* 141, pp. 55–8.

Fisk, H. N. (1959), 'Padre Island and the Laguna Madre Flats, Coastal South Texas', *2nd Coastal Geography Conf.* Baton Rouge, pp. 57–101.

Folk, R. L. (1959), *Petrology of Sedimentary Rocks,* Austin, Tex., Hemphill.

Folk, R. L. and Ward, W. C. (1957), 'Brazos River Bar: A Study in the Significance of Grain-Size Parameters', *Journ. Sed. Petrol.,* 27, pp. 3–26.

Fox, F. A. (1959), 'Some Problems of Petroleum Geology in Kuwait', *Journ. Inst. Petrol.*, 45, pp. 95–110.

Friedman, G. M. (1961), 'Distinction between Dune, Beach and River Sands from their Textural Characteristics', *Journ. Sed. Petrol.*, 31, pp. 514–29.

Friedman, G. M. (1962), 'On Sorting, Sorting Coefficients, and the Lagnormality of the Grain-size Distribution of Sandstones', *Journ. Geol.*, 70, pp. 737–53.

Friedman, G. M. (1967), 'Dynamic Processes and Statistical Parameters compared for Size Frequency Distribution of Beach and River Sands', *Journ. Sed. Petrol.*, 37, pp. 327–54.

Frye, J. C. and Willman, H. B. (1961), 'Continental Glaciation in Relation to McFarlan's Sea-level Curves for Louisiana', *Bull. Geol. Soc. Am.*, 72, pp. 991–2.

Fuchs, W., Gattinger, T. E. and Holzer, H. F. (1968), *Explanatory Text to the Synoptic Geologic Map of Kuwait*, Geologic Survey of Austria.

Fuller, A. O. (1961), 'Size Characteristics or Shallow Marine Sands from the Cape of Good Hope, South Africa', *Journ. Sed. Petrol.*, 31, pp. 256–61.

Gees, R. A. (1969), 'Sampling of Laminated Beach Sands', *Maritime Sediments*, 5, pp. 40–3.

Geographical Section of the Naval Intelligence Division, Naval Staff, Admiralty (1918), *Geology of Mesopotamia and its Borderlands*, London, HMSO.

Glennie, K. W. (1970), *Desert Sedimentary Environment*, Amsterdam, Elsevier.

Godwin, H., Suggate, R. P. and Willis, E. H. (1958), 'Radiocarbon Dating of Eustatic Rise in Ocean-level', *Nature*, 181, pp. 1518–19.

Godwin, H. and Willis, E. H. (1959), 'Cambridge University Natural Radiocarbon Measurements I: Radiocarbon 1', *Am. Journ. Sci. Radiocarbon*, Supplement, pp. 63–75.

Griffiths, J. C. (1967), *Scientific Methods in Analysis of Sediments*, New York, N.Y., McGraw-Hill.

Griffiths, J. C. and McIntyre, D. D. (1958) 'A Table for the Conversion of Millimeters to Phi Units', Pennsylvania State University, Mineral Ind. Expt. Sta.

Guilcher, A. (1969), 'Pleistocene and Holocene Sea level Changes', *Earth-Sci. Rev.* 5, pp. 69–97.

Haas, F. (1954), 'Some Marine Shells from the Persian Gulf', *The Nautilus*, 68, pp. 46–9.

Harrison, J. V. (1941), 'Coastal Makran', *Geogr. Journ.*, 97, pp. 1–17.

Henson, F. R. S. (1951), 'Observation on the Geology and Petroleum Occurrences of the Middle East', *3rd World Petroleum Congr.*, The Hague, Sec. 1, pp. 118–40.

Higginbottom, I. E. (1954), *Report on the Surface Geology of Kuwait, with Reference to the Natural Resources of Building Materials*, Ministry of Public Works, Kuwait (Unpublished Report).

Hodgson, A. V. and Scott, W. B. (1970), 'The Identification of Ancient Beach Sands by the Combination of Size Analysis and Electron Microscopy', *Sedimentology*, 14, pp. 67–75.

Holm, D. A. (1960), 'Desert Geomorphology in the Arabian Peninsula', *Science*, 132, pp. 1369–79.

Holmes, A. (1944), *Principles of Physical Geology*, London, Nelson.

Houbolt, J. J. H. C. (1957), *Surface Sediments of the Persian Gulf near the Qatar Peninsula*, The Hague, Mouton.

Inman, D. L. (1949), 'Sorting of Sediments in the Light of Fluid Mechanics', *Journ. Sed. Petrol.*, 19, pp. 51–70.

Inman, D. L. (1952), 'Measures for Describing the Size Distribution of Sediments', *Journ. Sed. Petrol.*, 22, pp. 125–45.

Inman, D. L. and Chamberlain, T. K. (1955), 'Particle Size Distribution in Nearshore Sediments in Finding Ancient Shorelines', Society of Economic Paleontologists and Mineralogists, spec. publ. 3, pp. 99–105.

Ionides, M. G. (1954), 'The Geographical History of the Mesopotamian Plain', *Geogr. Journ.*, 120, pp. 394–5.

Irani, R. R. and Callis, C. F. (1963), *Particle Size: Measurements, Interpretation and Application*, New York, Wiley.

Iriondo, M. H. (1972), 'A Rapid Method for Size Analysis of Coarse Sediments', *Journ. Sed. Petrol.*, 42, pp. 985–6.

Jelgersma, S. and Pannekoek, A. J. (1960), 'Post-glacial Rise of Sea-level in the Netherlands (A Preliminary Report)', *Geol. en Mijnbouw*, 39, pp. 201–7.

Jensen, H. (1972), 'Holocene Sea-level and Geoid-Deformation', *Bull. Geol. Soc. Denmark*, 21, pp. 374–81.

Johnson, D. (1931), 'The Correlation of Ancient Marine Levels', *C. R. Congr. Int. Geogr.*, Paris, 2(1), pp. 42–54.

Kapel, H. (1967), *Atlas of the Stone-Age Cultures of Qatar*, Aarhus, Denmark, University Press.

Kassler, P. (1973), 'The Structural and Geomorphic Evaluation of the Persian Gulf', in *The Persian Gulf: Holocene Carbonate Sedimentation and Diagenesis in a Shallow Epicontinental Sea*, B. H., Purser (ed.), Springer-Verlag, pp. 11–32.

Keller, W. D. (1945), 'Size Distribution of Sand in some Dunes, Beaches, and Sandstone', *Bull. Am. Assoc. Petrol. Geologists*, 29, pp. 215–21.

Kendall, C. G. St. C. and Skipwith, Sir Patrick, A. d'E. (1969), 'Holocene Shallow-Water Carbonate and Evaporate Sediments of Khar al Basam, Abu Dhabi, Southwest Persian Gulf', *Bull. Am. Assoc. Petrol. Geologists*, 53, pp. 841–69.

Khalaf, F. I. (1969), 'Geology and Mineralogy of the Beach Sediments of Kuwait', Univ. Kuwait, M.Sc. Thesis (unpublished).

King, C. A. M. (1967), *Techniques in Geomorphology*, London, Arnold.

Krinsley, D. and Donahue, J. (1968), 'Environmental Interpretation of Sand Grain Surface Textures by Electron Microscopy', *Bull. Geol. Soc. Am.*, 79, pp. 743–8.

Krinsley, D. and Doornkamp, J. C. (1973), *Atlas of Quartz Sand Surface Textures*, Cambridge, England, Cambridge University Press.

Krinsley, D. and Funnel, B. (1965), 'Environmental History of Sand Grains from the Lower and Middle Pleistocene of Norfolk, England', *Quart. Journ. Geol. Soc. Lond.*, 121, pp. 435–561.

Krinsley, D. and Margolis, S. (1969), 'A Study of Quartz Sand Grain Surfaces with the Scanning Electron Microscope', *Trans. N.Y. Acad. Sci.*, 31, pp. 457-77.

Krinsley, D. and Takahashi, T. (1962a), 'The Surface Textures of Sand Grains; An Application of Electron Microscopy', *Science*, N.Y. 135, pp. 923-5.

Krinsley, D. and Takahashi, T. (1962b), 'The Surface Textures of Sand Grains, An Application of Electron Microscopy: Glaciation', *Science*, N.Y. 138, pp. 1262-4.

Krinsley, D. and Takahashi, T. (1962c), 'Applications of Electron Microscopy to Geology', *Trans. N.Y. Acad. Sci.*, 25, pp. 3-22.

Krumbein, W. C. (1934), 'Size Frequency Distribution of Sediments', *Journ. Sed. Petrol.*, 4, pp. 65-77.

Krumbein, W. C. (1936), 'The Use of Quartile Measures in Describing and Comparing Sediments', *Am. Journ. Sci.*, 32, pp. 98-111.

Krumbein, W. C. (1953), 'Statistical Designs for Sampling Beach Sand', *Trans. Am. Geophys. Union*, 34, pp. 857-68.

Krumbein, W. C. (1954), 'Application of Statistical Methods to Sedimentary Rocks', *Journ. Am. Statist. Assoc.*, 49, pp. 51-66.

Krumbein, W. C. and Pettijohn, F. J. (1938), *Manual of Sedimentary Petrography*, New York, Appleton-Century-Crofts.

Krumbein, W. C. and Slack, H. A. (1956), *Relative Efficiencies of Beach Sampling Methods*, Beach Erosion Board, Tech. Memo, 90.

Kuenen, P. H. H. and Perdok, W. G. (1962), 'Experimental Abrasion, 5: Frosting and Defrosting of Quartz Grains', *Journ. Geol.*, 70, pp. 648-58.

Larsen, C. E. (1975), 'The Mesopotamian Delta Region: A Reconsideration of Lees and Falcon', *Journal Am. Oriental Soc.*, 95, pp. 43-57.

Lees, G. M. (1928), 'The Physical Geography of South-eastern Arabia', *Geogr. Journ.*, 71, pp. 441-70.

Lees, G. M. and Falcon, N. L. (1952), 'The Geographical History of the Mesopotamian Plains', *Geogr. Journ.*, 118, pp. 24-39.

Lees, G. M. and Richardson, F. D. S. (1940), 'The Geology of the Oil-field Belt of South-west Iran and Iraq', *Geol. Mag.*, 78, pp. 227-52.

Libby, W. F. (1946), 'Atmospheric Helium Three and Radiocarbon from Cosmic Radiation', *Phys. Rev.*, 69 (11/12), pp. 671-72.

Libby, W. F. (1955), *Radiocarbon Dating*, 2nd ed., Chicago, Ill., Chicago University Press.

Libby, W. F., Anderson, E. C. and Arnold, J. R. (1949), 'Age Determination by Radiocarbon Content: World-wide Assay of Natural Radiocarbon', *Science*, N.Y. 109, pp. 227-8.

Lloyd, S. (1943), *Twin Rivers*, London, Oxford University Press.

Loftus, W. K. (1857), *Travel and Researches in Chaldaea and Susiana*, London, James Nisbet.

MacLaren, C. (1842), 'The Glacial Theory of Prof. Aggassiz', *Am. Journ. Sci.*, 42, pp. 346-65.

McCammon, R. B. (1962), 'Efficiencies of Percentile Measures for Describing the Mean Size and Sorting of Sedimentary Particles', *Journ. Geol.*, 70, pp. 453-65.

McFarlan, E. Jr (1961), 'Radiocarbon Dating of Late Quaternary Deposits, South Louisiana', *Bull. Geol. Soc. Am.*, 72, pp. 129-58.

McIntyre, D. D. (1959), 'The Hydraulic Equivalence and Size Distribution of some Mineral Grains from a Beach', *Journ. Geol.*, 67, pp. 278–301.

Mason, C. C. and Folk, R. L. (1958), 'Differentiations of Beach, Dune, and Aeolian Flat Environments by Size Analysis, Mustang Island, Texas', *Journ. Sed. Petrol.*, 28, pp. 211–26.

Melvill, J. C. (1897), 'Descriptions of Thirty-four Species of Marine Mollusca from the Arabian Sea, Persian Gulf and Gulf of Oman', *Mem. Manch. Soc.*, 12, pp. 1–25.

Milner, H. B. (1962), *Sedimentary Petrography*, London, Allen and Unwin.

Milton, D. I. (1967), 'Geology of the Arabian Peninsula, Kuwait', *US Geol. Surv. Prof. Paper* 560–F, pp. 1–8.

Mina, P., Razaghnia, M. T. and Paran, Y. (1967), 'Geological and Geophysical Studies and Exploratory Drilling of the Iranian Continental Shelf, Persian Gulf', *Proc. 7th World Petrol. Congr.*, pp. 872–901.

Mitchell, R. C. (1957a), 'Recent Tectonic Movements in the Mesopotamian Plains', *Geogr. Journ.*, 123, pp. 569–71.

Mitchell, R. C. (1957b), 'Notes on the Geology of Western Iraq and Northern Saudi Arabia', *Geol. Rundschau*, 46, pp. 467–93.

Mitchell, R. C. (1958), 'Instability of the Mesopotamian Plains', *Bull. Société de Géographie d'Egypte*, 31, pp. 127–40.

Moody, J. D. (1947), *Notes on the Surface Geology of Kuwait*, Kuwait Oil Company (unpublished report).

Mörner, N. A. (1970), 'Isostasy and Eustasy, Late Quaternary Isostatic Changes in Southern Scandinavia and General Isostatic Changes of the World', in B. W. Collins (ed.), *Recent Crustal Movements and Associated Seismicity*, Proc. Intern. Symp., Royal Society of New Zealand.

Mörner, N. A. (1972), 'Isostasy, Eustasy and Crustal Sensitivity', *Tellus*, 24 (6), pp. 586–92.

Moss, A. J. (1962), 'The Physical Nature of Common Sandy and Pebbly Deposits. Part I', *Am. Journ. Sci.*, 260, pp. 337–73.

Moss, A. J. (1963), 'The Physical Nature of Common Sandy and Pebbly Deposits, Part II', *Am. Journ. Sci.*, 261, pp. 297–343.

Newton, R. B. (1905), 'An Account of some Marine Fossils contained in Limestone Nodules found on the Makran Beach, off the Ormara Headlands, Blauchistan', *Geol. Mag.*, 11, pp. 293–302.

Otto, G. H. (1938), 'The Sedimentation Unit and its Use in Field Sampling', *Journ. Geol.*, 46, pp. 569–82.

Otto, G. H. (1939), 'A Modified Logarithmic Probability Graph for the Interpretation of the Mechanical Analysis of Sediments', *Journ. Sed. Petrol.*, 9, pp. 62–76.

Owen, R. M. S. and Nasr, S. N. (1958), 'Stratigraphy of the Kuwait-Basra Area', Habitat of Oil, A Symposium, *Am. Assoc. Petrol. Geologists*, pp. 1252–78.

Page, H. G. (1955), 'Phi-millimeter Conversion Table', *Journ. Sed. Petrol.*, 25, pp. 285–92.

Parsons Corporation, Engineers-Constructors (1963), *Ground-water Resources of Kuwait*, vol. I and II, Los Angeles (unpublished).

Penck, A. (1913), 'Die Formen der Landoberfläche und die Verschiebung der Klimagürtel', *Sitzungsber. d. K. Preuss. Akad. d. Wiss*, no. 4, p. 11 (87).

Perry, J. T. O'B. and Al-Refai, B. H. (1958), *Notes on the Geology of the Coastline North-west of Ras Al-Jilai'a, South-east Kuwait*, Kuwait Oil Company. (Unpublished Report.)

Pilgrim, H. G. E. (1908), 'The Geology of the Persian Gulf and the Adjoining Portions of Persia and Arabia', *Mem. Geol. Surv. India.*, 34, pt. 4, pp. 1–177.

Porter, J. J. (1962), 'Electron Microscopy of Sand Surface Texture', *Journ. Sed. Petrol.*, 32, pp. 124–35.

Powers, R. W., Ramirez, L. F., Redmond, C. D. and Elberg, E. L. Jr (1966), 'Geology of the Arabian Peninsula: Sedimentary Geology of Saudi Arabia', *US Geol. Surv. Prof. Paper*, 560–D.

Privett, D. W. (1959), 'Monthly Charts of Evaporation from the Northern Indian Ocean (including the Red Sea and the Persian Gulf)', *Quart. Journ. Roy. Met. Soc.*, 85, pp. 424–78.

Purser, B. H. and Seibold, E. (1973), 'The Principal Environmental Factors influencing Holocene Sedimentation and Diagenesis in the Persian Gulf', in *The Persian Gulf: Holocene Carbonate Sedimentation and Diagenesis in a Shallow Epicontinental Sea*, B. H. Purser (ed.), Springer-Verlag, pp. 1–9.

Rawlinson, H. C. (1857), 'Notes on the Ancient Geography of Mohamrah and the Vicinity', *Journ. Roy. Geogr. Soc.*, 27, pp. 185–90.

Reineck, H. E. and Singh, I. B. (1973), *Depositional Sedimentary Environments*, Springer-Verlag.

Robinson, G. P. G. and May, H. P. (1974), 'The Musandam Expedition: Scientific Results, Part II', *Geogr. Journ.*, 140, pp. 94–104.

Sarnthein, M. (1972), 'Sediments and History of the Postglacial Transgression in the Persian Gulf and North-west Gulf of Oman', *Mar. Geol.*, 12, pp. 245–66.

Schneider, H. E. (1970), 'Problems of Quartz Morphology', *Sedimentology*, 14, pp. 325–35.

Schott, G. (1908), 'Der Salzgehalt des Persischen Golfes und der Angrenzenden Gewasser', *Annalen der Hydrographie und Maritimen Meteorlogie*, 37, pp. 296–9.

Schwarzbach, M. (1963), *Climates of the Past*, New York, Van Nostrand.

Shepard, F. P. (1963), 'Thirty-five Thousand Years of Sea-level', in *Essays in Marine Geology in Honour of K. O. Emery*, T. Clements (ed.), Los Angeles, Calif., University of South California Press, pp. 1–10.

Shepard, F. P. (1964), 'Sea-level Changes in the past 6,000 years: Possible Archaeological Significance', *Science*, N.Y., 143, pp. 574–6.

Shepard, F. P. and Curray, J. R. (1967), 'Carbon-14 Determination of Sea-level Changes in Stable Areas', *Progr. Oceanogr.*, 4, pp. 283–91.

Shepard, F. P. and Suess, H. E. (1956), 'Rates of Postglacial Rise of Sea-level', *Science*, N.Y., 123, pp. 1082–3.

Shepard, F. R. and Young, R. (1961), 'Distinguishing between Beach and Dune Sands', *Journ. Sed. Petrol.*, 31, pp. 196–214.

Shinn, E. A. (1973), 'Sedimentary Accretion along the Leeward, South-east Coast of Qatar Peninsula, Persian Gulf', in *The Persian Gulf: Holocene Carbonate Sedimentation and Diagenesis in a Shallow Epicontinental Sea*, B. H. Purser (ed.), Springer-Verlag, pp. 199–209.

Shotton, F. W. (1967), 'The Problems and Contributions of Method of Absolute Dating within the Pleistocene Period', *Quart. Journ. Geol. Soc. Lond.*, 122, pp. 357–83.

Shuwaikh Port Authority, (Undated), *Temperature and Analysis of Seawater of Shuwaikh*, Kuwait.

Sieber, R. (1968), In *Explanatory Text to the Synoptic Geologic Map of Kuwait*, W. Fuchs *et al.* (eds.), Geological Survey of Austria.

Sindowski, K. H. (1957), 'Die Synoptische Methode des Korn Kurven – Vergleiches zur Ausdeutung Fossiler Sedimentations Raume', *Geol. Jahrb.*, 73, 235–75.

Smith, S. (1954), 'The Geographical History of the Mesopotamian Plain', *Geogr. Journ.*, 120, pp. 395–6.

Snead, R. E. (1970), *Physical Geography of the Makran Coastal Plain of Iran*, University of New Mexico, Dept. of Geography.

Solohub, J. E. and Klovan, J. E. (1970), 'Evaluation of Grain-size Parameters in Lacustrine Environments', *Journ. Sed. Petrol.*, 40, pp. 81–101.

Soutendam, C. J. A. (1967), 'Some Methods to Study Surface Textures of Sand Grains', *Sedimentology*, 8, pp. 281–90.

Spencer, D. W. (1963), 'The Interpretation of Grain-Size Distribution Curves of Clastic Sediments', *Journ. Sed. Petrol.*, 33, pp. 180–90.

Steininger, F. (1968), 'Special Investigations: Recent Marine Molluscs', in *Explanatory Text to the Synoptic Geologic Map of Kuwait*, W. Fuchs *et al.* (eds.), Geological Survey of Austria, pp. 37–49.

Sugden, W. (1963), 'The Hydrology of the Persian Gulf and its Significance in respect to the Evaporate Deposition', *Am. Journ. Sci.*, 261, pp. 741–55.

Taylor, J. C. M. and Illing, L. V. (1969), 'Holocene Intertidal Calcium Carbonate-Cementation, Qatar, Persian Gulf', *Sedimentology*, 12, pp. 69–107.

Thompson, W. O. (1937), 'Original Structures of Beaches, Bars and Dunes', *Geol. Soc. Am. Bull.*, 48, pp. 723–52.

Tooley, M. J. (1974), 'Sea-level Changes During the last 9000 Years in Northwest England', *Geogr. Journ.*, 140, pp. 18–42.

Trask, P. D. (1932), *Origin and Environment of Source Sediments of Petroleum*, Houston, Tex., Gulf Publishing Co.

Udden, J. A. (1898), *The Mechanical Composition of Wind Deposits*, Augustana Library Publ., 1.

Udden, J. A. (1914), 'Mechanical Composition of Clastic Sediments', *Bull. Geol. Soc. Am.*, 25, pp. 655–744.

US Waterways Experiment Station (1939), 'Study of Materials in Suspension, Mississippi River', *Techn. Mem.*, 122–1, Vicksburg, Louisiana.

Van Andel, Tj. H., Heath, G. R., Moore, T. C. and McGeary, D. F. R. (1967). 'Late Quaternary History, Climate and Oceanography of the Timor Sea, Northwestern Australia', *Am. J. Sci.*, 265, pp. 737–58.

Visher, G. S. (1965), 'Fluvial Processes as Interpreted from Ancient and Recent Fluvial Deposits', in *Primary Sedimentary Structures and their Hydrodynamic Interpretation*, G. V. Middleton (ed.), Soc. Econ. Paleontologists Mineralogists, Spec. Publ. no. 12, pp. 116–32.

Visher, G. S. (1969), 'Grain-size Distributions and Depositional Processes', *Journ. Sed. Petrol.*, 39, pp. 1074–1106.

Vita Finzi, C. (1969), 'Late Quaternary Alluvial Chronology of Iran', *Geol. Rundschau*, 58, pp. 951–73.

Vita Finzi, C. (1973), 'Late Quaternary Subsidence', in P. F. S. Cornelius *et al.*, The Musandam Expedition 1971–72: Scientific Results, Part I, *Geogr. Journ.* 139, pp. 414–21.

Vita Finzi, C. (1975), 'Quaternary Deposits in the Iranian Makran', *Geogr. Journ.*, 141, pp. 415–20.

Voute, C. (1957), 'A Prehistoric Find Near Razzaza (Karbala Liwa): Its Significance for the Morphological and Geological History of the Abu Dibbis Depression and Surrounding Area', *Sumer*, 32, pp. 1–14.

Walcott, R. I. (1972), 'Past Sea-level, Eustasy and Deformation of the Earth', *Quaternary Res.*, 2, pp. 1–14.

Walcott, R. I. (1974), 'Recent and Late Quaternary Changes in Water Level', *7th GEOP Research Conference on Coastal Problems related to Water Level*, Columbus, Ohio, Ohio State University.

Wentworth, C. K. (1922), 'A Scale of Grade and Class Terms for Clastic Sediments', *Journ. Geol.*, 30, pp. 377–93.

Wentworth, C. K. (1927), 'The Accuracy of Mechanical Analysis', *Am. Journ. Sci.*, 13, pp. 399–408.

Woolley, Sir C. L. (1938), *Ur of the Chaldees*, London, Pelican Books.

Zeuner, F. E. (1952), 'Pleistocene Shorelines', *Geol. Rundschau*, 40, pp. 39–50.

Zeuner, F. E. (1953), 'The Three "Monastirian" Sea-levels', *Actes Congr. Int. Quaternaire*, Rome-Pisa, 4.

Zeuner, F. E. (1959), *The Pleistocene Period*, London, Hutchinson.

# Index